PLACING JOHN HAINES

PLACING JOHN HAINES

James Perrin Warren

UNIVERSITY OF ALASKA PRESS
Fairbanks

Published by
University of Alaska Press
P.O. Box 756240
Fairbanks, AK 99775-6240

Cover design by University of Alaska Press
Interior design by Publishers' Design and Production Services, Inc.
Cover image: "Mountain Road" from *The Last Road North*, by Ben Huff

Library of Congress Cataloging-in-Publication Data

Names: Warren, James Perrin, author.
Title: Placing John Haines / James Perrin Warren.
Description: Fairbanks, AK : University of Alaska Press, 2017.
Identifiers: LCCN 2016025205 (print) | LCCN 2016044506 (ebook) | ISBN 9781602233096 (paperback) | ISBN 9781602233102 ()
Subjects: LCSH: Haines, John, 1924-2011--Criticism and interpretation. | Poets, American--20th century--Biography. | Nature in literature. | Ecology in literature.
Classification: LCC PS3558.A33 Z89 2017 (print) | LCC PS3558.A33 (ebook) | DDC 811/.54 [B] --dc23
LC record available at https://lccn.loc.gov/2016025205

CONTENTS

ACKNOWLEDGMENTS

THIS STUDY WOULD NEVER HAVE HAPPENED without the encouragement of John Luther Adams, who opened his studio and shared his passion for the poetry of John Haines in the summer of 2012. For fifteen months in 2013–2014, colleagues and friends in Fairbanks, Alaska, opened their hearts and homes to my wife Julianne and me. I thank especially Len Kamerling and Julie Kaufman, Phyllis Morrow and Chase Hensel, Phil Marshall and Jan Lokken, Larry Kaplan and Jan Dawe, Carolyn Kremers, Eric Heyne and Alexandra Fitts, Ned Rozell, Birch Pavelsky, Karen Brewster, and Dave Klein—the core of a very special community surrounding the University of Alaska Fairbanks. Many of us gathered together for Gretel Ehrlich's memorable reading of Haines's poetry at the Richardson homestead in summer 2014.

During those same fifteen months, I depended constantly on the expertise and goodwill of Charles Hilton, Rosemarie Speranza, Lisa Morris, Robyn Russell, and Nicholas Evans at the Alaska and Polar Regions Collections and Archives, Elmer E. Rasmuson Library, University of Alaska Fairbanks. I was also helped by staff during shorter visits to the Special Collections libraries of the University of Minnesota; Ohio University, the University of Vermont, and the Berg Collection at the New York Public Library. The librarians at the Kentucky Historical Society were especially gracious while I delved into multiple boxes in the Wendell Berry Collection.

I received important financial support in the form of three Lenfest Summer Research Grants and a Lenfest sabbatical leave grant from Washington and Lee University. The Alaska Humanities Forum provided me with a grant that supplemented my research during the sabbatical year. I gratefully acknowledge the help of these institutions. My colleague and dean of the college, Suzanne Keen, recommended that I apply for the Alaska Humanities Forum grant and supported my work through her good offices.

Steven B. Rogers, trustee of the literary estate of John Haines, has provided invaluable counsel and ready permissions throughout the project.

Dana Gioia gave helpful comments and guidance on chapter 6 and on his collaboration with Scott Walker and Haines in the 1980s. John Knott and Bernard Quetchenbach, colleagues from the Association for the Study of Literature and Environment, gave me important readings of the whole manuscript in its final phases. Their suggestions were precise and insightful, and I have tried my best to incorporate them all. Along the way, Eric Heyne taught me much about the literature of the North in the spring of 2014, and we found many opportunities to discuss Haines in relation to other writers of Alaska and Canada.

James Engelhardt, Amy Simpson, and Krista West at the University of Alaska Press have given me the very best of professional treatment during our work together in bringing the book to press. Ben Huff kindly gave permission to reproduce the photograph on the cover, and Dan O'Neill provided the photograph of John Haines at the Richardson homestead. I'm very grateful for both of these adornments to the book.

Finally, without the passionate intelligence of Julianne, we would never have lived in Alaska, and I would never have written this book. I dedicate *Placing John Haines* to her.

Dedication

To Julianne Lutz Warren

"All wrong turns get left behind."

John Haines in 2010, by the cabin he built on 160 acres southeast of Fairbanks, Alaska. Photo courtesy of Dan O'Neill.

INTRODUCTION

PLACING JOHN HAINES

MY ALASKA

John Haines (1924–2011) was the most important literary writer to come out of Alaska after World War II. Haines himself evoked the importance of Alaska to his work in one of his most resonant sentences: "As a poet I was born in a particular place, a hillside overlooking the Tanana River in central Alaska, where I built a house and lived for the better part of twenty-two years" (*Living Off the Country*, hereafter cited as LOC, 4). He first came to Alaska in 1947, after service on a US Navy submarine chaser in the South Pacific and a year of art school on the GI Bill. For over fifteen months in 1947–1948, he homesteaded near the former gold-mining camp of Richardson, some seventy miles southeast of Fairbanks on the road to Valdez. In 1954, following three more years of art school, he returned to the Richardson homestead for fifteen years, remaining there till he sold the property in 1969. It was during this second, prolonged period that Haines began to develop his gifts as a poet and essayist. At the same time, he learned, in fine detail, how to hunt, trap, fish, gather berries, and garden vegetables in the Far North, becoming adept at many aspects of subsistence living. Haines differs from outside writers like John Muir, Jack London, Robert Service, Robert Marshall, and John McPhee in that he settled in Alaska and wrote about the place from the inside. Though he was not a birthright Alaskan, for over fifty years Haines stood for a particular kind of authentic inhabitation.

From 1970 until his death in 2011, Haines led the itinerant life of an artistic journeyman, holding writing fellowships and teaching at a variety of universities. In a relentless search for a stable living, he moved to California soon after selling the homestead, and over the years he taught for short periods in Washington, Montana, Ohio, Tennessee, and Washington, DC, among other places. He also taught and lived in Anchorage, and periodically he returned to the Interior. Despite his persistent movements and sojourns, the Richardson homestead once again became his principal residence from 1980 to 1994. Moreover, Haines lived in Fairbanks for most of the last decade leading up to his death, teaching small seminars for the honors program at the University of Alaska Fairbanks.[1]

The patterns that emerge from Haines's biography are seemingly contradictory. Largely self-educated, especially in reading and writing literature, Haines nonetheless pursued and held a series of academic literary positions for much of his mature career. Finding his voice as a writer on an isolated wilderness homestead, Haines was also closely connected to major contemporary poets of the 1960s and 1970s, especially the Deep Imagism community associated with Robert Bly, Donald Hall, Louis Simpson, William Stafford, and James Wright. A neglected, largely unknown Alaskan writer, Haines regularly published poems and essays in prestigious national magazines and presses in California, Washington, Minnesota, and Massachusetts; he gave countless poetry readings all over the Lower 48 and abroad during his forty-year career. Perhaps no contemporary American poet is more associated with the idea of place, and yet Haines is also one of the most restlessly peripatetic writers of the late twentieth and early twenty-first centuries. One of his most long-lasting friendships was with Kentucky writer Wendell Berry, but the sense of place in the two writers' lives and careers could not be more different.

This abiding sense of contradiction is extremely productive in many ways. Whatever its origins may have been, it kept Haines from settling into one place or pattern of writing, so that we constantly find him reinventing himself and his work. Moreover, the apparently contradictory ideas of place and movement work in dialogue with each other, so that a larger pattern of constant change and development emerges from his life's work. Haines defined this pattern in a 1981 interview with David Stark and Robert Hedin entitled "Living Off the Country." In a kind of double synecdoche, Haines uses the phrase "living off the country" to figure his work as a writer; the phrase then becomes both the title of the interview and the title of his first book of essays, *Living Off the Country: Essays on Poetry and Place*:

> If I were pinned down to it, I might describe my work as a sort of homemade, pioneering effort of the kind we North Americans are sometimes noted for, using whatever comes to hand. Within the limitations of personal vision and talent, almost anything—Williams's efforts to rediscover the American grain, Chinese directness of vision, "deep" imagery—can be useful and nourishing. In its own way, it is a little like living off the country. Call it a search, an exploration, if you like—into the language as into the continent itself. (*LOC* 145)

The metaphor of pioneering exploration blends with the figure of foraging for something "useful and nourishing." Both evoke the hardscrabble homestead years as central to Haines's vision of his writing, so that Haines's "country" becomes a complex, "homemade" place. Indeed, the phrase "living off the country" also evokes the subsistence methods developed by arctic explorers in the late nineteenth and early twentieth centuries.

In other parts of the "Living Off the Country" interview, Haines describes this complex, homemade place as "my Alaska, that part of it I have known better than I have known any other place—the Interior, a very mysterious land. In my own case it is part actual, part myth, part wish, and so forth. And all of this says nothing of the geographical components of the place, and very little about the Alaska of the Indians and Eskimos, a very different place from the one we've known" (*LOC* 151). By "my Alaska," Haines clearly does not mean to suggest a domineering sense of ownership, for as he says elsewhere in the interview, "I sensed here in the North, quite early, a place that could be mine as no other could be. I don't mean exclusively mine, but mine in the sense of being a place of self-realization." According to Haines, this idea of self-realization is a necessary response to the silence of the land, which the poet figures as a call for an answering voice: "In this sense no country, no land really exists until it has been felt deeply enough to be written about or sung of" (149). For Haines, then, Alaska becomes a complex place of many visions and voices, and it becomes his place because he realized his vocation as a poet while homesteading there.

POETRY AND PLACE

In several important essays in *Living Off the Country*, Haines produces a richly complex, hybrid sense of the relationship between poetry and place. The book itself is a hybrid collection in four parts. The first two parts bring together some of Haines's deepest meditations on "Alaska and the Wilderness" and "Poets and Poetry." In the lead essay, "The Writer as Alaskan: Beginnings and Reflections," Haines develops a telling set of seven definitions of place, all in relation to his own origins as a writer. Some of these definitions find echoes in the extended interview that forms the third part of the book; all of them provide original insights into Haines's sense of place and poetry.

After the resonant first sentence about being born, as a poet, on a hillside overlooking the Tanana River, Haines explores the qualities of his homestead that made it into "a place of self-realization." The influences on the young homesteader are numerous, but finally it is "the place itself that provided the means of unifying all of these into a single experience" (*LOC* 4). The wilderness quality is paramount, a feature that from 1947 to 1969 would stay largely unchanged. Haines describes the Alaskan wilderness of the 1950s and 1960s as "open-ended" and marked by "limitlessness and mystery." He gives a sense of the wilderness by saying that he "could walk north from my homestead at Richardson all the way to the Arctic Ocean and never cross a road nor encounter a village" (5). The wilderness leads to a basic life of subsistence hunting and trapping, an "older and simpler existence" that Haines calls "a place to begin" (6), and the homestead is also a place "to learn in detail many things of a kind I could not have learned if I had stayed only briefly in the country or had lived there in easier circumstances" (6).

In at least three ways, then, Alaska as a physical place forced Haines to become an apprentice in fields both practical and poetic. He learned "the names of the things to be found there," learned "to make things for myself," learned "to hunt, to watch, and to listen, to think like a moose, if need be, or a marten, or a lynx" (6). He learned to read the river and the snow, to interpret the forms of frost, and to feed himself from the land. In short, he learned to live off the country, but the most fundamental lesson was that he "learned that it is land, *place*, that makes people, provides for them the possibilities they will have of becoming something more than mere lumps of sucking matter" (7). The place gave Haines the "possibilities" for becoming an accomplished woodsman and homesteader, living off the country in ways that reach far back toward the beginning of the twentieth century or much earlier. It also gave him a deep sense of connection to the old residents and their way of life, endowing Richardson with "the dimensions of myth" (9).

As Haines explores the origins of his identity as an Alaskan writer, he continually probes more and more deeply into ideas of place. Thus the local is more than a storehouse of good material, and Haines believes that one day the local must "include the continent, and finally the planet itself" (9). Likewise, Richardson is more than a collection of old-timers and their stories. It creates "an awakening, profound and disturbing," so that Haines feels he is entering "the original mystery of things, the great past out of which we came" (9). Thus Alaska becomes "the meeting of place and dream," and the immediate, seemingly natural result is that Haines begins to write poems. It would take nearly ten years before he would write anything that satisfied him, but from the very beginning the place is clearly as much imaginative as physical, reaching both into a deep past and into an ominous future. Haines quotes his own poem "Foreboding" to evoke those double senses: the poem registers the "nine long years" that the speaker has looked out onto an immense and lonely landscape, but ultimately the physical landscape leads to the speaker's imaginative vision of "manlike figures" approaching and passing on, the wind filling the ruts of the highway with dust, and the close of day arriving "like the closing of an inner door." As the poem closes, the day begins a dark journey into a spiritual night—"across nine bridges / wrecked one by one" (11).

At the end of Part I of "The Writer as Alaskan," Haines pauses to reflect on the Richardson homestead and its significance as a place. Even from a distance, it is "a place I go back to, in mind and in spirit, though it seems I cannot return to it fully in fact" (12). Although other experiences and places have added to the sum of Haines's life, he continually returns to central Alaska: "Behind all I write there is a landscape, partly idealized, perhaps, upon which the human figure, my own or another's, acts out a part of its life. That original place still sustains me" (13). The "original place" is partly a physical reality, the Alaska wilderness in the years before statehood and the oil boom, and it is partly an "interior place, formed out of dream and fantasy, and by intense imagination" (13). In all of its manifestations, the place is one of origins, and for Haines it acts as a metaphor for a personal and cultural odyssey:

> I believe that one of the most important metaphors of our time is the journey out of wilderness into culture, into the forms of our complicated and divided age, with its intense confusions and deceptions. The eventual disintegration of these cultural forms returns us once more to the wilderness. This journey can be seen both as fall and as reconciliation. And place, once again, means actual place, but also a state of mind, of consciousness. Once that place is established, we carry it with us, as we do a sense of ourselves. (13)

Other essays in the first part of *Living Off the Country* echo the language and ideas of "The Writer as Alaskan." In "Moments and Journeys," for example, Haines brings the two title ideas together by evoking a significant moment of reflection during a journey, a moment that joins dreams and actual life. Haines describes two key moments in a December crossing of the Tanana River (24–25) and in a hike to the Chumash caves of Pool Rock, near Santa Barbara, California (28–29). In both moments, Haines recognizes a profound connection to a place and "that hidden, original life we have done so much to destroy" (29). In "A Place of Sense," Haines uses the ironic reversal of the phrase "sense of place" to examine two contradictory patterns in the present: the break-up or atomization of life and lands, and global inclusiveness (39). As in the Pool Rock episode, Haines claims that landscapes conceal "a hidden place" and that this place is also "within us, a dreamscape" (40). This dual place, joining external and internal senses, will lead us, Haines believes, to a "poetry of the earth" (40–41). Finally, in "The Sun on Our Shoulders," Haines considers the idea of wilderness as both external and internal (51–52) and picks up the two opposing impulses—to return to the past and to a wilderness life of origins, and to move beyond and extend life's boundaries (57). By adopting a middle position between the two impulses, Haines discovers two abiding responsibilities as a writer and as a culture: to save what we can of land and wilderness, and to see in wilderness both a refuge and a warning (59). The responsibilities accompany all of us on a particularly significant journey, "not toward some shining destination, but toward a fullness of understanding" (58–59).

In Part II of "The Writer as Alaskan," Haines develops a broader but more specifically American context for his visionary ideas of place. He reflects on the "spirit of place," a phrase he takes from D. H. Lawrence's *Studies in Classic American Literature* and applies to his own assertion that "place makes people" (7, 14). Next, he cites William Carlos Williams's *In the American Grain* as an attempt to break through the conspiracy of silence concerning the relationships of people to places, especially in Williams's sense of "what he felt had gone wrong with America from the start—the inability or refusal to recognize what was actually under our feet, or in the air, and live by that. Instead we fell back on the old names for things, familiar responses to whatever lay beyond our power to see. The meaning of what he found is still with us, as potent as ever" (14).

Haines exercises his own visionary authority in seeing this same inability or refusal in Alaska. The North is "a new country" for Americans, but Haines still looks for the "real literature" that can enhance the place and the people who live there (14–15). Instead of this authentic writing rooted in the land, Haines believes that we see Alaska through a market of clichés for tourists and therefore reduce it to a generic anywhere that bespeaks an "impoverished inner world" (16). Like Lawrence and Williams, Haines employs the extreme rhetoric of the jeremiad, pronouncing the absolute negation in a sentence: "There is no place called Alaska, just as there is hardly anything today that can be identified as California" (15). As in "The Sun on Our Shoulders," however, even while he renounces the "shining destination" of our journey, Haines holds out hope for an authentic poetry of place that will bring a fullness of understanding: "I think that there *is* a spirit of place, a presence asking to be expressed; and sometimes when we are lucky as writers, and quiet in a way few of us want to be anymore, a voice enters our own, becomes mingled with it, and we speak with a force and clarity not otherwise heard" (19). Most important for this sense of origins and beginnings, Haines brings his idea of hope to the specific place of modern Alaska in the years after statehood and the oil boom:

> Perhaps in Alaska is an opportunity to deepen that understanding. It is another *place*, where we can stand and see the world and ourselves. The literature that is to come will bear the mark of an urgency, a seriousness that recognizes the dangers and choices held out to us by our

> involvement with the earth. And it may now and then be possible to recover, in a new land, something of that first morning of existence, when we looked at the world and saw, without motives, how beautiful it is. (20–21)

In this passage, Haines joins Alaska and the world in an urgent literature of place. It is a place of great beauty and grave dangers, and it calls for our deepest awareness of our responsibilities to the earth.

MOMENTS AND JOURNEYS

This discussion of "The Writer as Alaskan" suggests, at the very least, how powerful John Haines can be as an essayist. He develops ideas in concrete terms, advancing them with care and authenticity drawn from personal experience. As profound as the ideas about place may be, we can also see that they tend to stay close to a few thematic patterns and to deepen moments of insight and reflection. That is the sense of the episodes in the essay "Moments and Journeys," just as it is the sense one gains from the essays on poetry and place in the second part of *Living Off the Country*. Thus an essay like "Roots" is valuable both for defining poetry as establishing a "place of conviction" (85) and for retelling the story of Pool Rock as a renewed discovery of the place of conviction within ourselves (88–89). To take another example, without any announced thesis or line of argument, the essay "Poems and Places" (123–35) uses five poems to show how a human figure appears in a landscape and gives concrete form to ideas of place. As Haines puts it in one of the poems, "Listening in October":

> There are silences so deep
> you can hear
> the journeys of the soul,
> enormous footsteps
> downward in a freezing earth.

Here, Haines develops paradoxes of silence and sound, movement and stasis, soul and earth in a pattern that deepens the meanings of place.

In *Placing John Haines*, I argue that the best way to understand the signal achievements of Alaska's first great writer is to focus on place, especially on

John Haines's often solitary experiences in the wilderness of Alaska. But I also argue that Haines's sense of his role as a writer owes important debts to other writers and to the capacious, multidimensional concept of place I have begun to trace in this introduction. Haines is a solitary Alaskan homesteader, but he is also part of a larger constellation of place-based writers. This productive tension in Haines's writing career makes him a rigorously independent poet and essayist. It also tends to mark his overwhelmingly environmental, ecocentric vision.

Haines carries ideas of place with him for his whole life. He returns to Alaska, and to Richardson, over and over again during his fifty-year career as a writer. At the same time, he engages repeatedly with the "complicated and divided age" of contemporary America after World War II, and his work can seem both complicated and divided as a result. In Haines's own terms, is the journey a fall or a reconciliation? Is it an odyssey, an epic of departure and return for the heroic wanderer? Is "wilderness" the proper term for what the Richardson homestead and "my Alaska" signify, both for Haines and for modern readers? What place do Haines's poetry and prose occupy in contemporary American culture, especially if we view his work as more than simply nature writing? More broadly, what place does literature occupy in relation to the major postwar social movements of civil rights, women's rights, peace, and environmentalism? What are the relations of Haines's environmental poetry to other arts, especially to the visual arts and to contemporary music? These are some of the fundamental questions I carry through *Placing John Haines*.

MAPPING JOHN HAINES

The six chapters of this book are organized in an overlapping, roughly chronological pattern. I have found it productive to move around within the stages of Haines's career, examine prose and poetry in concert with each other, and place unpublished manuscript materials in the foreground in order to shed light on published texts. In Part 1, "Alaska," three chapters focus on the manuscripts of early poems and essays in order to show how Haines develops his lyric style, both in poetry and in prose.

In chapter 1, "Discovering Richardson," I look at Haines's homestead as the place of his birth as a poet, but I also argue that he found important mentors and supporters in correspondents like William Carlos Williams, Robert Bly, Donald Hall, and others. The early poems from the 1940s and 1950s reveal a young writer searching for his own voice, a search that is not always successful but is always interesting. Unpublished manuscript materials show how in the early 1960s Haines began experimenting with classical Chinese poetry of the eighth and ninth centuries, adapting poetic forms to Alaskan subjects. From short, two-quatrain experiments to longer, more complex forms, Haines's voice begins to emerge, always in relation to the complicated dimensions of Richardson as a place. In *Winter News* (1966), Haines's first book of poems, the spiritual, dreamlike quality of wild animals strongly suggests that Haines is discovering an early form of ecopoetry.

Chapter 2, "Inside America," broadens the geographical scope to show how Haines moved from the specific, local place of Richardson to the large social and cultural concerns of a turbulent, changing nation. In six books of poetry published during the 1970s, Haines searches repeatedly for what he calls "a place of conviction," as much a vision or stance toward the hollowness of contemporary America as it is a style of writing or a way of life. In this prodigious search, Haines works through uneven achievements to create a new poetry of the earth, most clearly seen in the poems of *Cicada* and *In a Dusty Light*, both published in 1977. Through commentary on volumes, individual poems, and two significant sequences—"Homestead" and "News from the Glacier"—I argue that Haines figures his place of conviction in a new poetry of the earth.

Chapter 3, "Shadow Language," retraces Haines's art of memory by examining his prose memoirs from 1947 to 1989. For over forty years, Haines wrote and rewrote stories relating his Richardson experience and ideas of place both to the past lives of old-timers and to the shadowy lives of wild animals. As an essayist, Haines develops a plangent, often tender style, evoking the shared mortality of all beings in a common journey. The shadow language reaches its deepest beauty in the essays of *The Stars, the Snow, the Fire*, a book that effectively evokes the realities of homesteading in Alaska in lyric, visionary prose. As in chapters 1 and 2, I argue that Haines's investment in the local leads to a profoundly planetary vision of the earth.

Part 2, "Another Country," parallels the first in form, featuring two chapters that focus primarily on poetry and a final chapter focusing on prose. Rather than survey a number of texts, however, I closely examine some of Haines's most challenging works of the 1980s and 1990s. As in Part 1, archival material plays a fundamental role in understanding Haines's mature vision.

In chapter 4, "The Changed Pastoral," I examine the six major poetic sequences of *New Poems, 1980–88*. Two unpublished typescripts from Haines's collaboration and friendship with composer John Luther Adams shed light on the poet's theory of mimesis and the power of poetry to mediate between nature and culture. The roles of history and art are especially important in sequences such as "Meditation on a Skull Carved in Crystal," "Death and the Miser," and "Days of Edward Hopper," but they also figure significantly in the sequences focused more particularly on nature: "Rain Country," "Water of Night," and "In the Forest Without Leaves." These last two sequences, the last in *New Poems*, integrate the elements of art, nature, history, and poetry to create a new pastoral vision and a new expansion of Haines's poetry of the earth.

In chapter 5, "The Place of Conviction and the Public Voice," the relationship between Haines's early and late work becomes especially important. The essay collection *Fables and Distances* (1996) is closely related to *Living Off the Country* (1981) in both theme and form. Moreover, many of the essays in the later volume echo the two unpublished typescripts that provide such sharp insights into the poetic sequences of *New Poems*. For Haines, essays and poems are expressions of the place of conviction made by the poet who speaks in a public voice. We see those two key ideas at work in the final fifteen poems of *The Owl in the Mask of the Dreamer* (1993) and in four poetic sequences that appear in *For the Century's End: Poems, 1990–1999* (2001). Thus, as Haines nears the end of his writing career, he summarizes his central ideas and deepens their significance in both essays and poems.

In chapter 6, "Somebody There," I reconstruct Haines's career through his letters with six important correspondents. The early correspondence with Robert Bly reveals a productive but testy relationship, whereas Haines's long correspondence with editor Scott Walker was marked by a common passion for contemporary literature. Walker's Graywolf Press became a crucial supporter of Haines's work in the 1970s and 1980s. As Haines grew in stature and maturity, he forged two strong friendships with younger artists. The poet Dana Gioia and the composer John Luther Adams gave support and advice that proved crucial to Haines's development as a mature writer about the spirit of place. Finally, two near contemporaries, Hayden Carruth and Wendell Berry, were lifelong correspondents, giving Haines their careful, respectful friendship in letters that reveal deep trust and insightful criticism for over forty years. In their different ways, the six correspondents became the "somebody there" to whom Haines could say what he wanted with some assurance that it would be understood.

I close the book with a short conclusion, "John Haines's Place as Ecopoet," reflecting on four phases of Haines's career and arguing that his major work as a writer defines a place for him in the canon of major American ecopoets of his generation. He belongs, I argue, with the generation of environmental poets like Robert Bly, W. S. Merwin, Gary Snyder, and Wendell Berry.

PART 1

ALASKA

CHAPTER 1

DISCOVERING RICHARDSON

Place and Voice in Winter News *(1966)*

THE ROAD TO RICHARDSON

In poems from the early 1950s, the young John Haines openly imitates writers like Walt Whitman, Edgar Allan Poe, and Stephen Crane, as well as modernist poets Ezra Pound, Wallace Stevens, and T. S. Eliot. Most evident in the early poems, however, is the abiding influence of William Carlos Williams. Haines never tired of telling how he sent some poems to Williams in 1952. Despite having suffered a stroke, Williams wrote back to Haines on April 21, 1953, encouraging him to continue writing. The manuscript letter in the John Haines Papers at the University of Alaska contains praise that many poets would covet: "I'm certainly glad you wrote and sent me your poems for by doing so you revealed the most authentic talent for verse that I have encountered in your generation. . . . Continue as you are going, read, read, read all the examples of the verse you admire—and some that you do *not* admire—and you'll be in another ten years, if you have what it takes to survive, top dog."[1] Williams praises the young poet for his voice, his sense of lively detail, and his "unaffected sense of rhythm." In his own characteristic terms, Williams admonishes Haines to pay attention to "measure," for that is the way that the young writer can "write the next chapter in the history of verse" (John Haines Papers Box 5, Folder 20; hereafter cited as JHP). Free verse, he adds, "is not enough," and "instinct is not enough." On the back of the letter, Florence Williams adds a postscript from "Bill": "Widen your scope—Don't be satisfied with being labeled '*regional*.'" One can see why Haines, a few years out of the navy and art school, and newly committed to writing poetry, would be vitally encouraged by Williams's letter. In his essay "Homage to the Chinese," however, Haines recalls that he stopped writing poems for some three years while working on the homestead at Richardson, only beginning again when he discovered Kenneth Rexroth and the ancient Chinese poets (*LOC* 120).

Perhaps the three-year silence occurred in part because of a second, less famous letter from Dr. Williams. Writing on May 7, 1959, in response to a packet of recent poems from Haines, Williams finds little to praise: "What the hell am I to say: I doubt that you have written a single one that can be called a poem. There is a general feeling of a poem about what you send me but it never comes to a focus as any piece of writing must do to bear the name 'poem.' You must bring your writings to a head. Your images must focus nearer than 'a music, very distant music of the sea'" (JHP Box 5, Folder 20).

Looking for helpful words, Williams throws up his hands in the letter, saying, "I'm really at a loss to know what to say to you. You've got me stumped. . . . Maybe it's the infinite distances with which you are very evidently surrounded that has cut you off from any possible communication." In Williams's reading, the "infinite" qualities of Alaska as a physical place battle against the poet's urge to communicate. It is as if Williams is consigning Haines to a vast silence because of the vast, silent landscape Haines inhabits. Frustrated, the elder poet would like to say "at least SOMETHING that would be of help to you" and that might "get you out of the rut you seem to be in," but what that might be is "beyond me."

What poems did Haines send to Williams in the first place, and what poems did he send six years later? How did Haines lose the focus and rhythmic control that Williams detected in the earlier poems, and what came to take their place? These are ultimately questions without definitive answers, but we can nonetheless arrive at some good ideas about the difficulties Haines experienced in the 1950s. There are dozens of early typescript poems in the John Haines Papers, many of them never published (JHP Box 7, Folders 1–16). Beginning in 1994, Haines also published three books of early poems, reaching deeper and deeper into the archives of his early poetry. The first, *Where the Twilight Never Ends*, prints fifteen poems, some of which were originally published in magazines. These poems date from the early 1960s and show the influence of Chinese, Spanish, and German poetry.[2] The second, *At the End of This Summer*, prints forty-three titles, dated 1948 to 1954 and organized according to Haines's sojourns in Washington, DC; New York City; Provincetown; and California. Haines notes in the preface that the poems are apprentice work, and he once again recalls Williams's 1953 letter of encouragement as restoring "a good deal of my faltering confidence."[3] The third, *Of Your Passage, O Summer*, retrieves eighteen poems from the late 1950s and early 1960s; Haines notes that these poems date from his "renewed passion" for writing poems after his three-year silence.[4]

At the End of This Summer is especially helpful because of its general availability and the range of poems it prints. In an early experiment like "To Remember Another Time," we can readily hear Poe's influence, perhaps mingling with early Yeats: "Helen, beyond all accustomed beauty I place you, / Shining alone." A later sequence, "Pictures and Parables," seems modeled on Stephen Crane's portentous imagism, with a dash of early T. S. Eliot: "This is the sea, and I / have come to know a great / deal about it, noting / its moods, counting the tides, listening / to the many voices / that are at last but one voice." In both poems, the speaker's profession of special knowledge and authority merges with a flat-footed, prosaic truthiness. Later poems are more successful because Haines resists the urge to characterize and editorialize upon his subjects, presenting them with more concrete detail and less evaluative language. "In the Natural History Museum," "Totem," and "Interview," three poems set in New York City's American Museum of Natural History, describe particular scenes or objects for their own value, not for what they might mean. In ways reminiscent of Williams, the restrained technique of "no ideas but in things" makes these poems among the most effective of the collection. Even so, the collection certainly does not reveal any clear progression of a young writer in his craft. Thus the poems from California, 1952–1954, verge on the frankly embarrassing at times, as in "Pawnee Dust" and "Ghost Town."

The final poem of the collection, "Lineage," directly faces the question of poetic authority in terms of "the songs and praises of poets who died." The poem presents a real dilemma, as if the speaker were entering into a frozen world of death and silence, but Haines remains optimistic:

The earth they knew remains. Despite the
swollen lives of men, I see the grass before
me and believe the dead could stand in

recognition there, braving another season.
Their words shape mine, their hearts expand again

in this remembered sun. And I am still,
and face the changeless autumn with a smile,
knowing that resurrection.

The strong lineage of Wallace Stevens appears in these stanzas, evident in the imagery of the "remembered sun" and Stevens's theme of "death is the mother of beauty," both of which echo "Sunday Morning." The young writer's blank-verse tercets and doublets, moreover, directly recall Stevens's versification. Still, Haines's sense of lineage is general, the lineage of poets decidedly plural. The real point is that the speaker, in his singularity, embodies the resurrection of the sun. If that stance bespeaks artistic bravado, it also may suggest real bravery in the face of death.

Rather than presenting an image of steady progress, then, the cumulative evidence of dozens of poems, published and unpublished, supports a narrative of prolonged, somewhat haphazard experimentation from 1948 to 1960. Even though Haines wrote that he was "born as a poet" in 1947–1948, during his first winter at the Richardson homestead, he actually served a long apprenticeship in the service of earlier poets. In fact, he spent over half of those apprentice years as a journeyman of uncertain vocation, traveling as an art student across the country to urban centers along the eastern seaboard, to the Atlantic and Pacific Oceans, and finally back to Richardson. As the selections in *At the End of This Summer* suggest, the poems of the 1950s provide clear echoes of Poe, Whitman, Stephen Crane, Eliot, Williams, Pound, and Stevens. But Haines was unable to do more than imitate these important American precursors rather randomly. None of them—not even Stevens or Williams—gave him a sure path to his own voice and place. Indeed, Williams's 1959 letter shows that the mentor was "stumped" and the younger poet in a "rut." In short, even though Haines read and appreciated the great modernist poets like Williams, Stevens, and Pound, he had a difficult time assimilating the lessons of modernism and finding his own voice in his early poems.

Despite these mixed results by an inexperienced writer, Haines never lacked for confidence in his own opinions. On November 19, 1959, for instance, only five months after Williams's "what the hell" letter, Haines wrote his first letter directly to Robert Bly, focusing on Bly's rejection of his poem "Descent" for publication in the poetry magazine *The Fifties*. Bly had roundly lectured "Mr. Haines" in a letter of September 18, telling him that his poems were "too talkative" and disputing the younger writer's admiration for Dr. Williams's views of the American language. In his reply to Bly, Haines defends the poem, calling it "in its own small way . . . as perfect a poem as I've ever written." He then discusses Williams as leading the way in thinking about "the poem as a technical matter lying outside the metaphysical and philosophical," and he shows a thorough knowledge of Williams's *In the American Grain* (1925): "He *has* been right in insisting on beginning with the local elements, the *American language*." Haines then forthrightly tells Bly the story of the two letters from Williams and concludes that he is very "puzzled" by the second one. In response to Bly's recommendation of the poetry of Antonio Machado, Juan Ramón Jiménez, and Federico García Lorca, Haines offers his view of translation as "rewriting the original in your own language as if you were the original poet thus writing. And to succeed you may have to cut down considerably or change something here or there to make it contemporarily alive" (JHP Box 1, Folder 15). At the very outset of this important poetic friendship, Haines actively resists Bly's advice and attempts to impose his own views on the more accomplished writer.

The title "Descent" for Haines's rejected poem is intriguing, though I have not been able to locate the text. The word "descent" reverberates strongly. First of all, in reading Haines as a young, unknown writer, we should recall the chapter "Descent" in Williams's *In the American Grain* (New Directions, 1925), for Haines returned to this chapter many times throughout his career. The chapter presents Williams's short meditation on Sam Houston, who ran away to live with the Cherokee in western Tennessee as a young boy. Houston became governor of Tennessee in 1829 but soon divorced his wife and resigned his office, returning to live with the Cherokee. As Williams puts it, Houston "took the descent once more" (213). In a seemingly different vein, Williams argues that the poet must be the means to "aesthetic satisfaction" in the country, but most of America's aesthetic productions remain vibrant, superficial, and artificial. The authentic poetic genius is, Williams maintains, "shy and wild and frail" (214). The genius finds that "it is imperative that we *sink*," avoiding conformity such as one finds in the universities: "Those who come up from under will have a mark on them that invites scorn, like a farmer's filthy clodhoppers" (215). Houston emerges as an exemplar of the need to descend into the soil and avoid the blindness of America's supposedly "manifest" destiny. In the last paragraph of the chapter, Williams broadens the cultural lesson yet further: "However hopeless it may seem, we have no other choice: we must go back to the beginning; it must all be done over; everything that is must be destroyed" (215).

This apocalyptic message is the source for Haines's 1969 poem "'It Must All Be Done Over'" in *The Stone Harp*. Haines also quotes the Williams text in the essay "The Sun on Our Shoulders" in *Living Off the Country* (50). Finally, Haines returns to the ideas and the Williams text in his brief essay "Descent" (1995) in the 2010 volume by the same name (*Descent* 3–7). Haines's essay "Descent" focuses on his reading as a young poet and student in the 1950s; Williams's *In the American Grain* is certainly all-important to him, gaining, he says, "a life interest for me" (3). Haines fastens on Williams's sentence "It is imperative that we *sink*," and he connects it to his own decision to "let go, to sink into that country, accept it on its own terms, and make of it what I could" (4). Then Haines expands on his sense of the "country" he means: "Among those steep hills of birch and aspen, on the fire-scarred spruce ridges and windswept domes, in the bogs and alder-tangled creek bottoms; in the Tanana River islands, sandbars, and channels; in the early snowfall and late spring, the long nights of midwinter and the long light of midsummer—in its scattered, transitory human history also—I found my place in which to settle, in the true sense, and everything has grown from that" (4–5).

The translation of Williams's public, renegade history of American genius to Haines's personal, renegade history of an Alaskan homesteader is an important, characteristic strategy. It suggests one way in which Haines translated Williams's poetic "news" from the late love poem "Asphodel, That Greeny Flower" into the place-based poems of *Winter News*:

> It is difficult
> to get the news from poems

yet men die miserably every day
for lack
of what is found there.

In the reading I am proposing, Williams emerges in Haines's imagination as the larger-than-life poet of place, the model for Haines's own sinking into place at the Richardson homestead. That is the dual meaning of the word "settle" in Haines's sentence: "I found my place to settle, in the true sense, and everything has grown from that." Moreover, in another doubling, Haines characteristically draws a parallel between the Interior of Alaska and the interior of his imagination, just as he does in "The Writer as Alaskan." He notes that to descend means that one must then re-ascend, in his case coming out of the wild setting of Alaska and emerging from his own "interior country" (6). He relates that ascension to entering into contemporary America, "that other America" of wealth and hierarchy, the "industrial maggot" burrowing into Alaska (6–7). Ultimately, Williams's text means that Haines must renew his own "country of imagination, that knows no geographical or political boundaries, and where a writer, a poet, is free to roam, to settle and build as he can" (7). Through all of these doublings, Haines begins to find his sense of poetic place and direction. The place is at first defined as Alaska, but it does not remain a "settled" place; instead, Haines keeps redefining the place as a free, imaginative country without boundaries. The doublings thus reveal a fundamental tension in Haines's sense of place.

SINKING INTO CHINESE POETRY

In addition to the profound influence of William Carlos Williams, Haines's commitment to sinking into place by homesteading in the late 1950s and early 1960s coincides with his discovery of classic Chinese poetry. Pound's 1915 book *Cathay* was one important source for the discovery, but even more decisive is Kenneth Rexroth's 1956 translation *100 Poems from the Chinese*. Haines writes incisively about Rexroth and the Chinese influence in his short essay "Homage to the Chinese," which first appeared in a festschrift for Rexroth and was reprinted in *Living Off the Country* (120–22). In just eight resonant paragraphs, Haines describes his own isolation on the Richardson homestead in the late 1950s after his first wife had left him. As he says, "I felt out of things entirely, a long distance from anything going on in the world of letters. I had my life in the woods, and that was enough" (120). A chance reading of an essay by Rexroth about the Beat poets, followed by finding William Carlos Williams's "enthusiastic review" of Rexroth's anthology in *Poetry* magazine, led Haines to a deep study of Rexroth's translations. The effect was immediate: "It was for me a time of renewal and rediscovery. I began to write poems again, hesitating and unsure. I wrote a few things that were direct (and weak) imitations of Chinese poems as I understood them from Rexroth's versions; but these were only trials" (121). The galvanizing effect of Rexroth's anthology allowed Haines to return to his own poetry, suggesting that the Chinese poems gave him a path out of silence and pointed a way to his own voice. Indeed, Haines asserts that Chinese models abound in *Winter News*, especially the work of the eighth-century Tang poet Tu Fu. He notes qualities of simplicity, brevity, clarity, solitude, quiet, and a "direct link to nature" in this work, and he recalls feeling that all of these qualities were like "the substance of my own life. How often do we find this to be so, when the book and the life make one sound within us?" (122).

"Homage to the Chinese" in effect describes how Haines discovered his own voice by hearing it echoed in ancient Chinese poems. As he writes in concluding the essay, "It is as if in order to hear anything at all we must silence the world around us and its agitation within us" (122). By silencing the world and hearing the ancient voices of Tu Fu, the nature poet Wang Wei, and others, Haines began to hear his own voice more clearly.

The Haines archive at the University of Alaska Fairbanks contains many early experiments with Chinese poems, and it suggests some of the ways Haines learns to make the experiments into the poems of *Winter News*. In addition, the archive shows that through the early 1960s, Haines was in close contact with Robert Bly, Donald Hall, and Louis Simpson, all of whom strongly influenced his style in the poems of *Winter News*. As the early correspondence indicates, Robert Bly was an especially strong mentor for Haines. Aside from direct criticism of Haines's poems, Bly introduced Haines to the surrealist poetry of Machado, Lorca, and Pablo Neruda, all of whom opened up possibilities for his own writing. At the same time, during the years of his closest friendship with Bly, Haines discovered some of the principal subjects and themes of his early poetry: wild animals, deep time, the primary authority of the land, the "mind of winter" that Wallace Stevens knew. In his late thirties, moreover, Haines began to develop the style of his stanzas, with each stanza forming a short, complete sentence. He learned to write in short lines, and he came to understand the hoary dictum that less is more. He revised poems to make them terse, succinct, focused, and mysterious.

In a March 26, 1961, letter to Robert Bly, Haines reports on several poems he has revised, responding to Bly's commentaries. He adds the following paragraph on Chinese poems:

> These poems from the Chinese fall generally into two groups. Some, like "The Autumn Mountain," in fact most of those of Wang Wei and Li Po, are very close in feeling to the originals. Words, some of the elements have changed, but the poems are close enough that their origins could be recognized. Others, like the Li Shang-yin here, are very remote. The last poem here, "Beyond," comes out of Li Shang-yin also, but is so remote from its starting point that I didn't bother to make the reference. Of the others, "Old Men of December" and "Fountain of Old Poems" owe something to the very early Chinese. I forgot to say that "Foreboding" got its start from a poem of Li Ho [Li He], but it is not much like it. Sometimes, in the case of short poems like those of Wang Wei, I am able to relate the whole poem to my own experience. More often, it is a line, or a few lines, or just a phrase that sets me off. I find that the further I go on with it the more remote my poem is from its beginning. Well, maybe this will be interesting to you. (JHP Box 5, Folder 37)

Both the substance and tone of this letter are interesting, for they suggest that Haines was willingly working with Bly on improving his poems by translating or adapting Chinese models. In fact, Haines wrote a suite titled "Six Poems after Wang Wei," and the archives contain both worksheets and fair copies, with autograph corrections of line breaks. In addition to "Morning," "Departure," and "The Long Rain," there are three unpublished experiments in two-stanza poems. These three poems are modeled on the poems of Wang Wei, but they blend Chinese imagism with Richardson realities. Wang Wei, master poet and painter of the eighth century, was known especially for his quatrains and for his landscape paintings of mountains and rivers. Haines mentions the first (of three) poems, "The Autumn Mountain," in the letter to Bly, and the other two are similar in form, technique, and tone:

THE AUTUMN MOUNTAIN

The barren dome
has turned red and brown,
the autumn wind
has ice in its throat.

Leaning on my stick under
the heavy pack,
far below I hear the call
of a lonely moose.

THE BERRY PICKERS

Dark cranberries grow
on the northern hills,
they glisten in
the frost of a clear morning.

Come, let us pick all we can,
for soon the birds
will eat them, and snow will
bury the withered vines.

IN THE HILLS

White birches edge
the ascending path
and yellow leaves drift
in the quiet air.

There has been no rain
for many days,
but my trousers cling
in the evening mist. (JHP Box 7, Folder 2)

In all three experimental poems, Haines uses quatrains analytically: the first quatrain gives a physical description of quasi-objective details of landscape; the second brings in the speaker's humanity, feelings, and perspective.

Each line is often a self-contained clause or phrase, such as a prepositional phrase or a subject-verb clause. Enjambment, where it occurs, is not radical, staying within predictable syntactic boundaries. The diction in all three poems is clear, monosyllabic, concrete, and utterly simple. The details are Alaskan, as is the subject matter. Here we clearly see that Haines is working toward finding his own voice and subject within the classic Chinese style.

The other two poems that Haines mentions by title in the letter to Bly explore the blending of Richardson themes with Chinese poetry, and both develop new experimental forms. In "The Old Men of December," the debt to "very early Chinese" is evident in the imagery of preindustrial beggars, especially in the third stanza; Haines joins that imagery with a supple variation in stanzas:

> All grass is yellow
> on the cold frontier.
>
> We are not wolves or foxes,
> why do we wander
> desolate on this road?
>
> With crooked staff
> and begging-bowl
> we prowl the empty village—
>
> our jaws hang loose,
> we babble of the dead.
>
> By day and night,
> we greet
> the withering year. (JHP Box 7, Folder 2)

The first and last stanzas create an envelope of poverty and aging, but in the first stanza the landscape itself is yellow and cold, while in the last the old men "greet / the withering year" because they recognize its kinship with them. Even though they refuse to be compared to "wolves and foxes," the old men "prowl the empty village," unable to speak like human beings. In both relationships, Haines combines nature and culture in provocative ways. The stanzas may recall “Lineage,” but in this poem Haines works with a loose, short-lined free verse rather than Stevens’s masterful blank-verse cadences.

The five short sections of “From the Fountain of Old Poems” resemble haiku in their brevity and focus. In order to create a sequence, Haines arranges the sections in a rough chronology, following times of day: dawn, day, evening, midnight, and departure from earth.

> I
> Go, bring me
> those few white blossoms
> that tremble at
> the brink of dawn.
>
> II
> Interminable,
> the roads of the earth;
> I will not die
> before I climb
> that lonely hill.
>
> III
> Fragrance of the southwind,
> comfort my anger.
>
> Be good to me,
> flower of the evening.
>
> IV
> At midnight
> I feed the dark cattle
> and hear their horns
> against the
> stones of my grief.
>
> V
> Earth, goodbye!
> return to yourself—

> the heavy tree
> that falls and finds
> the abiding worm. (JHP Box 7, Folder 2)

As in the earlier imitations, Haines experiments with the relationship between nature and humanity, but the relationship is not treated as analytically or as statically as it is in "The Autumn Mountain" and other Wang Wei quatrains. Instead, the chronological arrangement suggests that the speaker confronts a different stage of life in the moment of each imagistic poem. The sections also suggest that different senses—such as sight, sound, and taste—connect the speaker to the landscape, but that is not a rigid scheme. Instead, the speaker's aged perspective connects the sections to form a suggestive pattern of leave-taking. The lines occasionally break off into a true enjambment, a technique that Haines rarely employs in a consistent way but one that works well in four of the five sections.

Both of Haines's two collections of retrieved manuscript poems—*Where the Twilight Never Ends* (1994) and *Of Your Passage, O Summer* (2004)—are dedicated to the Richardson homestead, to "the time, the place, and the life lived—that which gave me the poems," as he puts it in the introductory note to *Of Your Passage, O Summer*. The poems are clearly superior to anything printed in *At the End of This Summer*, and they show the great gains Haines made as a poet from the late 1950s to the publication of *Winter News* in 1966. Many of the poems could easily rank with the poems in *Winter News*, and it may be that Haines excluded them simply because of the wealth of material he had on hand for his first collection. *Where the Twilight Never Ends* includes two Chinese poems, "After Tao Yuan-Ming" and "The Long Rain." In the former, the speaker imagines sleeping in his wilderness grave, and the tone of solitude and silence matches perfectly that of many poems in *Winter News*. Other poems are beautiful observations, such as "Shadows," a poem about bats that anticipates the subject and title of the essay "Shadows" in the prose memoir *The Stars, the Snow, the Fire* (1989).[5]

Perhaps most remarkable in these poems from *Where the Twilight Never Ends* is the way in which the poet refuses to evaluate his experiences from an emotional distance and still manages not to fall prey to sentimentality. A poem like "Dead Horse Gulch" strikes that balanced tone, marking the history of horses in the Alaskan mining stampedes:

They came up from the sea,
wearing a harness of galls;
those who fell were unloaded
and pitched into the ravine.

"Departure," in which the poet reflects on the space race of the early 1960s, is just as balanced, with a blend of observation and critical acumen:

One day from an incredible distance
will come the voices from cities
plunging silently through space:

new races with armored thoughts,
machines whose remote, steering hands
stretch out between the stars,
holding the future, terrible and strange.

The speaker's critical distance from the military and technological future only emerges after he registers the "incredible distance" between the imagined space cities and our home planet. Physical reality thus opens the way to the poet's reflection on a possible future. The analytical structure of earlier experiments like "The Autumn Mountain" appears here in an altered but recognizable form.

In *Of Your Passage, O Summer*, Haines digs more deeply into the manuscripts, and the poems strongly resemble those of *Where the Twilight Never Ends*. There are several political poems, along the same lines as "Departure." Poems like "The True Shepherd," "Signs," "La Revolución," "America," "A Short History of the Republic," "The Vanishing Americans," and "Spring Evening on a Hill Above a Northern River" use the distance of a speaker at one or two removes from the subject to comment ironically on current or past events. The poems are not uniformly subtle or successful, but in all of them Haines embraces the authoritative role of the poet as a commentator on political and social realities. As Haines notes in the introductory preface, it was "an intense and foreboding time," one in which the future "seemed at certain moments seriously in peril."

A suite of five Chinese poems reaches back to the period of 1958–1960, the time in which Haines returned to writing poems after a three-year hiatus.

The formal experimentation of "The Autumn Mountain" is less mechanical or predictable in poems like "A Letter" and "Untitled," which strike a delicate tone. Moreover, it is difficult to distinguish between "political" and "Chinese" elements in a poem like "Animals in the Night":

> They move in a world not ours,
> filling the moonlight
> and open trees
> lighted by the borealis,
> feeding on frozen bark
> and the hidden blood.
>
> Night thickened with shadows,
> when we kept our fires burning
> in the dread of a field
> beyond death—
> of spirits
> waiting in cover of nightfall,
> souls of dead men
> and slaughtered beasts.
>
> Blood spills from the veins,
> the bones crack within.
> The hearts of men contract
> and have no room for ghosts
> that climb in the darkness
> beside us, going to sleep.
>
> Twilight shivers in the mind.
> A breath out of the north
> shakes the icy branches,
> and a dog's howl drifts downwind
> to the edge of the world,
>
> lost among stars.

Dated 1963, this poem fits well into a national period of intense foreboding; it creates that tone by focusing on the relationship between animals and humans in a northern landscape. The scene established in the first stanza is clearly Alaskan, marked by images of the aurora borealis and frozen bark. The "hidden blood" of predators and prey lies on the edge of vision. In the second stanza the landscape broadens into "the dread of a field / beyond death," eventually evoking an overarching apocalypse. Yet Haines contains the effects of dread within the human body and psyche, as if our bodies and souls were under siege, invaded by the ghosts who climb into bed beside us, the twilight that shivers in the mind, or a breath out of the north that shakes in the branches outside. Even the dog's howl becomes larger than a mere sound, drifting to "the edge of the world, / lost among stars." The poem enacts an effective haunting: intense dread seems to inhere in the landscape, heightened by the potential effects of a world beyond the present, despite the leaky barriers humanity creates to wall out our fears.

The poems I have been discussing suggest that Haines developed Chinese models of short, two-stanza poems into longer, more elaborate forms. But that is only part of the story. To see other lessons that Haines draws from the Chinese masters, compare the draft poem "Death in the Frost" (January 1961) to the printed version, "Dream of the Lynx," from *Winter News*:

DEATH IN THE FROST

I
The lynx in the depth of the forest
knows the depth of my heart
where the hunter springs at dusk
and his prey expires at dawn.

II
Beside a narrow trail in the blue
cold of evening the trap is sprung,
and a growling deep in the throat
tells of life risen
to the surface of darkness,
held fast in hunger.

III
The moon in my dream has the form
of those who walk by its light

and never sleep, whose yellow eyes
are certain of what they seek.

IV
Sinking, floating beneath the eyelid,
adrift on a snowy field,
I see the hairy shape of the slayer;
the shadow that crouches
hidden in a thicket of alders,
nostrils quivering,
poised at the brink of fear;
and the ever-deepening track
that follows its strange desire,
mark of the unseen, feeding host.

V
A world of midnight, death and magic,
blood of the returning victim,
light of the fading star—revealed to me
as I stalk the slow November sunrise
and, astride that reddening hill,
stand in wonder.

VI
Now by the frozen trail
life falters and listens, hears only
a distant wind,
the sigh of lifting branches,
retreating ghosts of the night.

VII
The lynx asleep at the foot of the tree
knows the depth of my heart
where the padded footfall stops,
and the caught breath
glitters in a gaze of ice. (JHP Box 8, Folder 2)

DREAM OF THE LYNX

Beside a narrow trail in the blue
cold of evening the trap is sprung,
and a growling deep in the throat
tells of life risen
to the surface of darkness.

The moon in my dream takes the shape
of animals who walk by its light
and never sleep, whose yellow eyes
are certain of what they seek.

Sinking, floating beneath the eyelid,
the hairy shape of the slayer appears,
a shadow that crouches
hidden in a thicket of alders,
nostrils quivering;
and the ever-deepening track
of the unseen, feeding host.

Haines revises masterfully in the interest of compression and reduction. The core of the printed poem "Dream of the Lynx" appears in Sections II, III, and IV of "Death in the Frost." But even in revising those three sections, the poet deletes the sixth line of II ("held fast in hunger"), changes "those" to "animals" and "form" to "shape" in III, and thoroughly rewrites IV to make seven tight lines out of the ten lines in the draft. The other material in Sections I, V, VI, and VII becomes commentary on the actual poem. Thus Sections I and VII are repetitions of the frame, connecting speaker and lynx as hunters. Section V comments on the speaker's point of view or tone, the wonder he feels for the "world of midnight, death, and magic." Section VI gives an abstract version of the moment of death, which, given the plain title, is not really necessary.

With the change in title to "Dream of the Lynx," we gain the ambiguity of whose dream it is, the poet's or the lynx's, and that appears to be the real point of connection. The first stanza describes the moment in which the lynx is caught in a snare. In the second stanza, it seems that the poet snares the lynx through dream or imagination as the lynx seeks its prey. But in the third stanza the lynx enters the poet's dream as "the hairy shape of the slayer," and it is at first unclear just which one, lynx or poet, leaves the "ever-deepening track." Who, moreover, is the "unseen, feeding host"? The draft poem reveals an underlying narrative structure: the lynx is caught in a trap at evening, the poet/trapper dreams of the lynx, at sunrise the poet/trapper goes his rounds and ultimately finds the (dying) lynx. But narrative is not the focus of "Dream of the Lynx."

The compression and reduction help the revised poem achieve several important sound effects. Haines employs persistent assonance in the poem. He uses the /i/ sound of "deep," "dream," "sleep," "seek," "ever-deepening," "unseen," and "feeding" as a musical way of emphasizing key words. The present participle, ever a marker of ongoing action, abounds in the final stanza. The fact that the assonance and participle come together in the phrase "unseen, feeding host" once again raises the question of how to read the final word of the poem. On one level, there might be a sense of host/parasite, but then the adjective "feeding" would seem misplaced. Another reading would see "host" as a synonym for "multitudes," and there could even be an ironic echo of the biblical "heavenly host." In this interpretation, the single, visible lynx multiplies into an invisible multitude, signaled by the "ever-deepening track." Section IV of "Death in the Frost" may suggest that the "mark of the unseen, feeding host" refers to the tracks left by the multitude of unseen prey, most likely mice and voles. But in still another direction of reading, could "host" even suggest the heavenly bread of communion? Instead of answering these questions, the poem ends in a haunting suspension, evoking actions that continue beyond the borders of our perception, and those effects render the experience of an intriguing, unsettling dream.[6]

THE ROAD TO *WINTER NEWS*

By any measure, *Winter News* (1966) stands as an impressive debut collection of poems, but it had quite a long foreground. Most of the poems in the book date from the early 1960s, and nearly all of them had been published in literary magazines during that time. The copyright page acknowledges fifteen separate journals for permission to republish; several are quite prestigious, including *San Francisco Review*, *Hudson Review*, *Epoch*, *Massachusetts Review*, *Kayak*, and *The Nation*. Haines was by no means unknown, then, when Wesleyan University Press published *Winter News* in its distinguished poetry series. As we have already seen, the archives indicate that Haines was both isolated and well connected during the late 1950s and early 1960s. On the one hand, as homesteaders, Haines and his second wife, Jo, were surviving on barely $500 of annual income during the 1960s, much of the money and postage stamps sent to them by Haines's mother. On the other hand, Haines was conducting a rich correspondence with a host of writers and editors, including Wendell Berry, Robert Bly, Alan Brilliant (of Unicorn Press), Donald Hall, George Hitchcock (of the *San Francisco Review* and *Kayak*), Bert Meyers, Don Olsen (of Ox Head Press), Charles Simic, Louis Simpson, William Stafford, and Henry Taylor. The network of correspondents widened and deepened over Haines's career, but already in the beginning Haines sought and found a host of strong literary connections.[7]

Several of these correspondents exercised a healthy influence on the making of *Winter News* as well as later books, like *The Stone Harp* (1971), *Twenty Poems* (1971), and *Cicada* (1977). In the early 1960s, both Robert Bly and Donald Hall encouraged Haines to submit his manuscript, which bore the working title "Floating Homeward," to Wesleyan University Press. Hall wrote to Haines on September 4, 1964, for example, saying that Bly had sent him the manuscript and that he would like Haines to submit it to Wesleyan for publication. In the letter, Hall complains about Denise Levertov's critical reading of manuscripts at Wesleyan, and then he advises Haines to work hard on cutting "a lot of clichés and dead metaphors, sloppy words with no power" (JHP Box 8, Folder 5). Likewise, Bly was writing often to Haines in the early part of the decade. He does so at length on July 17, 1965, advising Haines in detail about dropping some poems and revising many others (JHP Box 1, Folder 18). Louis Simpson, who had won a Pulitzer Prize in 1964 for *At the End of the Open Road* (Wesleyan University Press, 1963), was a third reader of the manuscript. In a letter of April 1, 1965, he advises Haines to include recent poems like "The Cave of Animals," "The Invasion," "The Traveler," and "Watching the Fire" in the book. (Haines complied.) He praises Haines for his "powerful poems" and admonishes him, "Don't worry about the book's being 'already long enough.' A book of this quality can never be too long" (JHP Box 4, Folder 27). These three poetic advisors probably exercised more influence on *Winter News* than anyone else, but editorial readers at journals in the early 1960s had offered much excellent advice and encouragement as well. A. R. Ammons, for instance, then poetry editor for *The Nation*, commented in a letter of April 10, 1963, on a half dozen of Haines's poems, accepting "South Wind" and "On the Road" (JHP Box 3, Folder 35).

The complete first typescript of *Winter News*, with annotations and revisions, gives subtitles for the four sections of the book: I. In Alaska; II. Hunting; III. Dreams; IV. Preparing for Winter (JHP Box 8, Folder 6). The subtitles set the theme for each section, but they also establish somewhat arbitrary boundaries. Thus Section III: Dreams contains "Dream of the Lynx" and "The Dream of February." Of course it is possible to read other poems in the section as dream visions, but it would be a mistake to confine the oneiric effects of Haines's poems to the third section. A poem like "Divided, the Man Is Dreaming," from Section II, evokes both dreams and hunting. Similarly, and rather obviously, the poems of the second section clearly belong "in Alaska" as much as do those of the first section, and the entire book seems to be engaged in "preparing for winter." Still, the subtitles do suggest a thematic logic to Haines's organization, and he repeats this pattern of organization in subsequent volumes of poetry, always dividing the collection into significant groupings of poems. In the published *Winter News*, however, the subtitles are omitted.

Letters from March 1963 show that the original title of the typescript, "Floating Homeward," was in fact Robert Bly's suggestion. The phrase comes from the first poem in the book, "If the Owl Calls Again," in which speaker and owl meet, fly together, and then return to their respective homes in mutual silence. Haines at first considered calling the book "This Dark Water" or "Poems for a Cold Journey," but Bly won Haines over with his overwhelmingly constructive criticism of the individual poems and the book as a whole. When Haines submitted the typescript to Wesleyan University Press in the late summer of 1963, it bore Bly's suggested title. But Wesleyan rejected the book in October 1963, a blow that Haines took personally and attributed, in a letter to Bly of December 15, 1963, to Denise Levertov being "against me" (JHP Box 5, Folder 37). The most important result of the rejection, however, was that Donald Hall, Bly, and Louis Simpson all took another turn at reading the book in 1964 and 1965. Among loose papers with drafts of poems for the revised typescript of *Winter News*, Haines has an autograph "Acknowledgement Page—(tentative)" in which he writes, "I wish to record a special debt of gratitude to Mr. Robert Bly for his help and encouragement in preparing the manuscript of this book." He also has a typed version without title, where he writes, "I wish also to thank especially Mr. Robert Bly for his criticism and encouragement in preparing the manuscript of this book" (JHP Box 8, Folder 6). On April 5, 1965, Willard A. Lockwood, director of Wesleyan University Press, wrote to Haines accepting the revised typescript and urging him to submit a clean copy for the Lamont Prize (JHP Box 3, Folder 7).

Haines notes in the essay "Homage to the Chinese" that a "careful reader" of *Winter News* can "find ample evidence of the Chinese models" (*LOC* 121), and he even cites "Saying Goodbye on the Yukon" as a specific example of a Chinese poem (122). The early drafts of this poem date from January 1961, and the poem appears on the same sheet with drafts of "Winter News" and "Break-Up" (JHP Box 8, Folder 2). The early drafts of "Saying Goodbye on the Yukon" are nearly identical to the published version, which follows the final revisions of the typescript by inserting "northern" in the first line (JHP Box 8, Folder 6). All of the drafts strike a mournful tone, preparing for an emotional winter as the speaker begins "to shape / this lonely summer." The three stanzas follow the analytical pattern of Haines's Chinese experiments: first, a description of a gently erotic spring scene, tinged with a figurative gesture of farewell; second, the addressee placed on "the long / south road," leading to a landscape where "snow never falls"; last, the speaker in "an old garden," shaping what little remains to him. In their divisions, moreover, the three stanzas enact the distance between two lovers. One must wonder, when reading this fine poem, why Haines decided to omit it from the 1993 collected poems, *The Owl in the Mask of the Dreamer*.

One of Haines's trial titles for the collection, "This Dark Water," appears as a poem in the draft typescript of "Floating Homeward." He marks the text "OMIT" and follows his own advice. But the poem itself, published in *Poetry* in January 1964, is well worth reading, especially for the overarching plainness of statement and the clear evocation of the Alaskan Interior as a place and a poetic situation:

THIS DARK WATER

Reading in another man's book
of voyages in a tropic sea

and strange thoughts
under the green silence of
an equatorial forest,
I found this passage:
"You, in the hard and bitter
north, on the exposed summit
of the world where Polaris
glitters in the forehead of a
frozen god . . ."

And it spoke to me of ourselves
here in the vast, lonely
twilight of Alaska
with the rumors of war steadily
pulsing against the hillside.

The friends we have
are few and distant,
their words reach us through
the onrushing season
like the hurried sentences
of those about to depart.

Shadows grope
among the trees outside.
An animal
crawls through the grass
to stand on hairy legs
and stare unblinking
through the window.

We have drawn in the flesh
and gripped against our bones
the warmth of our
troubled companionship. (JHP Box 8, Folder 6)

No one will claim that this poem is as tersely effective as "Winter News," but both poems function as synecdoches for the entire collection. "Winter News" is Chinese in tone and technique, and like "Saying Goodbye on the Yukon," it wraps its perspective in the coldest of northern imagery. "This Dark Water" is more discursive and "talkative," as Bly might have it. It begins with a bookish frame, quoting H. M. Tomlinson's popular travel book *The Sea and the Jungle* (1912). The quotation and second stanza together evoke the extremes of southern and northern climates, and the opening of "This Dark Water" is in that way similar to "Saying Goodbye on the Yukon." Here, however, the complex of "ourselves," the "vast, lonely / twilight of Alaska," and "rumors of war" makes the situation apply explicitly to Haines during the escalation of the Vietnam War. The last three stanzas evoke a plural speaker and situation, rendered so by friends and curious animals, but the plural friends are present only in hurried words of departure, while the plural speaker provides only "troubled companionship." Indeed, the speaker is ultimately bereft of friends and family, and even a wandering bear seems to stare "through the window" at nothing.

An omitted poem like "This Dark Water," as good as it is, makes a well-known poem like "Winter News" exceptionally bright in its cold beauties:

They say the wells
are freezing
at Northway where
the cold begins.

Oil tins bang
as evening comes on,
and clouds of
steaming breath drift
in the street.

Men go out to feed
the stiffening dogs,

the voice of the snowman
calls the white-
haired children home.

There are at least a dozen drafts of this short poem among Haines's manuscript papers, and they suggest that he worked persistently to place the elements of the poem in a rigorous, dynamic pattern. Carolyn J. Allen comments especially well on "Winter News" as using "literal references to evoke universal meanings," and her commentary illuminates the role of extreme cold in evoking death.[8] In the early drafts, Haines already has the first stanza, but he has to discover the image of the oil tins banging as the evening comes on and the cold deepens, and he at first uses the imagery of "clouds of / steaming breath" to close the poem. By bringing the two images together in the second stanza, Haines increases the power of the literal cold, so that the first two stanzas create an overwhelming sense of "Northway" as a place so cold it is emptied of human figures. The place-name clearly functions symbolically, since the literal place is a small village southeast of Richardson on the Alaska Highway. In the third stanza, the speaker finds human beings, for "Men go out to feed / the stiffening dogs," and in the fourth stanza, "the voice of the snowman / calls the white- / haired children home." There is surely another echo of Wallace Stevens here, but Allen rightly insists on the literal quality of the snowman, evoking in its voice the call of death. In some drafts, Haines at first called the children "frost-furred," but the images of "white- / haired children," like the "stiffening dogs," push the poem into the place of dreams. We are still in "the vast, lonely / twilight of Alaska," but we are also recognizably in the country of the imagination.

A LONG-SLEEPING ANIMAL PRESENCE

Animals figure strongly in the poems of *Winter News*. Nearly half of the poems in the volume focus specifically on wild animals of the Interior, animals like bear, moose, lynx, fox, and caribou. A sizable number of poems feature birds—sometimes identified, as in the case of "Prayer to the Snowy Owl," but often mentioned generically, as in "The House of the Injured" or "Victims." As we saw in "Dream of the Lynx," a second strong figure in the book is dream, especially a dream that takes the reader deep into the world of the unconscious. The two figures don't always appear together, but in some of the most powerful poems an animal takes on the imaginative force of the unconscious, becoming a psychological image as much as a physical one. That combination is Haines's singular contribution to the Deep Image school of American poetry, associated most closely in the 1960s with Robert Bly. As the *Princeton Encyclopedia of Poetry and Poetics* defines the Deep Image, "The base element of this poetry is the image, and its 'form' is a dreamlike, rather than objectively recognizable, progression of images, whose aim is not to dismantle the reader's sense of self and the world but to startle her into quiet, unwilled acts of recognition. . . . [T]he poet's inner self and the outer world become landscapes described and fused by images that treat both as physical yet highly charged phenomena."[9] In later years, animals and dreams would continue to be potent sources for Haines's poetry, but at the same time the "dreamlike progression" of the Deep Image becomes less obvious in his work.

My reading of the correspondence between Haines and Bly suggests that Haines benefited from Bly's mentoring but also resisted it. The complexities of the relationship over time are less important at this point than the sense of the relationship Haines comes to in later years. Two essays register that sense in terms that are much less angry and defensive than many of Haines's letters to Bly in the 1960s and early 1970s.[10] The first, "Robert Bly," was originally published in the *Westigan Review* in 1978 and reprinted in *Living Off the Country* (113–19). In that essay, Haines reviews Bly's work from *Silence in the Snowy Fields* (Wesleyan University Press, 1962) to *This Body Is Made of Camphor and Gopherwood* (Harper & Row, 1977). He praises the first book in terms that any writer would wish to hear: "Driving through that country, the names and places have come back to me, still fresh, given life by the grace of a poet. It is a gift, perhaps the finest a writer can make to his country" (*LOC* 114). In terms of place, country, and poetry, Haines lavishes his highest praise on Bly's first book. After that book, however, Haines finds Bly's images "stalled and static," the rhetoric overcharged with a "denunciatory tone" and a "moral fervor spoken into the silence" (114). Haines remains uneasy with Bly's public stance: "The voice of the missionary, intent on teaching, fails to reach me" (115). When he discusses more private poems in a book like *The Morning Glory* (Harper & Row, 1975), Haines offers careful praise for the poet's ability to "see and to inhabit the world, and not just to live in one's head and its imaginary ecstasies" (115–16). Like many of Bly's readers, Haines finds "a mixture of brilliance and obscurity" in the poetry, and he gravitates strongly toward the perceptive observations of the poet:

> Finally we come back to the fields, to the snow, to the deserted main streets, to the windy spaces, and to things at home. The emptiness is still there; it may never change, but it is the place where we act out whatever we can do in our lives. The porch in the summer storm, a water glass filling with rain: scattered things, watched and recorded, brought together. Much of it will seem beyond naming, ready to leave us, to fly away forever. But a few things stay, fixed in the language. And something still of potential joy in the heart that continues to search, "for we cannot remain in love with what we cannot name." (*LOC* 119)

Haines ends the paragraph and review by quoting Bly's final prose poem in *This Body Is Made of Camphor and Gopherwood*, "The Cry Going Out over Pastures." The quotation sounds like a gentle warning to Bly himself, as if the reviewer were warning Bly to stay within the transitory but namable world. After all, Haines seems to say, this emptiness is hard to understand, love, and express, but "it is the place where we act out whatever we can do in our lives." Therefore, the earth is the authentic place for poetry and for potential joy in the heart.

The second essay, "Robert Bly: A Tiny Retrospect," exists as a typescript in the John Haines Papers, and I have not found it in any published form. It dates from the 1980s, or perhaps even later, and it takes the form of an elegiac remembrance of earlier days, in keeping with the tone of Haines's other prose memoirs from that period. Haines opens the essay with the memory of first seeing Bly's magazine *The Fifties* in the fall of 1958, when he was beginning a new life with his second wife, Jo, and was embarking on his writing career with renewed commitment. He affectionately recalls Bly's letters, along with James Wright's poems and translations: "It would be difficult to exaggerate the importance of that contact for me at the time; for someone as isolated as I had been and was still to be, that correspondence, intermittent but generous, was a rare and cherished thing" (JHP Box 27, Folder 8, page 2). He also recalls the books and magazines that Bly sent to him, especially the work of Georg Trakl, Machado, and Jiménez, and how the poems brought his own situation into a newly significant light: "Reading those poems as they came to me, issue by issue and page by page, I became aware of something brooding in the sub-arctic twilight, in the long nights; nature became saturated with something like its old spiritual vitality—a long-sleeping animal presence awakened in the cold snows and the deep timbered shadows. That time will always be associated in my mind with darkness and frost, with clarity and richness; with deep reading and the slow coming together of thought and style, of word, perception, and deeply held emotion" (2). This evocative description of poetic awakening combines the real time of reading successive pages with the dream time of "old spiritual vitality." The "long-sleeping animal presence" that Bly's pages awaken in Haines's Alaskan landscape is his own imagination, his own thought and style, his own deepening awareness of vocation. Voice and place merge in the "sub-arctic twilight" to form the "long-sleeping animal presence."

As he continues his retrospect, Haines names three books as marking a poetic watershed, establishing what we now call Deep Image poetry or American Surrealism: Bly's *Silence in the Snowy Fields*, James Wright's *The Branch Will Not Break* (Wesleyan University Press, 1963), and his own *Winter News*. Almost immediately after the publication of these three books by Wesleyan University Press, he notes sardonically, "a second- and third-hand pastoral surreality manifested itself, and all kinds of people began writing poems crowded with stone and earth images and a forced imagery of darkness. Small, tousled animals were creeping out of all kinds of castles in the oaks and maples, and from little houses in the grass. Moose were sighted in the suburbs of Los Angeles, as I recall, and wolves were baited on the rooftops in San Francisco" (3). By belittling the animal presence and its effects on the landscape of cities and suburbs, Haines dismisses the work of those with "a swift talent here for seizing upon anything innovative and fresh, turning it into an item for sale and duplication" (3). The animal presence, in all its spiritual vitality, deserves special protection. For Haines, it is a highly charged and malleable imagery, evoking the vibrant otherness of the Alaska wilderness, the dream imagery of psychological depths, and the awakening of a new poetic movement in American literature.

The poems of animal presence in *Winter News* resonate with this "old spiritual vitality" in a number of ways. In "A Moose Calling," "Horns," "The Field of the Caribou," "Book of the Jungle," and "The Cave of Animals"—all from the second section, devoted to hunting—the animal is associated with sudden, forceful sounds of the rut. Roaring, thumping, bellowing animals call in the night, as much to the poet as to their potential mates. Just as often, the animal presence invades the speaker's dreams. "The Dream of the Lynx" and "The Dream of February" are good examples of that mode, as is "On the Divide":

> I am haunted by
> the deaths of animals.
>
> Their frozen, moonlit eyes
> stare into the hollow
> of my skull; they listen
> as though I had
> something to tell them.
>
> But a shadow rises
> at the edge of my dream—
>
> No one speaks;
>
> and afterwhile the cold,
> red mantle of dawn
> sweeps over our bodies.

This poem enacts the invasion of the speaker's unconscious by the animal presence, specifically by means of haunting. The imagery evokes the speaker's guilt for killing, a guilt that he cannot speak and therefore cannot appease. It is as if the animals wait at the edge of dreams for an answer they know will never come from the human dreamer. In that regard, the silence is utterly different from the unifying soundlessness of "If the Owl Calls Again." Here, on the divide between human and animal, there is no floating homeward. Instead, the fact of killing dawns like a "cold, red mantle" and "sweeps over our bodies" in a flood of awakening light. Haines marks the moment of anagnorisis with the colloquial word "afterwhile," a regional usage that disarmingly prepares for the overwhelming flood of recognition. But as in "Dream of the Lynx," the poem ends in questions rather than answers. Does "our" refer only to human beings, or, more likely, does the "red mantle of dawn" sweep over the bodies of animals and humans alike? As in "Dream of the Lynx," such ambiguity produces a richness of deeply held emotion.

As raw as many of the animal poems are, they also create a kind of spiritual vitality. A poem like "The Mole," for instance, sends signals of transcendence in the final lines, "as the rising sun slowly dries / his strange, unruly wings." Similarly, the meeting of poet and owl in the first poem of the collection, "If the Owl Calls Again," sends both figures flying away at the end, "fulfilled, floating / homeward as / the cold world awakens." It is a cold world, like that of William Carlos Williams's "Spring and All." And if deeply vital, it is a cold spirituality. Thus "The House of the Injured" begins with the literal discovery of a house in the forest, but with each stanza the discovery becomes darker, more and more surreal. The speaker smells a "suffocating odor of blood / and fur mixed with dung," then looks inside the house to see an injured bird fluttering against the walls and lunging toward the door. The bird is not simply trapped; it is nearly beat to death by its own panic:

> the beak was half eaten away,
> and its heart beat wildly
> under the rumpled feathers.
>
> I sank to my knees—
> a man shown the face of God.

Spirituality entwines with mortality. The vitality of the bird calls for the speaker's reverence, even if the worshiping poet recognizes the face of God in a beak "half eaten away."

Its beak half eaten away, the bird's silence reminds strangely of the poem "Horns." That poem focuses on the hunter calling in a rutting bull moose by rubbing an antler against a tree, imitating the sound of a rival bull polishing his antlers. That strategy does not work, at least not at first. The hunter's larger-than-life image of the "great, dark moose / . . . his eyes / on fire with the moon" does not appear until he is asleep in his old white tent. Then, as if called by the hunter's dream, the moose comes "roaring, / hoarse with rage and desire." The moose circles the camp, creating an explosion of wild sounds as he stalks by, but the hunter is still able to call him back with his horn:

> I called him back, and he came
> and stood in the shadow

not far away, and gently rubbed
his horns against the icy willows.
I heard him breathing softly.
Then with a faint sigh of warning
soundlessly he walked away.

I stood there in the moonlight,
and the darkness and silence
surged back, flowing around me,
full of a wild enchantment,
as though a god had spoken.

"Horns" is as surprising as "The House of the Injured," but in this case the surprise is consoling rather than weirdly Gothic. After three stanzas of explosive, violent sounds, the poem moves into the gentlest of silences. The moose is a figure of "wild enchantment," and like the frantic bird in "The House of the Injured," the animal presence reveals a spiritual image of divinity.

The old spiritual vitality speaks at the end of "Horns," but its power is not associated with violence or noise. In a book full of haunting silence, darkness, and cold, "Horns" strikes a telling balance. It is like the second stanza of "Divided, the Man is Dreaming," a poem that itself recalls the analytical pattern of Wang Wei. The first stanza is full of "sweat and tumult," meat and blood, the passion of killing; the second sinks into a place of rest and peace:

His other half
lies in shadow
and longs for stillness,
a corner of the evening
where birds
rest from flight:
cool grass grows at his feet,
dark mice feed
from his hands.

The old spiritual vitality is associated with wild animals, but that does not mean that it is necessarily part of hunting and killing wild animals. Instead,

Haines often moves away from the actual events of the hunting, trapping, or fishing in order to meditate more deeply on the relationship between wild animals and human beings. In that way, the animal poems of *Winter News* look forward to what we have learned to call the "more-than-human" dimensions of the earth.[11]

Those dimensions are especially apparent in "The Tundra," the final poem of *Winter News*. In four stanzas, Haines figures the subarctic tundra as the vital meeting place of humans and animals. Indeed, the tundra is itself an animal, a "living / body, warm in the grassy / autumn sun," but it exudes a mixed "odor of crushed / blueberries and gunsmoke." From the first stanza, the living place is threatened with death, and in the second stanza the "tangled lakes / of its eyes" reveal "a mirror of ice" and "frozen gut-piles" shining with a "dull, rosy light." Autumn on the tundra is the time of berries, but it is also the time of gunsmoke and gut-piles. The third stanza focuses on the "tiny campfires" of "coarse, laughing men / with their women." The wind picks up, and the campfires flare. Then, in the final stanza, the tundra seems to turn away, taking the form of a final, powerful presence:

> Full of blood, with a sound
> like clicking hoofs,
> the heavy tundra slowly
> rolls over and sinks
> in the darkness.

The power of place is at least one way to read this final image in *Winter News*, if we are persuaded that the tundra is more powerful than puny human beings laughing at their tiny campfires. But we should not neglect the crushed blueberries and gunsmoke of the first stanza, the frozen gut-piles of the second. The tundra is "full of blood," and the "clicking hoofs" specifically evoke the herds of caribou migrating across the tundra. In the manuscripts for the poem, Haines titled it "The Battlefield," and it may be that there is no clear victor in the place—only the struggle between the old vitality of wild animals and the newer vitality of the hunters. Such is the place that Haines creates in the poems of *Winter News*—tied to the physical landscape but evoking an ambiguously apocalyptic, inclusive place of darkness.

CHAPTER 2

INSIDE AMERICA

A New Poetry of the Earth

THE PLACE OF CONVICTION

In the opening paragraph of the 1978 essay "Robert Bly," John Haines starkly defines the particular difficulties of being a contemporary American poet: "It is hard to stay awake inside America, hard to stay alive. The soul feels empty there. After the sleep of ice, the buffalo hunt, the big plow, and the house on the plains, we walk around in our yards, survey our fences. The soul comforts itself with work, with business, with crop production, with money, and alcohol; it falls asleep at night before a dream, paid for and stale" (*LOC* 113). The particular duty of the poet is to remain awake somehow, but the fenced-in yards of contemporary America limit the poet's vision. Haines evokes a sweeping historical narrative in the catalog, reaching from "the sleep of ice" to the present, a sketch of imperialistic, continental conquest.

Perhaps more profoundly, however, the paragraph evokes the dream-like opening of Ralph Waldo Emerson's "Experience":

> Where do we find ourselves? In a series of which we do not know the extremes, and believe that it has none. We wake and find ourselves on a stair; there are stairs below us, which we seem to have ascended; there are stairs above us, many a one, which go upward and out of sight. But the Genius which, according to the old belief, stands at the door

> by which we enter, and gives us the lethe to drink, that we may tell no tales, mixed the cup too strongly, and we cannot shake off the lethargy now at noonday. Sleep lingers all our lifetime about our eyes, as night hovers all day in the boughs of the fir-tree. All things swim and glitter. Our life is not so much threatened as our perception. Ghostlike we glide through nature, and should not know our place again.[1]

For Emerson, the struggle to remain awake is a fundamental fact of human consciousness, but Haines connects the struggle more specifically to being "inside America." The story of American Manifest Destiny brings us to a never-ending series, like Emerson's stairs, but in Haines's version the series is made up of work, business, crops, money, and alcohol. The dreamy, grieving lethargy in Emerson's figure becomes, in Haines's view, a stale purchase. Emerson's last sentence is closest to Haines's vision of contemporary America. The effect of a suburbanized world is to make us glide ghostlike through nature, and we do not know our place because every place resembles every other. For Haines, the narrative of material progress and conquest declines into displacement and emptiness.

Inside contemporary America, all things swim and glitter. Much of Haines's biographical narrative can strike a reader as a restless search for place. In the late summer of 1969, Jo and John Haines sold their Richardson homestead and left Alaska for California. Haines left Alaska for the bigger arena of America, and he did so with a strong record of recent success. He had won a Guggenheim Foundation Fellowship in 1965, enabling him to finish his first book of poems. *Winter News* had come out the following year in the prestigious poetry series published by Wesleyan University Press, and the year after that Haines won a fellowship from the National Endowment for the Arts, making steady progress on a second book of poems, *The Stone Harp* (1971). In 1969, just as he was preparing to leave the state, Haines was named Poet Laureate of Alaska. As Emerson's staircase warns, however, the professional successes did not translate into a new kind of genius. By the end of 1970, Haines had divorced Jo and suddenly married a third wife, Jane McWhorter, though he lived only a few months with her and her four children. Over the decade of the 1970s, Haines lived in Pacific Grove, California; Anchorage, Alaska; Indianola, Washington; Missoula, Montana; and York, England. His residency and employment in all of these places were intermittent. He rented it. "By 1980, he had returned as a renter to Richardson and made the homestead and Missoula his quasi-permanent homes. In many ways, Haines seems to glide ghostlike through the decade of the 1970s, and he never again finds a fully permanent place—in Alaska or anywhere else.[2]

Despite the personal turmoil and unsettled life, Haines was immensely productive as a writer during the late 1960s and 1970s. In 1971, he published his second book with Wesleyan University Press, *The Stone Harp*, and that same year the prestigious publisher Unicorn Press brought out Haines's *Twenty Poems*. In 1974, Kayak Press published his *Leaves and Ashes*, and in 1976 Smokeroot Press published a chapbook, *In Five Years' Time*. Just a year later, Haines published a third major volume with Wesleyan University Press, *Cicada*. In that same year, 1977, Scott Walker's Graywolf Press brought out the limited edition of new poems, *In a Dusty Light*. These six books of poetry together represent Haines's journey from the work of *Winter News* to a broader and deeper engagement with contemporary America.

In notes he wrote for a tape recording of poems from *The Stone Harp*, made on July 2, 1970, Haines describes this new engagement in an interestingly provisional way:

> The poems contained in *The Stone Harp* begin more or less where *Winter News* ended and move from there through contemporary life as it has been experienced by someone who has shared inwardly in the general life of the latter half of the 1960s while living mostly at some physical distance from the actual events. . . . You might say *The Stone Harp* is a more outward book, though for me that would not be a good description. *The Stone Harp* could be said to describe a larger world, one which includes the world of *Winter News*, as a background, a source, perhaps even as a destination.[3]

Haines at first offers a characteristic tension between an intimate position inside America and his deeper sense of distance from actual events. Then he proposes the "more outward" description of *The Stone Harp*, only to retract and correct it. In the final sentence, he merges the "larger world" of the new poems with the world of the Richardson homestead, and he includes the homestead as "a background, a source, perhaps even as a destination." Thus

Haines's poetry opens up to a larger world in the 1970s, but it also keeps the imaginative possibility of the homestead as a place to which the poet can return.

The concept of place as background, source, and destination resonates strongly in Haines's writings. He describes *The Stone Harp* in similar terms in draft material for the essay "Roots," first published in *Quarry West* in 1972 and reprinted in *Living Off the Country*. Characteristically, he sees *Winter News* as rooted in a "physical place, but also an inner personal place," while the second book "shows me leaving that place, in more than one sense. The reality, let's say, was breaking up; I couldn't continue to pretend to myself that I was a hunter and trapper, nor did I believe in myself as Richardson's greatest living poet. My fame extended for thirty miles in one direction, and a hundred in another. I was becoming something else. And if the book presents a more fragmented vision, it is because the essential transitions in it couldn't be honestly disguised" (JHP Box 9, Folder 20). In the final version of the essay, Haines develops the idea of place as more than a geographical location: "The work, and the life, must have their origin in a place of conviction for the poet. It may be an entirely imaginary place invented for the poem, but it is nonetheless true. . . . It is a known place, full of meaning for the poet. What he is and does takes its vitality from that place, that certainty. The work itself may be a search for that place, an approach to it, or even an exit from it into or toward a more substantial reality" (*LOC* 85). The six books of the 1970s represent Haines's search for this place of conviction. Indeed, the search for the place of conviction operates centrally in Haines's thinking for the rest of his writing career.

The Stone Harp clearly reflects the tensions that arise from Haines's search for the place of conviction. The forty-five poems are presented in three sections of fifteen poems each, but this symmetrical order contrasts with the prevailing themes of decay, rebellion, apocalypse, and war. For example, the first section, "In Nature," begins with several poems set in Alaska—and animals in poems like "Lemmings" and "Wolves" project the kind of spiritual vitality that Haines develops in the animal poems of *Winter News*. In addition, place and its connections to deep time play significant roles in "On Banner Dome," "The Train Stops at Healy Fork," and "Choosing a Stone." All of these poems, however, develop a strong sense of the speaker's alienation and loss. The landscape of "On Banner Dome," for example, is powerfully evocative but threatening:

> The sunlight is never warm
> in such a place; to sleep there
> is to dream that the ropes
> that hold you to earth are letting go,
> and around the straining tent
> of your life there prowls and sniffs
> a fallen black star who overturns
> stones and devours the dead.

In this poem, as in the others, nature provides no pastoral escape. Indeed, the poem "In Nature" characterizes the natural landscape as a mirror image of human displacement: "Here too, neighborhoods / in revolt, revengeful columns; / evenings at the broken wall, / black armies in flight. . . . " The poem describes insects as human beings, and the clear implication is that human beings are no more (or less) significant than insects.

The title poem, "The Stone Harp," necessarily functions as a synecdoche for the entire book. The image figures the earth as a musical instrument, the strings being the telephone wires strung along the Richardson Highway near the homestead. But as Haines describes the scene in the 1976 essay "Poems and Places," the initial images of the harp and road open up dramatically, for the road "always seemed to me to be more than a state highway; a trail, a passage between Asia and America, flown over by birds, traveled by men and beasts long before the highway crews carved the hillsides and laid down their gravel and tar" (*LOC* 127). In Haines's imagination, the highway becomes a place for human and animal migrations, movements that occur over millennia, within deep time. Moreover, Haines insists on connecting the ancient road to the present world and its temporal concerns: "What else? There were events in the world beyond Mile 68. The Vietnam War was spoken of more and more. Men were going west by ship and plane to fuel and fight that war" (127). Finally, too, the ancient stone harp seems to require a bardic poet, perhaps a Scandinavian *skald* or Old English *scop*—"someone who might speak of these things in an adequate voice" (127).

The three figures of road, harp, and poet dominate "The Stone Harp," dividing the six stanzas into three movements. In the first stanza, the road at first appears to be the literal highway, but the image quickly turns to the figurative and visionary. The figuration leads to the next two stanzas, in which the sound of the harp becomes predominant:

> A road deepening in the north,
> strung with steel,
> resonant in the winter evening,
> as though the earth were a harp
> soon to be struck.
>
> As if a spade
> rang in a rock chamber:
>
> in the subterranean light,
> glittering with mica,
> a figure like a tree turning to stone
> stands on its charred roots
> and tries to sing. (1–12)

The key to the three stanzas may be the word "deepening." The road deepens in the north, and its resonance deepens as the first stanza becomes more and more figurative. Then the image of the earth-harp causes the figuration to deepen still further, plunging into the "rock chamber" and the "subterranean light." It is as if the poem were digging more and more deeply below the surface into the depths of the earth, finding the "charred roots" of the telephone pole, "like a tree turning to stone." The figure "tries to sing," but the implication is that it cannot.

The song requires a singer, as the harp requires a harpist. In the second half of the poem, Haines turns first to the sunset, evoking the war in the imagery of "all this blood / flowing into the west" (13–14), but as the sun sinks below the horizon, he finds the poet:

> And the only poet is the wind,
> a drifter
> who walked in from the coast
> with empty pockets.
>
> He stands on the road
> at evening, making a sound
> like a stone harp
> strummed
> by a handful of leaves . . . (17–25)

By naming the poet as the wind, or, rather, by insisting that the wind is the "only poet," Haines implies that the human voice pales in comparison to the sounds of the stone harp. But the Aeolian bard is a vagabond, "a drifter," and the sound that the poet makes becomes ever more figurative as the poem ends. Does that resolute figuration suggest, in fact, that the poet remains behind the poem, strumming the strings?

If "The Stone Harp" confers great power both on the poet and on the earth, it also seems to suggest that an even greater power might emerge from the combined force of the two. That is only a suggestion in *The Stone Harp*, but it becomes a conviction in later volumes. The problem in *The Stone Harp* appears to lie in the "fragmented vision" that Haines identifies in the drafts of the essay "Roots." While there are many fine poems in the book, the three sections do not create a sense of cumulative power and meaning. Even the first section, "In Nature," includes some comparatively weak poems about garden plants ("Cauliflower," "Marigold," and "Dried Poppy"). The second section, "America," focuses on political and social themes of revolution, materialism, racism, environmental waste, and government corruption. Three poems in particular address environmental issues: "The Legend of Paper Plates," "Dream of a Cardboard Lover," and "The Dollhouse." The section ends with two poems, "Poem Like a Grenade" and "From the Rooftops," that claim for poetry the power to "topple a government" or "take aim at the State." Unfortunately, none of the poems in the section attains the necessary authority for such claims, in part because of weak personifications.[4]

In the last section, "Signs," the required authority stems from more indirect treatments of these ideas. In "The End of the Street," for instance, the first stanza depicts a wintry cityscape, dominated by "the ruins of / a dynamited water tower" (5–6), then turns to a terse direct address:

> The car is out of gas;
> someone has gone to look.
>
> Your evening is here. (7–9)

That restrained warning verges on wry irony, a tone that recurs in other poems near the end of the volume. Poems like "Dürer's Vision," "The Middle Ages," and "The Wreck" set America of the Vietnam era within the context of European cultural history, implying that we are nearing the end of an apocalyptic narrative. Plain-spoken yet indirect poems like "Awakening," "The Turning," and "Cranes" end the book effectively because the earth confers authority upon the speaker, rather than the other way around, and the speaker responds with genuine humility. "The Turning" is especially resonant, partly because it deeply echoes "On Banner Dome" and "The Stone Harp." The first section of the poem describes a bear loping on a wooded road in front of the speaker then suddenly turning to disappear "with a sound like a sudden / shifting of ashes" (3–4). In the second section, the speaker turns to his own story, but the story echoes the sound of the bear and the wind:

> The wind thawing in a northern
> forest opened a leafy road.
>
> As I walked there, I heard
> the tall sun burning its dead;
> I turned and saw behind me
> a charred companion,
> my shed life. (9–15)

The "charred companion" recalls the sound of the bear, like shifting ashes, and the bear image echoes the "fallen black star" of "On Banner Dome." In addition, the road immediately recalls Haines's reflections on the "road deepening in the north" in "The Stone Harp." Indeed, reflection is the signal strength of all three poems, and that strength extends to others in the volume.

Given these readings, the poem "'It Must All Be Done Over'" achieves an especially deep resonance. As I noted earlier, the title echoes William Carlos Williams's essay "Descent," and the poem directly quotes the sentence from the last paragraph of Williams's essay: "However hopeless it may seem, we have no other choice: we must go back to the beginning; it must all be done over; everything that is must be destroyed" (*In the American Grain* 215). Because Haines interprets Williams's idea of descent or sinking as a way to settle into place, he finds in the image of necessary destruction a perpetual renewal, especially as a way of finding the place of conviction. All of these ideas of sinking into place come out strongly in the poem:

The houses begin to come down,
the yards are deserted,
people have taken to tents
and caravans, like restless cattle
breaking stride,
running off with their wagons
under a rumbling cloud.

There are too many stories,
rumors, and shadows;
like hordes of grasshoppers
they eat up the land,
columns of brutal strangers.

I leave my house to the wind
without baggage or bitterness;

I must make my life into
an endless camp,
learn to build with air,
water, and smoke . . .

The first stanza echoes the constrained, fenced-in yards of the "Robert Bly" essay, but here Haines portrays a post-apocalyptic scene of destruction already in progress. The houses and yards are being swept away, the people have already taken to tents and caravans, and they are running off with their wagons. There may be some sardonic wit in the comparison to "restless cattle," but the fact that the cattle are "breaking stride" evokes a certain liberty from constraint. The descent from a fixed life becomes most clearly positive in the last two stanzas, in which the speaker willingly leaves his house to the wind and makes his life into "an endless camp." In place of houses, he will learn to build with "air, / water, and smoke," the most immaterial of material things. It is no accident that the wind reappears, echoing the image of the wind as the only poet, "a drifter," in "The Stone Harp." The search for place thus becomes a search for a place of conviction, a place the poet can take with him anywhere, and "an endless camp" figures the place as open to perpetual renewal and movement.

The most successful poems in *The Stone Harp* combine at least three places. First, they locate themselves "inside America," or they gesture toward the large arena of social and political upheaval that marked America in the 1960s and 1970s. In addition, they give a sense of local, concrete place as the situation of the poem, often describing or implying the vast natural arena of Alaska. Last, they use the particular sensibilities of the poet's imagination to bring those two places together within the poem, characteristically in the form of figurative transactions or transitions from outer to inner worlds. Finally, the three places confer a sense of the poet's search for a place of conviction, even if that place remains elusive at the end of the poem.

These strategies appear as poetic principles in the headnote to Haines's essays in the section "Poets and Poetry" in *Living Off the Country*. In just three paragraphs, Haines argues that contemporary poetry takes on a necessarily "political color" and that the poet exercises an important cultural function inside America: "But whether we are concerned with war and peace, overpopulation, the disappearance of wilderness, pollution of the environment, or simply the survival of life on earth, we are confronted daily with decisions that must be made on a political level. The actual execution of these decisions is not, of course, within the grasp of the poet; but by an inner participation we may give these realities an imaginative or ideal existence, a life in spirit and thought, without which the more practical, day-to-day life of the culture will lack depth and meaning" (*LOC* 63). The catalog of political themes begins with the Vietnam War, but it expands to include four major environmental crises. Haines is clear in defining "political" as more than "the old politics of party and faction," and the poet's role is to deepen in "spirit and thought" the realities facing America in the 1970s. In fact, Haines is theorizing an early idea of what we now call ecopoetry, just as *Winter News* and *The Stone Harp* include visionary experiments in environmental poetry. Without any doubt, Haines's place of conviction has a decidedly environmental cast, one that bespeaks an active engagement between the poet and American culture.[5]

The volume *Twenty Poems*, published by Alan Brilliant's Unicorn Press in 1971, resembles *The Stone Harp* in structure and tone, and in its best moments it moves toward a similar place of conviction. Divided into three sections, the book opens with eight poems set in Alaska. The specificity of place gives a decided strength to many of these poems, and they use the indirect approach of "The Stone Harp" or "The Turning" to give an imaginative life to political realities. In "The Pitcher of Milk," for instance, the poet describes "the peace of this mist" as it mingles with the mist of battlefields and the smoke from "the homesteader's clearing." Homesteaders come to the doors of their cold houses and stand "with our brimming bowls, / called to where Peace awakens / in a cloud of white blood." The landscape of this poem is both physically literal and concretely figural: the mists and smoke, along with the brimming bowls, give birth to an allegorical figure that does not seem at all far-fetched. Like the homesteaders, we are called to witness a vision. Other poems in the first section, like "A Winter Light," "The Invaders," and "The Man Who Skins Animals," are as strong as any individual poem in *The Stone Harp*, and they create a singular, cumulative power within the context of a short book. "The Goshawk" is perhaps the only weak poem in the first section, mainly because the speaker turns out to be a scared little rabbit, causing the poem to veer too close to sentimentality.

The second section of *Twenty Poems* focuses on the advent of spring. It features no charismatic fauna like moose or bear; instead, the poems portray the renewal of the season through descriptions of flowers, mushrooms, and insects. None of the poems in this section creates the kind of complex combinations we find in the first part of the book, and several seem as fanciful and light in tone as "The Goshawk." The third section includes at least two weak poems, unfortunately the last two in the book, but it also presents two interesting ekphrastic poems that are signals of important work to come. "Ryder" describes the painting "Jonah" (1885) by American artist Albert Pinkham Ryder (1847–1917), while "Klee" presents a composite portrait of the Swiss painter Paul Klee (1879–1940). For Haines, with his academic training as a painter and sculptor, the two poems form a diptych, presenting two versions of the artist. Ryder's "Jonah" is a dark, mystical vision of divine power. The only source of light comes from the moon, "a pale horse of torment flying." The role of the visionary artist also appears to be a torment, as does "the shoal of a broken world." In "Klee," by contrast, Haines creates a blend of exotic and domestic images, alluding to the Swiss painter's breakthrough to color and abstraction on a trip to Tunis in 1914. Klee's "Tunisian patch" leads to other paintings, and "there are also disasters at sea, / compasses gone wrong." But unlike the vision of the tormented prophet/ artist in "Ryder," the last stanza of "Klee" turns to an entirely comic vision: "only because of a gentle / submarine laughter, / no one is drowning." Perhaps, then, these two figures of the artist stand for two kinds of poetry that exist side by side, even in a short volume like *Twenty Poems*. Both "Ryder" and "Klee" work in abstract, dreamlike forms, but Haines's desire to provoke "a gentle / submarine laughter" may account for poems like "Spilled Milk" and "The Goshawk."

THE PRODIGIOUS SEARCH OF APPEARANCES

My commentary on "Ryder" and "Klee" might suggest that I am biased against humorous, domestic, or personal poems and that I consider the only true poet to be some apocalyptic, visionary drifter who comes traveling on a godly whirlwind. But I am actually trying to take Haines on his own terms, even at their most demanding. In an incisive essay from 1975, "The Hole in the Bucket," Haines begins with a bold claim: "American poetry lacks ideas" (*LOC* 64). Always willing to provoke, especially in book reviews, essays, and letters, Haines also manages to make the claim more nuanced and persuasive as he proceeds:

> By "idea" I mean, among other things, some kind of conviction about the world and the place of poetry in it. It is an insight, let's say, that makes of experience and perception a particular way of seeing: what we sometimes call the poet's "vision." The insight may come as a sudden revelation, but it is more likely to be achieved slowly as a result of simply living and responding to things in the world, of reading and thinking, and of the daily work of writing poems and thinking about writing poems. After a while, if one is lucky, some pattern emerges; the substance of one's efforts begins to be clear. The process is all one piece, one way of being. And the value of the idea, once it is formed, is that it furnishes the means by which, in a world lacking unity, all that the poet sees and feels has meaning. Things fall into place. Every writer of poems seeks to accomplish something like this in single poems, or it seems to me that we would not write them at all. The task is to go beyond the single lucky poem, or even the single gift of a volume, and by a vigorous kind of self-exploration and a "prodigious search of appearances" (Wallace Stevens) develop and extend the meaning of the insight. (*LOC* 65)

For Haines, the "idea" organizes an entire career of writing, even as it develops over the years of that career. It is not a unifying thesis so much as an emerging pattern that shapes the writer's work. There is plenty of room for extraneous poems, even extraneous volumes of poems, but if the poet is extremely lucky and extraordinarily vigorous, she or he will create an overarching "conviction about the world and the place of poetry in it." This last phrase approximates, in its terminology and in its idea, the "place of conviction" Haines describes in "Roots."

Haines's conviction about place and the place of conviction form a core idea in his mature work, both poetry and prose. They also provide a standard for considering the relative success of a single poem, a volume of poems, and a career of writing. That is already the implicit standard I have used in discussing *Winter News*, *The Stone Harp*, and *Twenty Poems*. Haines makes the standard explicit in "Hole in the Bucket," and even though it is not the exclusive standard for judging the value of poems, it can be a good way to read Haines's work. As a critic, he is opposed to "the thinness, sameness, and dullness of so many contemporary poems," for he finds them "generated by a sporadic and shallow response to things, and not within the context of a unified outlook on life" (*LOC* 64). In addition to depth of thought and feeling, as well as skill with language, Haines demands that the significant poem deliver "the very sure sense that the moment we enter the world of the poem we are participating in another episode of the myth-journey of humankind; that a voice has taken up the tale once more" (70). The voice we hear in such a poem, he claims, is "at once contemporary and ancient" (71). Judged by such standards, Haines's first three volumes of poetry are sporadically brilliant, with moments of insight that attain the level of the "idea" or vision. Individual poems evoke the myth-journey of humankind, and the volumes in general seem to be moving in the direction of a career-long conviction about the world and the place poetry should occupy in it. But there is really no clear pattern of progress from one volume to the next. If Haines engages in vigorous self-exploration and a "prodigious search of appearances," his poems are most compelling when they combine those two modes to form a poetic place of conviction.

Leaves and Ashes (1974), Haines's fourth book of poems, follows the pattern established in the first three volumes. Published by Kayak Press as a small book, it distributes thirty-five poems in three untitled sections. The first section includes eleven poems, several of which are set in Alaska. The second section features seven poems, none particularly memorable. The third section presents fifteen poems, and while the quality is uneven, there are several poems that deserve notice. Perhaps most important, however, is the way that *Leaves and Ashes* consistently returns to the figure of the "prodigious search." The search takes place in the Alaska wilderness and in suburban houses, in physical landscapes and in dreamscapes, in figures that merge natural and human images. The first poem in the book, "The Ghost Hunter," speaks out of deep time, "the time of ice / and empty bellies," but the ghost hunter also stands in the present world, another poetic drifter: "I have come to this trampled ground / to stand all night in the wind / with a hollow bone in my hand." In the richly evocative poem "The Stone Bear," the speaker finds the remains of a sculpted stone bear on a gravestone, and in the second part of the poem he becomes the bear, sinking into "a grey shadow world" and becoming "in isolation, certainty and power / . . . / this hurt and hungry beast." In the third part of the poem, the speaker leaves the graveyard, feeling within himself "an aging strength" and vowing to live "in a wind spilling down / from wintry pastures." The search expands beyond Alaska, beyond nature, and beyond isolation; Haines continually places the search within contrasting temporal contexts. For example, the changing landscapes of Oregon figure strongly in "Men against the Sky," "The Oregon Coast," and "There Are No Such Trees in Alpine, California." In all three poems, the poet's recovery of a vanished past determines the description of the contemporary landscape of Oregon and "the leveled wreck / of California."

The consistent use of architectural imagery provides another measure of Haines's idea in *Leaves and Ashes*. The imagery recalls the essay "Robert Bly" and Haines's "inside America" narrative of continental pioneers declining into suburban backyards. In the third section, perhaps the strongest of the book, poems like "The Ravine," "The Tree That Became a House," "Circles and Squares," "Peter's Start," "Jane's Dream," "The Chase," and "March" present houses and rooms as confinements, an ever-present "prison and shelter," as the speaker of "The Ravine" calls "our house." Windows are dark or vacant; walls form tombs or boxes. Even a washing machine becomes a confining image, hiding a ghostly whale that comes out at night to roam the sleeping household:

Alone in the kitchen darkness,
looking through steamy windows
at the streets draining away in fog;

watching and listening,
for the wail of an unchained buoy,
the steep fall of his wave.

("The Whale in the Blue Washing Machine" 13–18)

If it is tempting to criticize the third section for repetitious, oversimplified, binary ideas, it is also worth remembering that *Leaves and Ashes* is still a relatively early book in Haines's career, appearing just eight years after *Winter News*. At the end of the decade, in both *Cicada* (1977) and *In a Dusty Light* (1977), Haines achieves a much stronger balance between vision and variety. Before such strengths, however, we must acknowledge the weakest collection of Haines's poems, the chapbook *In Five Years' Time* (1976). Fifteen poems, eleven previously published in magazines, appear in no particular order. Haines eventually reprinted nine of these in the 1993 collected poems *The Owl in the Mask of the Dreamer* in a section titled "Interim: Uncollected Poems from the 1970s." Perhaps the best one can say about the chapbook is that it includes a poem like "Tar," certainly the closest Haines ever came to an environmentalist rant and one of the nine poems retrieved in "Interim."

The third book that Haines published with Wesleyan University Press, *Cicada* both consolidates and advances the poet's prodigious search for a place of conviction. The draft materials for the book show that Haines was once again attempting to distribute the poems in thematic sections. One organizational scheme names four sections as "I: Personal," "II: People," "III: Impersonal/Abstract," and "IV: Family—Others." Another titles the four sections "I: Sleep and Death," "II: Family," "III: People/lovers," and "IV: Divergence." A third scheme titles the first section "from *Leaves and Ashes*" but gives no title for the other three sections (JHP Box 12, Folder 6). In the published version, the four sections are untitled. The book begins with a synecdochic title poem, "Cicada," and the first two sections reprint twenty poems from *Leaves and Ashes*. The only new poem, not reprinted from *Leaves and*

Ashes, is the beautiful lyric "Poem about Birch Trees." The third section is at best an interlude, gathering ten personal poems addressed to stepchildren and a lover. The fourth section, however, collects some of Haines's best work of the decade, combining personal and visionary styles in a coherent group of thirteen poems. In particular, the last five poems are new, and they show Haines actively renewing his search for the place of conviction.

The title poem, "Cicada," experiments with ideas of order, figuration, and organization, forecasting some of Haines's central formal concerns in the book. In theme, the poem strikes a note of renewal, somewhat akin to Section II of *Twenty Poems*. The renewal is related to the cicada's "song / of the absent and deaf" (2–3), and it is also related to the transformation from nymph to adult: "something I was, / something I might become" (10–11). Finally, it is related to sex and communion:

> I wanted wings and a voice,
>
> my own tree to climb,
> and someone else to answer,
> clear across
> loud acres of sun. (17–21)

At the close, the merging of sight and sound fits perfectly with the several kinds of renewal, perhaps most deeply with the renewed desire to sing at all. From the absent and deaf, the poem moves to loud acres of sun. If the speaker is a representative cicada, then, he is also a representative poet seeking an audience. Thus the fundamental hybridity of the poem is both synecdochic and significant, not least for its evocation of an ecopoetic vision.

As the title poem suggests, *Cicada* marks a significant stage in Haines's continuing search for a new focus in his poetry. In answering an author's questionnaire for Wesleyan University Press, he makes several important statements about the new volume. There are fundamental continuities with earlier work, as in the "conflict I have felt often between the part of me that has clung to the wilderness experience, and that other part of me absorbed with the difficulties of living among people in an urban world" (JHP Box 17, Folder 38). There are characteristic interests, such as dream and memory, which the volume shares with earlier work. There is also the focus on "the landscapes, the places we stand on, and our relation to the world we live in. The images that return to me again and again are those of the natural world, to which we owe our lives and deaths. If there is any salvation in our time, it may be found there in what remains to us of the wilderness, still fresh and full of meaning" (JHP Box 17, Folder 38). In the last paragraph of the statement, Haines gives a still more cohesive and significant account of the new work:

> It seems to me there is a poetry to be written in our time, though hardly written yet, that we might call a poetry of the earth, though that may sound too portentous. There are vast areas of our lives, and events in the world around us, which find little space in our poems. Places on our maps, things by which we are moved and dominated, and for which there are no words, or the words written are inadequate. Our poetry in recent years has been dominated by a subjectivity which, however necessary it may have been initially, has become so trivialized as to be nearly unreadable. The landscape inside our heads is much the same everywhere; but when the personal preoccupations common to all of us can be cleared away, the world outside—of individuals, the wilderness, the earth itself—gives us a fit subject to write of. (JHP Box 17, Folder 38)

Given this statement of purpose, the title poem "Cicada" suggests a new poetry of the earth, one that seeks to describe a new place for poetry and a new role that poetry might fill. The speaker is not subjective but a voice for "the world outside" or for "the earth itself."

The hybrid, four-part organization of *Cicada* is not an unqualified formal success, but the first two sections present some strong poems from *Leaves and Ashes*. The first section leads with "The Incurable Home," the last poem in Section I of *Leaves and Ashes*. "The Incurable Home" presents a claustrophobic nightmare within a "house of wood," the speaker bound on a "bed of wood" and the air smelling of "damp leaves and ashes." Whatever peace might lie in the final image of "the far country of sleep" seems very distant indeed.[6] Several poems appear in the same order as in *Leaves and Ashes*: "Skagway" (earlier titled "The Skagway Houses"), "The Mirror," "The Stone Bear," "Goodbye to the Flowerclock," "Men against the Sky," and "Dusk of the Revolutionaries." In addition, "There Are No Such Trees in Alpine, California" is another poem from the first section of *Leaves and*

Ashes, appearing in nearly the same sequence as the earlier book. Section II reprints ten poems from *Leaves and Ashes*, all but the sophomoric "The Windsock" taken from the third section of the earlier book. As in *Leaves and Ashes*, Section II develops the architectural imagery of confinement in a nearly relentless sequence of poems. Near the end of the section, "The Weaver" relieves the claustrophobia through the image of the poet's stepdaughter weaving "this house and the dusk / into one seamless, deepening cloth," but that beautiful image provides only a brief respite.

Some of the poems in Section III of *Cicada* may be thought of as similar respites. After all, it is part of any poet's mandate to write enduring love poems, and Haines is capable of writing very fine lyrics in that mode. "The Hermitage," in *The Stone Harp*, is a lament for a lost love, perhaps addressed to the poet's second wife, Jo. "Love among the Oranges," the last poem in *Twenty Poems*, is most likely addressed to Haines's third wife, Jane McWhorter. "Diane of the Roadways," in *Leaves and Ashes*, is probably addressed to a young woman, Diane Smith, whom Haines met in the early 1970s. In *Cicada*, Haines also publishes six poems to a woman named Daphne, creating a well-developed love sequence that tells a narrative of attachment, fulfillment, and loss.[7] While these lyrics are often affecting, they do not rise to Haines's level of an "idea" or vision. We might best think of them as domestic or occasional, and in that sense they are much like Haines's poems for his stepchildren. At worst, they seem to express the "sporadic and shallow response to things" that Haines critiques in contemporary American poetry (*LOC* 64). In any case, how they fit with a new poetry of the earth is far from clear.

The poems of Section IV differ from those of the Section III interlude in their greater focus and coherence, as if the poet were summoning up his imaginative vision to renew the prodigious search for a place of conviction and to create a new poetry of the earth. The section includes a variety of poems, from the elegies "Arlington" and "Certain Dead" to the love lyric "The Lake in the Sky," first collected in *Leaves and Ashes*. Haines also places "Circles and Squares" in the section, one of the best poems from the last section of *Leaves and Ashes*. Perhaps most important, he prints two powerfully dark poems inspired by the energy crisis of 1973–1974, "Driving through Oregon (Dec. 1973)" and "Things." Haines thought highly enough of these two poems to include them in the 1977 volume *In a Dusty Light*. Like "At

White River," he retitled "Things" for the 1993 volume of collected poems, *The Owl in the Mask of the Dreamer*, calling it "Rolling Back."

In "Driving through Oregon," the narrative begins with a realistic description of New Year's Eve on the road, the "gas pumps dry." But the narrative then moves into the poet's imagining a landscape of "the country we knew / before the cities came," a landscape that opens into an imagined journey to the end of the road, "past the rainy borders of Canada, / the wind-shorn taiga, / to the shore of the Great White Bear." On the imagined shore of the Arctic Ocean, the poet stops to regard "the last well / drained for a spittle of oil." Then his mind returns to the present scene, to Oregon on New Year's Eve, "deep in a continent vacant and dark." As in the Oregon poems from *Leaves and Ashes*, Haines juxtaposes contrasting visions of place and time, and his imagination bridges the gap between them in order to bring us to a moment of recognition. In "Things," Haines combines sharp, cutting intelligence and blunt statement: "the land will not forgive us." Since we are inside America, we may hide our sense of recognition in "a house at ease, a calm street / to walk on, and a sunset / in which the fire means us no harm," but finally we will awaken, with the deepest alarm, to our real place, and to the harm we ourselves do to that place:

> Rolling back from the blocked summit
> like an uncoupled train
> with no hand on the brake,
> gathering speed in the dark
> on the mountain grade. (25–29)

In both poems, Haines uses the imagery of nightmarish, unguided vehicles to evoke the idea of an impending disaster, and the disaster is a massive apocalypse of environmental, cultural, and political significance.

NEW POETRY OF THE EARTH

Cicada ends with five new poems, each powerful in its own right, which together represent a renewal of Haines's poetic vision. Like many of the poems in Section IV, the vision and tone evoke Haines's view of many growing environmental crises, but the poems also suggest the poet's conviction that humanity must somehow learn to belong to the earth. Indeed, the poems insist on merging the human and more-than-human in Haines's place of conviction, just as they merge the sense of deep time with a present-day contemporaneity. These mergings are the crucial elements of Haines's new poetry of the earth.

In "Fourth of July at Santa Ynez" and "Victoria," Haines contrasts the present situation of Native Americans with the deep past of a nearly vanished way of life. In both poems, a Native American individual sparks the poet's imagination. In fact, the two poems should be read together as Haines's meditation on the relationship between Native Americans and the land. The setting of the first poem implies a stark contrast between the patriotic holiday of "sweating whites" and an "old Indian seated alone / on a bench in the flickering shade." The old man stares at the celebration and smiles for an instant, the smile flashing "out of the ages of gold / and carbon." For the poet, the smile signifies division and distance, a feeling that is reinforced by the old man's departure: "Slowly, too slowly, as if returned / from a long and difficult journey, / the old man lifted his bucket /and walked away into the sunlit crowd." The departure echoes Haines's essay "Moments and Journeys," for it clearly suggests the disappearance of a "hidden, original life we have done so much to destroy" (*LOC* 29).

The subtext of this moment and journey lies in the regard of the old man, but in "Victoria" it seems to emerge most strongly from the poet's own perspective. The Native American figure is "a girl, half Indian" who is occupied threading beads. The girl must be the title figure, merging with a dream image in the second section of the poem. Using direct address to create a relationship, the poet sees her asleep beside a horse then awake and riding a horse "over stubble and waste allotments." The word "allotments" refers to the Dawes Allotment Act of 1887, which broke up Native American tribes by allotting parcels of reservation land to individuals and families. The law effectively enforced assimilation of Indians into the mainstream white American culture of small farm ownership by nuclear families.[8] Haines suggests that the "half Indian" girl is already a figure of Victorian moral codes, of assimilation and allotment, but in the dream sequence of the poem she escapes on horseback into a wilderness of the past. In that moment, Victoria's journey seems the reverse of the old man's.

In the final section, the poet addresses the girl as "dear friend at the continent's end" and makes a carefully worded statement about the relationship of humanity to wilderness:

> Wilderness survives at the camp
> we have made within us,
> a forest filled up with night,
> its ancient sounds
> and floating, starlit images.
>
> The sun climbs again, the landscape
> wrinkles into shadowy ranges
> and subsides; a plain of light
> kindles in the morning haze,
> dust from fallen pinnacles
> and milling of beasts in the sod.
>
> Will we ever again be at home
> on earth? Great bale of straw
> smoldering in the darkness,
> mire stuffed with singing bones.
>
> The green circle is broken,
> life and dream scattered
> through the flung constellations . . .
>
> This rain of particles,
> random sparks catching fire,
> blowing out in the stellar drifts,
> each one seeking the other. (34–55)

The first stanza immediately recalls the "endless camp" of "'It Must All Be Done Over,'" especially the idea that wilderness survives most surely within the dynamic imagination. The search for a home on earth appears doomed, but the burning off of the "great bale of straw" and the burying of "singing bones" in the mire may not be utterly destructive. Although the "green circle is broken" and the dreams of reunion are scattered, the poem ends with "random sparks catching fire, / blowing out in the stellar drifts, / each one seeking the other." The present participles suggest a perpetual searching for intimacy and community, despite inevitable losses. On the scale of "stellar drifts," a spark is infinitesimally brief, but the prodigious search remains, both within individuals and within communities. The two Native American poems emerge as elegies—recognizing losses, enacting a process of grieving, and pointing the way toward a provisional form of consolation.

Elegy affords moments of quiet affirmation in other poems. "To My Father" and "At White River" create such moments in subtle movements of return. "To My Father" begins and ends with the poet fishing in the Blackfoot River near Missoula, Montana. The body of the poem is the poet's memory of fishing with his father in Maryland, of his father's voice "steady and calm beside me," and of the trout rising to strike the lure. As a double image of return, the final stanza brings us back from death ("Night is on that water" [22]) to the present in Montana in order to reenact the remembered moment of fulfillment:

> Last evening I watched a rise
> break again on the still current;
> quiet as a downed leaf,
> its widening circle in the dusk. (23–26)

The ideas of descent and ascent, past and present, combine in the image of the widening circle. The poem also combines Haines's personal sense of loss at his father's death with a public act of memorializing the dead, capturing the father's voice at the same time that it evokes him through direct address. On many levels, "To My Father" is one of Haines's most gentle and moving elegies, a telling contrast to the claustrophobic nightmare of "The Incurable Home."

In "At White River," elegy appears at the roadside, a moment in a modern journey.[9] The speaker stops his car along the Alaska Highway, at Kluane Lake in the Yukon, and walks up a bluff to a grave, "a grey cross leaning there / and a name that was peeling away." Although he gives us the homesteader's name and dates, the description of the old homestead is marked by absence. We see a sign, but there is no sign of a person's life and works. Haines's imagination searches even further back in time, but he again finds no trace: "Not even the stone ring / of a hunter's fire, / a thin wire flaking in the brush." Even the possible remains of a subsistence hunter or trapper are absent; not even a stray piece of fencing. All he finds is the present landscape, "the Yukon sunlight warming a land / held long under snow, / and the lake water splashing." Caught in the present place, the poet characteristically reaches for the wind:

> From the narrow bridge in the distance
> a windy clatter of iron—
> billow of dust on a blind crossing,
> but a keen silence behind that wind.
>
> It was June 4, 1973. I was forty-nine.
>
> My ten-year-old daughter
> called to me from the road:
> she had found a rock to keep,
>
> and I went down. (25–33)

This may be Haines's happiest descent. Like the drifter in "The Stone Harp" and the voice singing along eroded wires in "Things," the sound of the wind on iron announces distance and isolation. The silence behind that wind is deeper and keener still. Then the poet realizes that it is nearly his birthday, that he stands at a bridge between decades, and that he can see across another bridge between life and death. His young daughter calls to him; she has found a rock to keep; he can go down from the grave, returning to life and the journey.

Haines's drafts and commentary on "At White River" place the poem precisely. It occurs south of the village of Burwash Landing, near the shores of Kluane Lake and close by the White River delta, as the tributary empties into the Yukon River. But the "idea" of the poem, as Haines calls it, is "above all a strong suggestion of the place, a vastness and emptiness, in which the cross and its words, the road and my car, the bridge, my daughter and myself, all took on the importance of things seen in a certain isolation. . . . Possibly some of the most authentic lines in the poem are in the sixth stanza: I felt keenly the silence behind that wind, and wanted to say something to fill it."[10]

Geographical place is transformed into the place of conviction, affording a bridge between life and death. Ultimately, moreover, that place is transformed a third time, into the poet's need to descend into life and its communal processes, into the reality and relationship of generations.

The last poem in *Cicada*, "Roadways," shows how Haines can transform a relatively weak poem into a visionary poetic statement. The original version of the poem, titled "Diane of the Roadways," appears in *Leaves and Ashes*, and it seems to be an effort to give a deep, timeless significance to a transient love affair. In the revised version, the figure of Diane disappears, replaced by a reflection on the long myth-journey of humankind. That is the overarching sense of the roadways, just as it was in Haines's description of Richardson Highway in his commentary on "The Stone Harp." The mythic idea of the road also resonates strongly with the imagery of "At White River." Here, the first two sections of "Roadways" repeat the earlier poem to Diane, developing dream images of "true / and fabulous journeys" and the speaker's memories of being "many times bound outward / from a house no longer mine." The perpetual journey becomes "an ancient track, / scar of the wilderness that sings / around lighted towns," and the poetic descent into the endless camp takes us "beyond / the dense prosperity of houses."

Given this strong recall of Haines's prodigious search for an endless place of conviction, the third and fourth sections of "Roadways" take on even deeper significance. Section III presents the memory of his father reading to him, "pages lit by the beastlight / in a mountain cave," and this personal memory becomes a memory taken from deep time. The personal journey merges with the perpetual human journey:

> And how we went, a tribe uprooted
> from ourselves, the road
> all voices and transformations;
> bewildering flux of shadows,
> spokes, and a rim, the one
> great mirror of water flashing. (33–38)

The journey does not end in a concrete destination or place. It continues, like a wheel, the sun flashing in the "one / great mirror of water."

Section IV delivers yet another return to the present, as in "To My Father" and "At White River." Here, the morning returns, "clear and radiant," and the final stanza delivers the wheeling sun once again. But what present, what past? The ambiguity creates a temporal permeability, a bridge:

> Over a bridge of land
> and restless water,
> where the ox-cart axles
> grind and wear,
> the sun rolls its wheels of fire
> through the squalor
> of awakening eastern streets. (47–53)

In a fine reversal, the end of the poem recalls the end of Section II. Earlier, the poet acknowledged the "dense prosperity of houses" only to envision "a stone planet rolling beyond" them. Here, the rising sun rolls its wheels of fire, a characteristic image of affirmation for Haines, even though the wheels roll through the squalor of human streets. The poem is all the more beautiful for such complex affirmation.

Even if *Cicada* cannot finally attain Haines's demanding idea of a unified vision, it shows the seriousness with which he pursues the idea. As he puts it in "The Hole in the Bucket," the idea will furnish "the means by which, in a world lacking unity, all that the poet sees and feels has meaning. Things fall into place" (*LOC* 65). The meaning is not unitary, but the pursuit of the idea can unify the poet's diverse projects. For Haines, another name for the "idea" is the "place of conviction." As Haines defines it, this place of conviction organizes a poet's career, and in Haines's case it leads toward a new poetry of the earth. Somewhat surprisingly, the best example of Haines's poetry of the earth comes in a beautifully letter-pressed, hand-set, limited edition of eleven poems, *In a Dusty Light*, published by Scott Walker at Graywolf Press in 1977, a few months before the publication of *Cicada*.[11]

THE DUSTY LIGHT OF EARTH

The poems of *In a Dusty Light* range widely across the western United States, from the Richardson homestead to North Dakota, Oregon, and Montana; many of them are set in and around Missoula, where Haines lived for much of the decade. Short lyrics present evocative moments of insight that depend, in some ways, on our previous understanding of Haines's vision and an appreciation for his ideas of place. In "The Blood Lake," for instance, the lead poem in the volume, the speaker and a companion are hiking on the Miller Creek trail near Missoula when they come upon "a runnel of blood / in the snow, and beyond it / a small red lake in the road." The description of the blood lake leads the poet to surmise that a deer had been shot the previous winter and that the hikers are now belated witnesses to the killing. After looking "long and deep," the hikers move on, arriving at the end of the valley, where they see "a great red barn / open to the weather, / belted and roofed with steel." The contrast is far from stark, but by now we know that architectural imagery tends to suggest confinement in Haines's work. The poem refuses to make any judgment on the barn, and the last stanza merges nature and culture in a complex suspension: "The cold red paint was fresh, / smell of turpentine and / ice in the wind." For Haines, the wind is always a talisman, suggesting the power of the "only poet, a drifter" to comment on the colors of human violence and the uses to which we put nature. If we are tempted to draw a causal connection between the red barn and the red lake, so be it; the restrained language of the poem allows this logic without insisting on it.

Other lyrics are equally restrained in their commentaries and equally evocative of concrete places. In "Alive in the World," Haines describes an ordinary evening in Missoula, but like every other place this one is full of "things that are smoke tomorrow." A "torrent of leaves" becomes a storm, darkening the streets, and the sun "comes briefly out of the storm, / lighting the alleyways, / their shingles and gleaming nailheads." As in "The Blood Lake," the moment of illumination is subtle and brief, but here Haines develops the larger implications of disappearances:

> [A]fternoon disappears into evening,
> full of ghosts, torn spirits
> in the wind, crying to be seen . . .
>
> Trees of the earth underfoot,
> what all of us walk on,
> shatter and pass through,
> going blindly into our houses. (15–21)

Ghosts and torn spirits cry out to be seen because the human world ignores them, losing sight of them in the constant disappearances of one moment into another. The poet first hears them crying in the wind, aligning himself with the poetic drifter and leading him to make the commentary of the final stanza. We are endlessly destructive—of the earth and of all the ghosts and spirits it contains—for we shatter and pass through every single thing in our path, and every path seems always to lead us "blindly into our houses." We bury the trees of the earth underfoot, just as we try to bury the ghosts and torn spirits that haunt us.

The last poem in the collection, "Missoula in a Dusty Light," functions both as a synecdoche for the volume and as an excellent instance of Haines's poetry of the earth. Like "Alive in the World," it is set during a twilight autumn walk in the city of Missoula, but in this poem the tone becomes apocalyptic in the second and third stanzas: "a cloud like a hill of smoke" descends upon the city and "the yellow air / [comes] full of specks and ash, / noiseless, crippled things." The visual stanzas shift to sounds, at first merely "a signal clanging" as a train goes by but then becoming truly frightening:

> And then a steady sound,
> as if an army or a council,
> long-skirted, sweeping the stone,
> were gathering near;
> disinherited and vengeful people,
> scuffing their bootheels,
> rolling tin cans before them.
>
> And quieter still behind them
> the voices of birds
> and whispering brooms:
> "This land
> has bitter roots, and seeds
> that crack and spill in the wind . . . "
>
> I halted under a blowing light
> to listen, to see;
> and it was the bleak Montana wind

sweeping the leaves and dust
along the street. (17–34)

The sweeping sound of the wind becomes an army of disinherited people, but perhaps more deeply appalling is the pronouncement of the birds and brooms, denying life to roots and seeds. The "whispering brooms" refer to the common tribe of plants as well as to the human tool for sweeping. Most alarming is the merely physical sensation of the "bleak Montana wind" in the street, sweeping away the poet's figurations and leaving only leaves and dust behind. It is only the wind, but we know the wind is the only poet. And what if the windblown leaves and dust are ultimately all there is? In this dusty light, the poet's windy place of conviction sweeps across the entire country, as if conviction carried with it a criminal sentence.

Animals are a second talismanic figure in Haines's poetry of the earth, and they evoke the connections of deep time in "The Eye in the Rock" and "The Head on the Table." Both poems are antiquarian, even paleontological, in their perspective. Both find ways to connect humanity to the old spiritual vitality of animals. In "The Eye in the Rock," the connection arises from the poet's journey to a "high rock face above Flathead Lake" and his clear vision of the eye "painted here by men / before we came, part of an Indian face, / part of an earth / scratched and stained by our hands" (4–7). This vision leads us back before our own destructive visitations on the earth, and it also leads inward, "as if the rock gave life" (15). The outcome of the journey back into deep time is the emergence of animals in the form of petroglyphs: "thin red elk and rusty deer, / a few humped bison, / ciphers and circles without name" (19–21). The art images persist, and nothing can erase them; their durability engenders a moment of magic, in which the poet recognizes more than one kindred spirit:

They who believed that stone,
water and wind might be quickened
with a spirit like their own,
painted this eye that the rock might see. (30–33)

The poem reaches back to the idea of "Fourth of July in Santa Ynez" and "Victoria," not only because of the focus on Native American art but also because the indigenous inhabitants provide models for living productively on the earth over thousands of years. That key idea combines community, reciprocity, and spiritual kinship in human beings' relationship with the land.[12]

"The Head on the Table," set in a museum, describes the preserved remains of a prehistoric steppe bison (*Bison priscus*). Today a visitor can see a splendid mummified specimen of a steppe bison at the Museum of the North on the campus of the University of Alaska Fairbanks. Although it is tempting to connect Haines's poem directly to the museum specimen known as "Blue Babe," the discovery of the animal came two years after the publication of the poem.[13] Haines devotes most of the poem to describing the head itself, but in the last three stanzas he turns the bison into a living creature, "listening with the deep presence / of matter that does not die, / while the whole journey of beasts on earth / files without a sound / into the gloom of the catalogues" (15–19). The animal evokes "the far tundra lying still" (20), and the poet imagines that "a rough blue tongue passes over teeth / stained by thirty thousand years / of swamp water and peat" (26–28). The bison thus becomes an emblem of deep time abiding among us in the present. We can, of course, explain away the vision of the bison's tongue passing over teeth as an optical illusion, but that is to ignore the living power of the head, a deep presence that Haines translates across thirty thousand years. For Haines, the head on the table functions as an art object, parallel to the petroglyphs of Flathead Lake. Thus "The Eye in the Rock" and "The Head on the Table" form a pair of ekphrastic poems about prehistoric animal art in which artworks become active, vital presences for us today.

In a third talismanic figure for *In a Dusty Light*, Haines's poetry of the earth takes on a new, open dimension in two sequences, "Homestead" and "News from the Glacier." As the titles suggest, the poems reach back to Richardson and to *Winter News*, and they do so in order to relocate Haines's vision in longer, more complex forms. The two sequences enact Haines's double idea of place as a quasi-mythic journey out of wilderness into culture, which he defines in "The Writer as Alaskan": "And place, once again, means actual place, but also a state of mind, of consciousness. Once that place is established, we carry it with us, as we do a sense of ourselves" (*LOC* 13).

The first four sections of "Homestead" focus on memories of Richardson in the 1940s. Even though these are short poems, they relish the images of the past and begin to form the outlines of a contemporary pastoral elegy.[14] The speaker suggests the subject of the elegy in Section II: "The land gave up its meaning slowly, / as the sun finds day by day / a deeper place in the mountain." Appropriately in a poem of loss, the slow process of discovering the place and its meaning contrasts with the rapidity of change. And given the poet's vision of contemporary America, I should note that Haines's Alaskan version of pastoral is anything but a retreat from a complex reality into a simplified fantasy of nature. Both wilderness and culture are complicated, transitory, and vulnerable. In Section IV, Haines recalls the "tales of Richardson / and Tenderfoot, names and antics / of the pathfinders and squawmen, / Jesus-workers, quick whores," but the stories do not leave any mark on the landscape:

> These shadows came and went.
> One still September day
> I knew their passing
> left no more sound in the land
> than a handful of berries
> tumbled in a miner's pail.

The transience of a momentary, muffled sound figures the transience of human endeavor and its effects. Perhaps this is not really unfortunate. In Section V, Haines meditates on the broader historical changes that have swept across the West, naming many of the states in which individual poems take place in order to portray a great swath of destruction, "a black hand mowing the plains" and "the sky littered / with shackled farms." The nostalgic images of the first four sections become "shade and a noise like death." Section VI is still darker in tone, beginning with an image of "half-rotted houselogs" and ending with a vague, ominous future:

> By oil-light and the glint of coal,
> forcing its way,
> a rougher spirit invades the land,
> this ruin carved by a plow.

The stanza clearly associates the "rougher spirit" with extractive industries, and the sequence arrives at a perilous moment of insight. The narrative of conquest, which we saw Haines critique in the essay "Robert Bly," once again becomes a story of invasion, ruin, and decline. Instead of pastoral, we have entered the country of the jeremiad.[15]

Haines backs away from the rhetoric of the jeremiad in Section VII, but the imagery of the poem does not sound a pastoral retreat. In fourteen lines divided into four stanzas, the poet once again retraces his arrival at the homestead, only this time he locates Richardson in the present. The effect is to restore, and perhaps protect, the homestead in the face of destructive changes to the land. The "steep camp" is in some ways absolutely temporary, "nailed to this hillside, by a road / that trails out of nowhere." Like "The Stone Harp" and "'It Must All Be Done Over,'" the first stanza presents the theme of the "endless camp," a descent into place that signals a new beginning. The second stanza is a gorgeous pastoral, full of clear, rain-washed light and the song of a thrush in the birch grove, and it is tempting to hear echoes in that stanza of Whitman's great pastoral elegy "When Lilacs Last in the Dooryard Bloom'd." The third stanza focuses ominously on architecture and the wind: "A door blows aside in the wind, / and a path worn deep to the spring / showers familiar leaves." The path seems to bypass the cabin door and lead back toward the spring. At such a moment we expect Haines, the antipastoral drifter, to break the movement and lead us blindly to our houses or leave us lost in windy streets. But instead he completes his own return:

> A battered dipper shines here
> in the dusk; the trees stand close,
> their branches are moving,
> in flight with the rustling of wings.

As plain as the language may be, it is a beautiful moment of nearly transcendent unity, even if the unity is horizontal, transient, and fragmentary, joining the battered dipper, the moving branches, and the sound of rustling wings. The description moves in a direction opposite to the subjective, surrealistic poetry of the Deep Image. Instead, Haines is performing exactly what he describes as a poetry of the earth: "The landscape inside our heads is much the same everywhere; but when the personal preoccupations common to all of us can be cleared away, the world outside—of individuals, the wilderness, the earth itself—gives us a fit subject to write of" (JHP Box 17, Folder 38).

"News from the Glacier" is even more ambitious than "Homestead," and it is also more given to the "world outside" than the Alaska poem. Draft materials reveal titles for the nine sections, most of which simply identify the subject or setting. Three of the titles refer to place-names within Montana's Glacier National Park, and place-names appear in the text of all nine poems. The draft titles correspond to the printed text in the following order:

I. Approach
II. Pack Train
III. Blue Lake
IV. The Cloud
V. The Goats
VI. Shape in the Rock
VII. Many Glaciers
VIII. The Herd
IX. East Glacier (JHP Box 15, Folder 7)

The nine poems are almost entirely devoid of any editorial commentary by the poet. It is as if Haines wished simply to present the "world outside" in and around Glacier National Park. The language of the poems is spare, direct, and descriptive. As in "The Blood Lake," the speaker always uses plural pronouns, perhaps referring to Gala Fitzgerald as a hiking companion, since he dedicates the sequence to her.[16] There is no clear narrative structure to the sequence as there is in "Homestead"; instead, each of the nine sections can function as a poem on its own. Together, they present an implicit journey toward Glacier Park from Missoula, then several visits to places within the park, and finally an exit toward East Glacier and the town of Browning, thirteen miles east of the park. The temporal coordinates are even less certain than the place-names: Section I takes place on a "mid-fall morning," but Sections III and IV seem to take place in summer. Rather than following a chronology, the sequence moves from the present into a series of poems about deep time, reemerging in the final poem to consider the contrast between the two temporal frames.

Sections I to V describe the landscapes of the present-day park, but they allude to a past world in a number of ways. In Section I, "Approach," the view of Flathead Lake in a "world of mist" gives the poet the impression of a landscape of "vague fossils / held still in the fog," even though the fossils take the shape of pine trees, roofs of barns and houses, and cattle. Similarly, Section II, "Pack Train," at first simply describes the horses and men beside the road at Marias Pass, but then it interprets them as "figures held over / from the day of stampedes / and vigilantes." The sudden appearance of a coyote bounding out in front of the travelers and "gone in the smoky thickets" dispels the visionary moment and ends the poem. Sections III and IV describe a hike to Blue Lake, at nine thousand feet, and the vision of a cloud forming over the water. The two poems are nearly without implication, it seems, save for the image of the poet throwing a rock over the ice of the lake and an echoing sound "like a creature that cries in the dusk, / warning of night and the cold." In Section V, the titular goats are nearly invisible and silent, grazing away from tourists, except for "one old billy / who stood alone on the ridge, / his beard in the wind, / watching the watchers who / waited and stamped their feet." Like the coyote in Section II, the goat seems to give a silent commentary on human beings and their actions, as if comparing their purposes to his own.

This sense of the landscape as a source of inscrutable authority resurfaces in Sections VI to IX, and as the sequence continues Haines develops and clarifies the theme of deep time more explicitly. Section VI, "Shape in the Rock," describes "the eroded shape of a whale" made visible in a rock wall near St. Mary, on the Going-to-the-Sun Road. The whale leads the poet to the fact that the "deep lake of the west is gone," probably an allusion to the great glacial lakes formed by the Cordilleran ice sheet some twelve thousand years ago.[17] The meditation resembles "The Eye in the Rock" and "The Head on the Table," which immediately precede "News from the Glacier" in *In a Dusty Light*. The whale's "bleached bones break / into fragments that cut our fingers," implying our inability to grasp the meanings of deep time. Such implications accumulate in Section VII, "Many Glaciers." The poet imagines the whorled granite like a thumbprint of a giant who paused to look out onto the "watery east" and, like the poet in Section III, skid a "mighty stone / over the flooded continent." In Section VIII, a herd of bison remains from the Pleistocene steppes, where the mastodon, great horse, and bison suffered "the cold, starved / in the great earth changes." The landscape reveals both the immense herd and the immense changes that led to its destruction; by steady accumulation of meanings, the landscape also reveals our own future.

In Section IX, the poet reemerges from the "twenty thousand year / siege of rain and ice" to visit the present-day "sprawling / settlement" of Browning. Not surprisingly, he figures a moment of recognition in terms of the wind:

> No great encampment stands in view
> at Browning. We are awake
> in our own desolate time—
>
> clotheslines whipping the air
> with sleeves and pockets,
> little fists of plastic bags
> beating the stony ground.

Once again the only poet, a drifter, walks in from the coast with empty pockets, but here the empty sleeves and pockets whip in the bleak Montana wind. The plastic bags are empty, too, and though the "little fists" are "beating the stony ground," the poet does not seem to believe that they will ever outlast it. Rather than predict a future, Haines insists that we be "awake / in our own desolate time," for the poetry of the earth depends most deeply on our being alert. If we are awake, even the empty sounds are full of meanings; if we open our fists, perhaps we can make something more lasting than plastic bags.

CHAPTER 3

SHADOW LANGUAGE

Practicing the Art of Memory

OUTLINES

From his very first days at Richardson in 1947, John Haines was practicing the art of memory. Some of the earliest material in the John Haines papers includes a draft piece called "Somebody's Country," written in a style somewhere between verse and dramatic prose, in which the young writer attempts to portray the community of old-timers at the Richardson roadhouse as a country that is already disappearing. The young "John Norton" of the drama, like Haines himself, acts as a kind of apprentice to the older miners, gardeners, hunters, and trappers of Richardson (JHP Box 7, Folder 12). In a later form, dating from about 1950, Haines called the work "Somebody's Country: A Short Novel," with four sections arranged by season (JHP Box 9, Folder 1).

Other prose from the early years puts the Richardson experiences into narrative form. An essay called "After the Hunters," for instance, is a straightforward story of the narrator and a friend on a caribou hunt along the Denali Road in October. The road is jammed with hunters, and the climax of the humorous tale comes when a taxi pulls up behind the hunters' vehicle and the occupants tell them that there is a dead bull for the taking farther down the road. Then one of the taxi cab riders shouts, "There's your caribou now, man!" Eight caribou are trotting up the road toward the men. As the animals approach, five vehicles roar up, hunters jump out, guns at the ready, spooking the caribou and ruining the hunt. The narrator and his friend go back to their camp, leaving the other road hunters to the wind and darkness (JHP Box 9, Folder 2). A more pensive two-part essay from the early 1950s, "Twilight in Richardson," describes the town as it was from around 1905 to Haines's arrival in 1947 then reflects on the value of knowing the old-timers and recounts several anecdotes from Haines's first encounters with them (JHP Box 9, Folder 2). From the beginning, Haines was strongly aware of the transience of the Richardson community, and he sought to capture the past in the very moment of its passing.

The practice of memory is complicated by Haines's abiding interest in lyric forms of dream and the imagination. In another early prose piece, an eight-page draft essay called "To Think in Winter," Haines imagines returning to the Richardson homestead after a long journey, accompanied by landscapes of dream: "And on the last hill, with all the sight and familiarity got from the journey, with the dream blown to its fullest and blessed with amazing light, you look down upon a country that stretches far away, now beyond any horizon, the road losing itself before you under a sky marvelously dark and like the first you knew when you began; so your dream sheds superfluous light on a dark country you have not the further strength to penetrate, and you rest upon a wayside stone, waiting for the dark wind to snuff your lamp and hush you with sleepy songs" (JHP Box 7, Folder 13). The Faulknerian syntax mirrors the turns of dream, memory, perception, and imagination. In a clear parallel with Haines's early poetry, moreover, the metaphor of the journey is a key to the passage and to the writer's developing vision of place. Even as he returns home from the journey, the landscape is leaving him behind, as if the land itself were traveling beyond the horizon, disappearing down a road that is also losing itself in the present moment. Perhaps these multiple complexities were too much for Haines to capture in the early days at the homestead, but he would return to them repeatedly during the next forty years and more of his writing career.

While living at the homestead from 1954 to 1969, Haines continued to think in terms of a prose memoir about his life in Alaska, even though the majority of his writing during those years took the form of short poems. In October 1969, for example, Haines drafted "An Outline of a Prose Work on my life in Alaska, 1947–1969," and though the project did not have a working title, it did have a full table of contents (JHP Box 9, Folder 14). A two-page preface contrasts Richardson of the present day with the Richardson of a lost past, as Haines describes it in the book. Then Haines gives a chronological outline with thematic subjects as chapters and some sketches of probable contents.

The technique recalls Haines's practice of organizing his collections of poems into significant groupings or parts. In the draft "Outline," Part I is called "First Days" and recounts the young navy veteran's trip north to Fairbanks in May 1947. Part II begins with "Return," indicating Haines's return to the homestead in the spring of 1954. Then follow the thematic chapter titles "Richardson," "Gardens and Greenhouses," "The River," "Fishing," and "Buckeye and Beyond." Part III lists "Woodcutting," "Hunting," "Sleds and Dogs," "Trails," "Shelters," "Trapping," and "Other Days." Eventually, "Other Days" would become an important title for Haines; here, it refers to "Winter. Tanning skins. Making moccasins and harness. Watching the snow come down. Reading, waiting for the weather and the sun." Part IV lists "People," "Campbell," "Places," "The Roadhouse," "The Bag of Bones," and "Tenderfoot." "The Bag of Bones" would not become a full-fledged essay until it was published as "The Sack of Bones" in *The Stars, the Snow, the Fire* (1989). Part V lists "Seasons," "Mosquitoes," "Animals and Birds," "Snow and Ice," and "The Sun." Part VI lists "Other Days" once again, this time described as "Berry picking. On the road, waiting for a ride."

As he nears the end of the outline, Haines adds two important topics: "Writing—Dreams and Events" and "Last Days." The first topic includes "How I began writing poems, my life interwoven with the subject, the land and the animals. The ground of happiness." The second is still closer to the present moment of writing: "Decision to leave Alaska and sell the homestead. Last summer, traveling around, seeing parts of the country. The life had been lived, the sap was gone? Still it was hard. I felt like a tree tearing myself up by the roots and moving to a different hillside, another watershed. Would it be any better there? Would the roots reach down again? I locked the gate, left the key under a rock for the new owners, and we headed down the highway for California. October 1, 1969" (JHP Box 9, Folder 14). In a sense, the outline begins and ends with loss, and the prose work that Haines imagines is clearly meant to combat the loss of Richardson as a significant, fruitful place in the writer's imagination.

Another way of reading Haines's outline is to see it as a metaphorical journey, beginning with the arrival at Richardson and ending with an inevitable departure. Although rich details of the homesteading years appear in the full list of chapters and their possible contents, Richardson remains a way station on some larger journey. The poetry of the 1960s and 1970s supports this reading because of the centrality of the "myth-journey" metaphor in Haines's vision. In addition, the essay "Moments and Journeys," originally published in the Wilderness Society's magazine *Living Wilderness* (1978), shows how Haines uses the art of memory to develop a large sense of "the movement of things on this earth" (*LOC* 22). The central theme of the essay is that everywhere we look we find "moments and stages in existence" (22). For Haines, the homestead years are particularly important because they retain "an aura of deep and lasting significance," one that he links with "a life much older than mine" (23). In the essay, the significance resides in stories of journeys over the Alaska landscape.

In "Moments and Journeys," Haines gives four brief scenes or "moments" of reflection in the middle of a journey. In the first, his aged mentor Fred Campbell accompanies Haines and his first wife, Peg, on a late-summer hike to Buckeye Dome, the highest viewpoint near Richardson, and the moment belongs to Campbell, "an entire history told around the figure of one man" (24). In the second, more mythic scene, Haines and Campbell are on another journey together, and the younger man pauses to look at his elder, ahead of him on the trail and surrounded by his dogs, as "the embodiment of an old story." In the third, Haines and his unnamed wife (probably his second wife, Jo) are crossing the Tanana River on midwinter ice, and they pause to reflect on the dangers and possibilities of living by a large river through the seasons, in which "other seasons were stations on the journey" (24). Finally, the fourth moment begins with the simple phrase "Other days" and describes the rising of a full moon on an arctic evening. Then Haines recalls an earlier day, in which the old-timer Billy Melvin told him of a still-earlier moonrise, the full moon on the trail "as big as a rain barrel" (25). The last moment thus figures three mythic moments within one. Journeys, moments, myths, and memories: these elements combine and recombine in a host of significant patterns.

One characteristic pattern in "Moments and Journeys" is the accumulation of stories. The four moments of reflection form one version of the pattern. In the second half of the essay, memories create yet another version. Between those two versions, Haines reflects on what it takes to make a journey and what role dreams play in creating significance. Those two ideas come together in Haines's meditations on "some ancient human activity" in relation to "the turning of a great wheel" of seasons (27). A moment within a journey is valuable because it allows the traveler to discern a meaningful pattern linking events. In order to illustrate the idea of accumulating stories and memories, Haines moves to the second pattern, recounting three memories of wilderness scenes involving children.

The significance of memories accumulates as the stories expand, until Haines tells a full-blown narrative of hiking to Pool Rock in the San Rafael Wilderness north of Santa Barbara, California, with his daughter and a friend. The hike itself is uneventful, but when the three arrive at Pool Rock, Haines describes the place as "a great sandstone pile rising out of the foothills like a sanctuary or a shrine to which one comes yearly on a pilgrimage" (29). The three explore the caves and view Chumash petroglyphs painted and gouged into the rock; finally, they climb to the top of the rock, eat their lunch, and drink from the pool of water there. When a storm blows up, they descend and hike back to the trailhead, talking of what they have seen and feeling "strangely happy" (29). The story of Pool Rock recalls "The Eye in the Rock" from *In a Dusty Light*—as if Haines were somehow remembering a poem within the memory of a previous hike. The links are clear in the use of Native American petroglyphs and the images of cultural myth-journeys. In Haines's view, such links resonate most fully in the context of a life led in intimate contact with wilderness, especially with the spiritual vitality of wild animals, but even in our present world the links "are present nonetheless, available to imagination, and of the same character" (28). The final link, then, connects the deep, prehistoric past of the Chumash to the present-day hikers, for that reason making them "strangely happy." As Haines points out, the hike to Pool Rock, in effect, links "the dream journey and the actual life" (27).

"Moments and Journeys" is significant in yet another way: as we saw already in the introductory chapter, the hybrid essay appears in the collection *Living Off the Country*, which in turn appears in Donald Hall's series *Poets on Poetry*. The subtitle of Haines's collection, *Essays on Poetry and Place*, suggests that the entire collection is a hybrid, including more than critical reflections or manifestos on poetic craft. Even though Haines claims in the preface that his aim is to "offer some encouragement toward a fuller, more exacting criticism," only one section of the volume is devoted explicitly to literary criticism. The role of place is central to the first section, "Alaska and the Wilderness," and memory is of primary importance in the fourth section, "Autobiographical Sketches."

The three autobiographical essays in the fourth section—"Nineteen Thirty-two," "The Yard," and "Nothing to Do"—are most significant for their form, not for the actual content of the narratives. The three essays focus on the years between 1932 and 1941, portraying Haines's migratory navy childhood from age seven to sixteen. In the headnote to the section, Haines calls the sketches "a beginning" and sees them as expressing his "desire to give imaginative shape to a period whose meaning may not ever be known completely, but whose force in my life, as background and preparation, can never be discounted" (*LOC* 163). They are most successful in providing thematic links to the idea of the journey. Thus "Nineteen Thirty-two" recounts the upheaval of the Haines family following an earthquake near Long Beach, California, leading to their journeys north to Bremerton, Washington, and east to Washington, DC (164–67). "The Yard" and "Nothing to Do" sift through "the eternal moving from place to place" (169) and Haines's adolescent fascination with boats and cars (180–85) to suggest a timeless journey toward adulthood, ending with the specifics of time and history: "At the end of the summer, my mother and Bob and I drove south to San Diego, where we were to spend the next two years. My father was once more at sea, where he liked best to be. It was September, 1941. The Japanese raid on Pearl Harbor was three months away" (188). The ending marks the passage between childhood and adulthood, and in several ways it strongly recalls Elizabeth Bishop's poem "In the Waiting Room," first published in the *New Yorker* in 1971.[1] Most important, however, is the way the essays suggest Haines's abiding commitment to writing autobiography.

GATHERING SHADOWS

The manuscript materials in the John Haines Papers at the University of Alaska Fairbanks suggest that Haines was drafting autobiographical essays in 1974–1975 and that by the last years of the decade he had accumulated a substantial number of essays on the homesteading years in Richardson. The earliest manuscripts include the short essays "Other Days," "Sack of Bones," "Spring," "Shadows," "Richardson: The Dream," and "Lost," as well as a short story called "Dream of the Prisoner" (JHP Box 14, Folder 12). In February

1974, Haines had told a student reporter for the University of Washington *Daily*, "As far as writing goes I may tend towards prose in the next couple of years, but I definitely want to continue writing poetry and not just talking about it" (JHP Box 14, Folder 9). The publication of *Cicada* and *In a Dusty Light* in 1977 shows that Haines continued his disciplined work as a poet. Beginning in 1977, moreover, the poet and editor Hayden Carruth offered Haines his loyal support as a reader and unofficial agent, helping Haines to publish the essays "Spring" and "Lost" in *Harper's* in 1978 and providing his astute criticism of Haines's essays and poems for another three decades.[2] Along with Scott Walker of Graywolf Press, poet and essayist Wendell Berry, and the Vermont poet David Budbill, Carruth gave Haines the kind of critical support he had counted on from Robert Bly, Donald Hall, and Louis Simpson in the 1950s and 1960s.

Throughout the 1970s and 1980s, Haines steadily wrote essays and pursued magazine publication for them. In addition to the two essays published in *Harper's* in 1978, for which he was paid $500 apiece, Haines published "Snow" (1979) and "Of Wolves" (1981) in *Living Wilderness*, the magazine of the Wilderness Society, which had published "Moments and Journeys" in 1978. He also submitted a third essay, "A View from Buckeye Dome," to *Living Wilderness* and was ultimately paid a $200 "kill fee" for the essay.[3] Perhaps most significantly, he published four major essays in the fledgling journal *New England Review*, edited by Sydney Lea: "Three Days" (Autumn 1980), "Of Traps and Snares" (Autumn 1981), "Death Is a Meadowlark" (Summer 1983), and "Stories We Listened To" (Winter 1983). Meanwhile, other national literary journals, such as *Antaeus*, *Ironwood*, and *Kansas Quarterly*, published individual essays. Always in search of an audience, during the same period Haines reprinted "Snow" in the Canadian periodical *Northward Journal* (1981) and printed many essays, in whole or in part, in Alaska newspapers and journals, including the *Anchorage Daily News*, *Alaska Airlines Magazine*, *Alaska Magazine*, *Alaska Fish and Game*, *Alaska Journal*, *Heartland* (the magazine of the Fairbanks *Daily News-Miner*), *Homer News*, *Northern Line*, and *permafrost*, the literary magazine of the University of Alaska Fairbanks. The earliest prose publication appears to be "Richardson: The Dream" in the October 1977 issue of *permafrost*.

In addition to these magazine publications, during the 1980s Haines brought out three small collections of essays. Like Richardson itself, the three collections function as way stations on the journey toward the full-fledged memoir, ultimately published as *The Stars, the Snow, the Fire* (Graywolf Press, 1989). The first collection, *Of Traps and Snares*, was published by a small commercial company, Dragon Press, in Delta Junction, Alaska, in 1981. It includes the essays "Other Days," "Of Traps and Snares," and "Three Days." The book apparently uses the same plates as the *New England Review* printing of "Of Traps and Snares" and "Three Days," for the texts match exactly except for pagination.[4] The second book, *Other Days*, was published by Scott Walker at Graywolf Press in 1982. It collects six short essays and parts of two longer essays, all previously published in magazines or newspapers: "Snow," "Spring," "Other Days" (reprinted from *Of Traps and Snares*), "Wolves," "Lost," "Richardson: The Dream," and selections from "Three Days" and "With an Axe and an Auger." The third book, *Stories We Listened To*, came out in 1986 from Bench Press and includes a brief prologue (originally part of a long manuscript essay called "Shadows") and six short essays: "Stories We Listened To," "Out of the Shadows," "Burning a Porcupine," "Shadows," "Death Is a Meadowlark," and "Ice." As in *Other Days*, all of these essays had been published at least once before in magazines or newspapers. Finally, the memoir *The Stars, the Snow, the Fire* (1989) gathers the accumulated work of at least fifteen years, collecting eighteen essays that evoke, as the subtitle says, "*Twenty-Five Years in the Alaska Wilderness*." Sixteen of the eighteen essays had been published previously in *Of Traps and Snares*, *Other Days*, and *Stories We Listened To*. Only "The Sack of Bones" and "Mudding Up" were not previously collected; both essays date from Haines's earliest days in Richardson and his first attempts to capture his experiences in prose.

Like the poems of *Winter News*, *The Stone Harp*, *Cicada*, and other collections from the 1960s and 1970s, Haines takes the essays of *The Stars, the Snow, the Fire* through complex processes of compilation, expansion, condensation, and reduction. An especially instructive example is the essay "Shadows," which exists in several different forms. There are, in fact, at least two distinct essays published under the title "Shadows." One originally appears in *Stories We Listened To* (1986) and is structured as a series of memories of animals that appear as fleeting shadows—flying squirrels, a fox feeding at the Richardson roadhouse, a gaunt coyote, a pet woodchuck, a whimpering porcupine, a lynx raking its claws through the bark of a fallen tree. This affectionate, observational essay is retitled "Dusk" in *The Stars, the Snow, the Fire*. But before that title change, Haines published at least two other partial versions of the essay under the same title, "Shadows," in *Alaska Fish and Game* during 1985 and 1986.[5]

A second, more ambitious essay titled "Shadows" first appears in *The Stars, the Snow, the Fire*: it is composed of three very different parts. The first part begins "There are shadows over the land" and runs for five short paragraphs that reflect upon the human fear of mortality. The physical shadows "speak to the shadows within us, old ghosts that will not die" (*The Stars, the Snow, the Fire* 143; hereafter cited as SSF.), and they demand that we "think back through the silence, of the life that was and is not here now, of the strong pastness of things—shadows of the end and the beginning" (150). This part of "Shadows" was first published as the prologue to *Stories We Listened To* and later appeared in the pages of *Antaeus*. Part II begins "I stepped out into my yard on a warm October evening, just before dark," and the section becomes a brief natural history of the little brown bat, *Myotis lucifugus* (150–55).[6] The third part begins, "I speak much of twilight, of dusk and evening." Haines then develops a series of reflections on the deep human need for animals, even if they figure our inmost fears, ending with the wondrous thought that "so small and refined a creature [as the little brown bat] could fill an uncertain niche in the world; and that its absence would leave not just a momentary gap in nature, but a lack in one's own existence, one less possibility of being" (159). Thus, as the essay closes, the final shadow is cast over Haines's vision of a landscape devoid of animals: "To look, straining one's eyes, noting each detail of lake, meadow, and bog; and to find nothing, nothing alive and moving. Only the wind and the distance, the silence of a vast, creatureless earth" (160). That ending echoes the final image of "Of Traps and Snares," in which "the old hunter's dream of plenty" (28) gives way to "its sometime shadow: the country dead, and nothing to see in the snow. Famine, and the great dream passing" (29).

"Shadows" reveals the complicated, winding history of publication and the equally tortuous path of Haines's compositional process. But the complications do not end here. In fact, the two "Shadows" essays stem from a long manuscript essay that includes the texts of both "Dusk" and "Shadows" along with much else (JHP Box 27, Folder 3). For example, what Haines calls the "4th draft" of "Shadows I" runs to thirty-four typescript pages and includes material that later becomes "Dusk" and "Shadows," material that eventually becomes the essay "Burning a Porcupine," and descriptions of beavers and black bears that appear nowhere in *The Stars, the Snow, the Fire*. In another draft titled "Shadows III," Haines begins with the first four paragraphs as they appear in the published Part III of "Shadows," but then he drafts five new typescript pages on bears and adds several more pages of revised materials about bears. "Shadows II," by contrast, appears consistently in the draft materials as closely aligned with the published Part II of "Shadows," focusing on the little brown bat for some eight typescript pages. Still another early draft features an introductory reflection that becomes Part I of "Shadows," but Haines joins it with the story of a pet ermine, or short-tailed weasel, that he named Moo-moo.

As involved as this account of Haines's drafts may be, the story of his gathering shadows does not stop there. In yet another set of typescripts from 1979–1980, Haines includes the essay "(On) Wolves" as part of "Shadows: A Chapter on Animals" in five separate drafts, while another set of drafts called "Bear" and "Shadows" becomes the narrative essay "Out of the Shadows" when it is revised in October 1981 and published in *Antaeus* in 1982 (JHP Box 33, Folder 1). In loose manuscript materials included in an unlabeled folder (JHP Box 27), the typescript of "Shadows I" (eventually titled "Dusk" and Part I of "Shadows" in *The Stars, the Snow, the Fire*) is gathered with "Burning a Porcupine," "The Stories We Listened To," and "Ice," all of which eventually appear in *Stories We Listened To* (1986).

The typescripts suggest that Haines was attempting to join lyric and narrative essays to form a new kind of multisection essay or a collection of essays. Moreover, it seems safe to conclude that the long manuscript essay "Shadows" is the source for five separate essays published in *The Stars, the Snow, the Fire*: "Out of the Shadows," "Burning a Porcupine," "Wolves," "Dusk," and "Shadows." In other words, the long manuscript "Shadows" gathers Haines's versions of the idea of animals as a vital source of inspiration to the human imagination and as a reminder of our common mortality.

By breaking the manuscript "Shadows" into five shorter essays, Haines casts the shadow of mortality across the entirety of *The Stars, the Snow, the Fire*. Nor does the shadow of death appear only in those five essays. In the preface, for instance, he announces the major themes and strategies of the book—the ways in which he practices the art of memory—and the shadow already appears. Haines first defines his subject as "time—one's sense of time, and the time in which certain events take place. This journey in and out of time cannot be adequately expressed by any sum of calendar years. In the sense in which I write, there is no progress, no destination, for the essence of things has already been known, the real place arrived at long ago" (*SSF* ix). Haines requires that the surface chronology of the Richardson years, from 1947 to 1989, be held in the light of deep time, the "real place" that he also equates with "a kind of *dream-time* in the ancient tribal sense" (SSF x). Just as the early poems of *Winter News* deliver the experience of deep time through repeated dream journeys and encounters with wild animals, the essays of *The Stars, the Snow, the Fire* seek to recreate the experiences of "those days in the field, those treks with the dogs over snow and grass, the long hunts, the animal killing, and the rest of it," for these form "the inmost human experience on this earth" (SSF x). The relationship with wild animals is of particular importance as the most authentic path to the "real place":

> It is rank, it smells of blood and killed meat, is compounded of fear, of danger and delight in unequal measure. To the extent that it can even be called "experience" and not by some other, forgotten name, it requires a surrender few of us now are willing to make. Yet, in the brief clarity and intensity of an encounter with nature, in the act of love, and (since we are concerned with a book) in the recalling and retelling of a few elemental episodes, certain key moments in that experience can be regained. On these depends the one vitality of life without which no art, no spiritual definition, no true relation to the world is possible. (*SSF* x)

Even though Haines's art of memory tells much more than a story of primordial hunts, it is nonetheless clear that he considers the killing of wild animals a key to the Richardson experience. That is the fundamental "encounter with nature" he evokes in the preface. But how does the shadow of death give "the one vitality of life," how can it be part of an act of love, and what meanings reside in the recalling and retelling of such episodes?

A SHADOW LANGUAGE

In "Snow," the two-page opening essay of *The Stars, the Snow, the Fire*, Haines establishes a fundamental metaphor for the entire memoir. The snow, like many other elements of nature, is a book to be read; whatever aspect the snow shows, the language remains the same: "It is a shadow language, spoken by things that have gone by and will come again. The same text has been written there for thousands of years, though I was not here, and will not be here in winters to come, to read it" (*SSF* 3). The text is composed of animal tracks and the materials of scat, blood, and hair that American hunters and trackers call "sign" (*OED*). In all of the Richardson experiences, Haines functions as a reader of sign, an interpreter of the shadow language. His own ephemeral life, like that of the animals, accords with the ephemeral quality of tracks in snow. But the shadow language and its texts remain as a timeless, defining part of the landscape.

By reading the shadow language, Haines participates in the timeless stories told in the snow. The first of these stories is simply the "loping, two-toed track" of a wolverine that Haines follows for two miles, gaining a sense of the animal's "sure and steady" movement across the land (3). The second story is more complicated and dramatic. Haines discovers tracks and other fresh sign that he interprets as a running battle between a moose and three wolves. Through short, convincing interpretations, Haines brings the story to a climax in which the moose gets the better of the wolves, a mother and two nearly grown pups she is teaching to hunt (4). Haines functions as a kind of snow taphonomist, able to reconstruct events by reading the ephemeral sign left behind. Moreover, he also functions as a memorialist, or what he calls "the coldest scholar on earth, who followed each clue in the snow, writing a book as he went. It would be the history of snow, the book of winter. A thousand-year text to be read by a people hunting these hills in a distant time" (5). Reading the shadow language, the coldest scholar transcends individual death and produces yet another timeless book of winter, written in a human version of the shadow language. Haines's "coldest scholar," so reminiscent of Wallace Stevens, takes up the project of modernist poetry to transfigure the ordinary and ephemeral into a timeless sign.

The shadow language is not always so portentous, although much of *The Stars, the Snow, the Fire* strikes a sorrowing tone. In "Of Traps and Snares," the sense of learning to read animal sign can be rather joyous, "like beginning a new language, each detail and accent of which had its special meaning" (13). The exploration of the country leads to a parallel exploration within the novice trapper, who discovers "a passionate and tenacious longing—to put away thought forever, and all the trouble it brings, all but the nearest desire, direct and searching. To take the trail and not look back" (17). At the end of the essay, the trapper's ability to read the snow in the "strongly slanted shadows" of January awakens a deep wonder and "strange, mixed enjoyment," even when the work involves killing animals (28). Haines figures the experience of running a trap-line as occurring "far, far back in time, that twilight country where men sometimes lose their way, become as trees confused in the shapes of snow. But I was at home there, my mind bent away from humanity, to learn to think a little like that thing I was hunting. I entered for a time the old life of the forest, became part fur myself" (28). There is no grieving, no misgivings, over lost humanity here; instead, the ambiguity of entering the old life of the forest strongly recalls the early poem "Dream of the Lynx" and suggests a certain joy in transcending the confines of humanity. The old life also evokes the scale of deep time, the "real place arrived at long ago" that Haines invokes in the preface (ix). If there is a sense of the elegiac, it resides in "the old hunter's dream of plenty" and "its sometime shadow: the country dead, and nothing to see in the snow. Famine, and the great dream passing" (28–29). The dark nightmare, shadowing the dream of plenty, would be a real place without animals.

"Three Days" is in many ways a complement to "Of Traps and Snares." The two longest essays in the memoir both appeared in the *New England Review* before being published together in *Of Traps and Snares* (1981). Rather than being devoted exclusively to animals or to humans, they bring human life into rhythmic relationship with the Alaska landscape and its animals. "Three Days" recurs to the imagery of the shadow language written in snow, but here intimacy and affection become palpable: "The day passes, another hour, another mile. I walk, watching the snow, reading what is written there, the history of the tribes of mice and voles, of grouse and weasel, of redpoll and chickadee, hunter and prey. A scurry here, a trail ended there—something I do not understand, and stop to ponder. I find a trap sprung and nothing in it. I catch another marten, another male, so dark it is almost black. I am in luck today" (65). The paragraph includes the cruelty of trapping and the mixed enjoyment of success, but it also evokes the joy of reading the history of animals we do not trap or hunt—the mice and voles, redpolls and chickadees that often act like our curious companions. The lack of obvious pity does not mean that we enjoy cruelty; indeed, Haines often evokes pity and even dismay at the inherent cruelty of trapping and snaring animals. The paragraph seems to practice a paradoxical art of forgetting by bending away from humanity for a day or a part of the day. The events of the day form an all-inclusive, common journey: "The day passes, another hour, another mile."

Cruelty and killing are not necessary for the trapper to bend away from humanity. In Part II of "Three Days," Haines arrives at a remote cabin along his trap-line and spends two days there, as if taking the time to answer his own questions:

> What does a person do in a place like this, so far away and alone? For one thing, he watches the weather—the stars, the snow, and the fire. These are the books he reads most of all. And everything that he does, from bringing in firewood and buckets of snow, to carrying the waste water back outdoors, requires that he stand in the open, away from his walls, out of his man-written books and his dreaming head for a while. As I stand here, refreshed by the stillness and closeness of the night, I think it is a good way to live. (71)

This passage illustrates the restrained beauty of Haines's prose style. The theme of standing "away from his walls" echoes the manuscript essay about Robert Bly and the difficulties of living inside suburban America. It subtly echoes the stark beauties of *Cicada* and *In a Dusty Light*. One thinks of a poem like "Leaves and Ashes," for example, in which a woman stands "where the city and the forest / were walled together," standing alone with "the tall brown house of November / slowly unbuilding around her." This is the place occupied by the solitary walker in the Missoula poems, "Alive in the World" and "Missoula in a Dusty Light," who finds himself haunted by the wind and its warning voices, even though the real danger seems to lie within ourselves, "going blindly into our houses." At the trapper's cabin, by contrast, everything requires movement into the open. Here, too, reading the landscape opens up a deeper refreshment than the undeniable satisfactions of interpreting sign or successfully trapping marten and lynx. Even if it lasts no more than three days, the journey away from humanity leads, finally, to "a stretching kind of tiredness, the ease and satisfaction of the time well spent, and of the deep self renewed" (79).

Always tinged with a sense of mortality, the shadow language evokes a number of life-affirming realities. Several of the essays originally gathered in the long typescript "Shadows" illustrate that sense particularly well. In

"Out of the Shadows," for example, the story of a grizzly bear attack follows the track of violence as closely as possible but then turns aside. The narrator finds "no sign of blood" (48) and discovers that "a pervasive uneasiness seemed to divide the shadows and the sunlight" (49). Is the story marred by the fantasy of a final, intimate encounter and a maimed survivor? Perhaps the fantasy is an effective way of registering the narrator's relieved sense of an ordinary, inconclusive ending. The following essay, "Burning a Porcupine," is more telling as an educational, nearly comical process analysis than as a deep meditation on a "long-ago woods-spirit" and the ritual sacrifice of the wild animal (57). "Dusk," the original "Shadows" essay in *Stories We Listened To* (1986), is wholly given over to the joy of encountering wild animals in their own country and recognizing their vital otherness. In the final episode, the narrator is fishing on an October afternoon in a channel of the Tanana River when he becomes aware of a large lynx crouched on top of a fallen tree in the shadows at the edge of the woods behind him. The big cat is raking its claws in the dry bark of the tree, oblivious to the man below him. Then the two creatures experience an encounter: "The lynx paused in its raking. Its eyes opened, and it turned a wide yellow gaze upon me. There was no alarm in that look, no flash of recognition or fear. We looked at each other for a moment, each of us gazing into some dim shadow of ourselves. And then, not wanting to prolong my stare, as casually as I could I turned back to my fishing. When I looked again, the lynx was gone" (117). The balance of viewpoint bespeaks an essentially ecocentric perspective, one that avoids the inherent hierarchy of viewer and viewed. Two creatures gaze at each other, each one a "dim shadow" of the other. The human being returns to his fishing, an activity equivalent here to bringing in firewood and buckets of snow. The lynx ends the encounter, exercising the ultimate authority by vanishing from view.

The shadow language is not always subject to human translation. A fleetingly visible animal or a pack of invisible animals can be as meaningful as a clearly written story in the snow. In "Wolves," for instance, the relationship between wolves and dogs functions as a set of questions about wildness, as if the two groups of canids were discussing their deep past. For the human beings who keep the dogs, there is no answer, nothing clearly written in the tracks or in the occasional sighting of a wolf at the edge of the woods. The answer, or something like it, comes from sounds:

> Something like an answer came one night toward spring a few years later. We were awakened by a sound coming faintly through the walls of the cabin, like a distant singing. We got out of bed, and since it was a mild, clear night we went outdoors and stood in the snow to listen.
>
> Far across the Tanana, a mile or more to the south of us, a group of wolves was singing. I call it singing, not howling, for that is what it was like. We could distinguish three, perhaps four voices—wavering, ascending in pitch, each one following on the other, until they all broke off in a confused chorus. Their voices sank into distant echoes on the frozen river, and began again. A light and uncertain wind was blowing out there, and the sound grew and faded as the air brought it toward us or carried it away southward. It might have come across a thousand years of ice and wind-packed snow, traveling as the light of stars from a source no longer there. (92)

The word "singing" already implies beauty in the invisible chorus of wolves, but Haines carefully maintains a sense of distance and uncertainty in rendering human perceptions. The most certain aspect of the sounds is the timeless, infinite distance they travel across, reaching the human beings who stand in the snow to listen. Or is the most certain aspect the wind, more powerful than singers or listeners? Even the "light of stars" seems to waver on its way to us, and what we see is a track left by a vanished sun. Despite the uncertainties, the passage creates a tone of deep, abiding appreciation for the invisible, wild singing.

Invisible sounds lie at the origin of "Death Is a Meadowlark," though there is no direct echo of the shadow metaphor in the essay. Instead, Haines develops a childhood memory, much like the autobiographical sketches in *Living Off the Country*, and he uses metonymy to connect the thirteen-year-old boy's realization of death through his discovery of a freshly killed, eviscerated rabbit and the song of an unseen meadowlark (*SSF* 119–21). The essay is structured episodically, like "Dusk." The narrator dwells on the memory of the meadowlark and the rabbit, and the "ghost-image" that remains behind (120). Then he moves closer to the present and to Richardson, recalling a frozen redpoll at the entrance of the homestead road and then a worn skull of a caribou before he delivers a full story of killing a bull moose in early October. Only in the "dark eye" of the animal and in its "dark bulk" does Haines directly register his recognition of the shadow of death.

As he comments, immediately after the kill, "But now death was forgotten. A transformation had taken place, and what had been a vital and breathing creature, capable of perception and of movement, was now only meat and salvage—a hairy mound of bone and muscle" (124). If that description is cold—and perhaps evasive in its passive voice—it is also accurate, and the description of field dressing the moose is anything but evasive or cold. The episodes in the essay move from childhood fear to adult acceptance, but the movement is not figured as a progression. As Haines writes in "Three Days," "The day passes, another hour, another mile."

The most sustained meditation on the shadow language comes in Parts I and III of "Shadows." The opening reflections on "shadows over the land" quickly connect the physical, familiar shadows with "the shadows within us, old ghosts that will not die" (149). The shadows, both exterior and interior, tell us of "the strong pastness of things—shadows of the end and the beginning" (150). Part I ends with autumn leaves blown by the wind in the evening darkness, flying into our faces and scaring us with the recognition of death. Again we may hear the final stanza of "Missoula in a Dusty Light":

> I halted under a blowing light
> to listen, to see;
> and it was the bleak Montana wind
> sweeping the leaves and dust
> along the street.

Part II seems almost a merciful interlude, delving into the natural history of the little brown bat, but the interlude closes by lamenting the absence of the animal and missing its "rare kinship" on an October evening, when there is only the sound of "leaves in the wind" (155).

Part III traces the shadow of death and the figure of the bat through layers of folklore and literature, but the tracks always reveal the same shadow language. Still, Haines implies that the shadow language is the necessary origin for art: "The attitudes flicker and change, rehearsed continually on the screen of the wind. To be merely a creature on earth, to be left alone in an acre of grass, has seldom been sufficient—not since man the hunter scanned the open fairway, crouched in ambush, and took passionately to himself the skins of killed beasts, tore their meat from the bones, drank their milk and blood, and then by torchlight traced their outlines on a high rock face in soot and ochre" (157). Here, Haines reaches back as far as he can to an imaginative, primal scene of artistic creation, and his syntax suggests a causal sequence of human actions, in which artistic creation depends on hunting and killing animals. Haines willingly entertains the idea that "it is as though we require that evil exist, and that we find its faces in the world" (157). But even though "the mark of the forest is on us" (158), Haines ultimately turns away from "an old grip of terror" (159). The imagination will work upon experience, and it may create images we find horrible and frightening, but Haines also insists upon the primacy of the "familiar woodland": "And of the bats at Richardson, whose brown leaf-shapes crossed the twilight at such rare intervals, to speak now and then of companionship and delight is sufficient, for these may be found anywhere in the pure act of being, of pursuing one's way of daylight and dusk, filling by right that clearing, that space of air, that acre of soil and grass, undeflected by regret or thought of tomorrow" (159).

In the phrase "the pure act of being," as well as in the portrait of the bats as emblems of companionship and delight, Haines may well have Wallace Stevens in mind once again. But here it would not be the Stevens of "The Snow Man" and the "coldest scholar on earth" (*SSF* 5). Rather, one might think of the late poem "Of Mere Being":

> The palm at the end of the mind,
> Beyond the last thought, rises
> In the bronze distance.
>
> A gold-feathered bird
> Sings in the palm, without human meaning,
> Without human feeling, a foreign song.
>
> You know then that it is not the reason
> That makes us happy or unhappy.
> The bird sings. Its feathers shine.
>
> The palm stands on the edge of space.
> The wind moves slowly in the branches.
> The bird's fire-fangled feathers dangle down.

Stevens imagines a more foreign form of being than Haines, one that sings from the very edge of reason or "beyond the last thought," but the figure of the "gold-feathered bird" does resemble the bats of Richardson in its beautiful otherness. In both cases, the animal figures a form of being as more than merely human, occupying its rightful place in an absolute present moment. In both cases, too, the animal evokes in the writer a sense of beauty and delight.

Perhaps most telling is the fact that Haines imagines a more common, familiar form of mere being than does Stevens and responds with less rhetorical fire. Thus, as "Shadows" moves to a close, the bats function as "vanished companions," and they signify a potential loss in our own existence, our own imagination. They are the final shadows in Haines's memoir, recalling the writer's own dark nightmare, haunting the end of "Of Traps and Snares," that he might awake to find "the country dead, and nothing to see in the snow" (29). At the very end of "Shadows," too, the absence of bats on an autumn evening casts a deep shadow: "To look, straining one's eyes, noting each detail of lake, meadow, and bog; and to find nothing, nothing alive and moving. Only the wind and the distance, the silence of a vast, creatureless earth" (160).

VANISHED COMPANIONS

A second focus in *The Stars, the Snow, the Fire* is not a celebration of the "old hunter's dream of plenty" (29) but a memorial celebration of old hunters. As Haines's earliest attempts to capture Richardson in his writing suggest, he is devoted to the memory of the old-timers who introduced him to the subsistence life based on gathering, trapping, hunting, and fishing. These elders appear in a number of the essays focusing on the shadow language of animals, most especially "Of Traps and Snares" and "Burning a Porcupine." Moreover, they function as a second version of vanished companions, and in the six essays dedicated to their memory, Haines practices the art of elegy in remarkably tender ways. The essays begin with "Stories We Listened To," the third essay in the collection, immediately following "Of Traps and Snares." Much later, three consecutive short essays recur to the figure of sourdough homesteaders and evoke the earliest years of Haines's own homesteading:

"Lost," "The Sack of Bones," and "Mudding Up." Toward the end of the collection, Haines places "With an Axe and an Auger" just before "Shadows." "With an Axe and an Auger" is a major essay in four parts, one that went through several versions before its final publication in *The Stars, the Snow, the Fire.* Finally, Haines ends with "Richardson: The Dream," the shortest and most poetic essay in the collection.

The six essays devoted to vanished human companions employ, both explicitly and implicitly, a shadow language. Even the essentially domestic essay "Mudding Up," set in September 1947, keeps "the long dark" in mind, and the narrator finds "in the shadow of the stable wall" that "the air took on a deeper chill" (108). In "Lost," the dim imagery represents a more dangerous, alien place, even for the most experienced inhabitants: "Fred Campbell told me once of being shut in by fog on Buckeye Dome one fall day, a fog so thick he could not see the ground at his feet. He lost all sense of place and time, and wandered that day in an endless and insubstantial whiteness. It seemed to him at times that he was not walking on earth, but was stranded in a still cloud, far from anything he could touch or know. Toward evening the sun burned a hole in the mist, and he found his way down into familiar woods again" (95). Like the moment in the stable in "Mudding Up," the otherworldly quality of Campbell's experience is intensified by its nearness to the familiar and ordinary, as if any place could be transformed in a moment. That is precisely the quality that Haines discovers and describes in "Lost" as a "drowsy, half-wakeful menace": "I have felt it near me while kneeling in the snow, minding a trap on a ridge many miles from home. There, in the cold that gripped my face, in the low, blue light failing around me, and the short day ending, in those familiar and friendly shadows, I was suddenly aware of something that did not care if I lived" (95).

The ability to care leads the elders and Haines to storytelling. Storytelling lies at the heart of any memoir, of course, but here it functions as an explicit theme and literary strategy. Already at the end of "Lost," it appears in the final image of uncertainty: "But sometimes you can't be sure, and a thing will happen that remains so unresolved, so strange, that someone will think of it years later; and he will sit there in the dusk and silence, staring out the window at another world" (96). In the early manuscripts, Haines paired "Lost" with a story he first called "The Bag of Bones," here titled "The Sack of Bones" (97–103). A kind of Gothic detective story, the essay appears as a tale told by Hans Seppala to Haines, but unlike many of the old-timers' stories, this one is told only once. There is no clear moral to the unresolved mystery of Hans's discovery of a sack of human bones, bound with heavy wire, in a pile of driftwood on the Tanana River. Hans connects the bones to a man named Martin, an outsider who encroached on the trap-lines of old-timers Fred Campbell and Emory Hershberger, but there is no evidence to substantiate his idea. Martin had disappeared from his cabin one spring, and nobody knew what happened to him. As "The Sack of Bones" makes clear, Martin is simply a vanished character, not much missed. When Hans returns to the river to verify that the bones are human, the pile of driftwood and sack of bones are gone. There is no resolution to the story—only shadows within shadows.

The unresolved, uncanny moment lies at the center of "Stories We Listened To." In this essay, the main story within a story is Fred Allison's tale of two solitary trappers who meet at a remote cabin during a long winter, spend a night and day together, and never speak (30–35). Haines uses the story to create a "figure of darkness" sitting in the cabin, "looking out at starlight on the snow" (33). Like the figure at the end of "Lost," the trapper silently stares out the window and reflects on his "life of snow, of fur, of solitude and dogs" (33). He wonders how he chose this life, and he knows he could never explain it to his lost family and friends: "He could never say to them, the shadows whose forms now fill his darkening mind, why he came here, chose this life without company, without solace of children or ease for his age. He hardly remembers the reasons, the long-ago decisions. There was the finality of leaving, of saying good-bye; a landscape he would not see again, a people he would never hear from. All that has become part of an immense distance, part of a sleeping self" (34). Bill Melvin tells a humorous second story, about a crowd of impatient gold stampeders forced to walk slowly for three days on a narrow canyon trail behind an unhurried grizzly bear (36–38). Finally, Haines relates a story remembered from composite sources about a neighbor named Jim Chisholm who was badly burned in a cabin fire on Birch Lake and had to cross the frozen lake and walk two miles to the Richardson roadhouse, where two unnamed men saved him and his frozen feet (38–41). Together, the three stories form a legendary past, but the legends are not especially heroic or exemplary, nor do they offer a clear moral. Instead, in terms reminiscent of Jack London's Yukon tales, they seem to suggest the vulnerability of human beings in the Alaska wilderness and the final authority of the place and its animals. As Haines describes the grizzly bear when it decides to leave the stampeders behind, he sounds uncannily like Jack London: "The big, round face of the bear regarded them, his blunt nose searching the air. It was the assured and measuring look of the undisputed master of things" (38).

The most ambitious essay about old-timers is certainly "With an Axe and an Auger." The essay originally had five parts; an omitted Section II is a general reflection on the solitary men left behind "when the great outpouring of the stampedes receded and dried to the puddles of Dawson, Wiseman, Livengood, or Richardson" (JHP Box 33, Folder 5). The published essay begins with a description of an anonymous old man at his remote cabin, telling stories prompted by shadows: "The woods grown up around him are filled with shadows. These shadows have names and faces, but only a few of them have voices, shaken like leaves in the wind" (133). Part II focuses on the narrator's 1947 encounter at a store in Fairbanks with Tom, an old sourdough who is camping on church property along the Chena River. The narrator helps Tom move some of his outfit to the camp, getting one of his first insights into the stampeders left behind forty years before. In Part III, the narrator visits an anonymous old friend, living with his brother "in this rain-swept city on Puget Sound" (140). The three men drink and talk, "groping among memories—of places, events, and people we both have known," the burned and frozen Jim Chisholm among them (142). Together, they look out a window, "gazing into some far place. There is a fire there, warmth, and people we know. The names there have always fitted the things we could see and touch. This is the world we know, and we know ourselves as part of it" (145). Memory casts fitful light on a "shadowy place, to be recalled by a name, a voice, a face; and for a brief time light flickers upon a few images we understand. We are home again, and the known words come to our lips, to be heard and shared by a listener" (146). Part IV is a meditation spurred by the lead sentence, "The land lives in its people" (146), expanding into Haines's direct appreciation of having known the generation of sourdoughs and stampeders: "When I think of them now, it is of something hugely tender and forgiving, akin to a healing thingness in the world that assures the soil of its grasses, the earth of its sun" (147).

Like "Stories We Listened To," the loose episodic structure of "With an Axe and an Auger" creates an unresolved tone of nostalgia, but Section IV concludes with a positive image of the past. The land lives in its people because we remember the names, "names spoken from the shadows" (147). The names they gave the country count, too, no matter how amusing, ironic, or seemingly misplaced they might be. As the essay closes, Haines summarizes the meditation one last time, as if he needs to recur to the poetic rhythms of his own shadow language:

> A wandering spirit came home to the land. In the shape of a man, it cleared a space in the forest and built a shelter from the trees at hand. It came to learn the ways of this country; to sleep and awaken, to flourish and grow old; to watch the river, the clouds moving east, the frost in the grass.
>
> It will never die completely. Look for it in the trails you follow, in the amber blazes on black bark. You will find it in the settled forge, in the rotting windlass, in the cabin sill you come upon by a creek that has no name; in the green scar on that far hill. (148)

In this coda, the names vanish into the impersonal form of a "wandering spirit," but the anonymity of the wandering spirit does not negate the homecoming or the everlasting traces it leaves behind.

The last essay in *The Stars, the Snow, the Fire* is also the shortest as well as the first that Haines published: "Richardson: The Dream."[7] It may well be the most poetic and effective, too. The viewpoint is an anonymous, first-person plural, opening with a description of a midwinter night on the Richardson road, wind blowing a light and dry snow. The figure of a man approaches the Richardson roadhouse, and he is as anonymous as the "wandering spirit" in the "shape of a man" that closes "With an Axe and an Auger." The narrator conjectures as to a possible identity for the man, though "his face is hidden with the hood of his parka" (161). He names the names of old-timers—Hans, Melvin, Hershberger—even though the paradoxical figure appears to be "a stranger, and yet he knows his way." The roadhouse is empty, deserted, cold—but the man stubbornly climbs the porch and knocks on the door and windows.

The scene is completely empty, marked by the steady repetition of the word "no." No sound within, no dog barking, no light, no sheet of ice on the eaves, no fire in the house for a long time, nobody home. The man stands and listens, but besides the creak of the signboard there is "no other sound but the wind, quiet with snow in the forest. No stars can be seen, there are no lights anywhere in the distance. The entire landscape seems dark and empty, the vast Interior a place of snow and silence" (162). The wonder is that we see anything at all.

Haines's last dream of Richardson is far from the "old hunter's dream of plenty." It instead approaches a final version of that dream's "sometime shadow: the country dead, and nothing to see in the snow. Famine, and the great dream passing" (29). If the essay were to end with "the vast Interior, a place of snow and silence," it would cast a final shadow over the entire book and conclude definitively with the passing of the great dream. But that is not the actual ending. Instead, we read the following: "The man turns away, pulling his parka hood around him. He walks again on the road in the direction he came from, into the wind, toward Tenderfoot Hill. He disappears in the darkness. Snow closes around him, filling his tracks as he goes" (162).

The final paragraph is crucially filled with actions, even though the actions seem doomed to take place within shadows and an ultimate darkness. Indeed, the man vanishes in the darkness, and his tracks are erased by blowing snow, but in the last image he is continuing to walk into the wind, returning in the direction he came from, perhaps toward a home on Tenderfoot Hill. Yes, the entire landscape seems dark and empty, and the vast Interior is surely a place of snow and silence, but the wandering spirit in the shape of a man continues to search for a place of light and fire. If he knows his way, maybe he will remember how to reach home. Or perhaps the paragraph echoes most emphatically the final sentence of "Shadows": "Only the wind and the distance, the silence of a vast creatureless earth" (160). The essay is haunting precisely because it refuses to determine the identity and fate of the hooded, vanishing figure. In any case, the "real place" we seem to have arrived at stretches equally into the past and into the future, and it is a "country that is both specific and ideal" (*SSF* ix). Rather than being a place of reductive oppositions, however, it seems to be a place of possibilities. Finally, in our journey and arrival, the place speaks a shadow language, and we—Haines and his readers—must always speak a shadow language in return.

PART 2

ANOTHER COUNTRY

CHAPTER 4

THE CHANGED PASTORAL

New Poems, 1980–88

COLLECTING THE NEWS

Some basic tendencies in John Haines's composition process emerge from reading the early poetry and prose in the light of the manuscript drafts and correspondence. Haines works most often from direct observations, constructing a landscape that combines memory, dream, and imaginative projection with concrete, physical details. He drafts poems and essays through a complex process of collection, expansion, and concentration. In chapter 3, for example, we saw how Haines collects stories from the very beginning of his Richardson homesteading, patiently holding a story like "Bag of Bones" for decades before he is prepared to publish it as "The Sack of Bones" in a strategic pairing with the reflective essay "Lost." In chapter 1, we followed another trail: An early poem like "Dream of the Lynx" begins as a realistic narrative of trapping in the draft poem titled "Death in the Frost," but through the process of condensing and concentrating the language of the draft, Haines creates a richly oneiric experience in which the trapper and the lynx deepen into one another. In chapter 2, we encountered a third process, similar to collecting, in which Haines patiently gathers stories or images that are somehow related to one another, eventually discovering a way to clarify the relationship. In the essay "Poems and Places" (*LOC* 123–35), for example, Haines comments on several of his early poems, relating most of them to his experiences at the Richardson homestead and showing how an event or a set of images can gestate for years until it finds a role in a poem. "The Stone Harp" emerges from Haines's discussion as a gathering of images, each element forming a separate stanza and the whole poem creating, according to the poet, "a metamorphic figure, something trying to become another thing, and the ghost of a sound" (*LOC* 128).

This complicated process of gathering materials leads to a variety of results. The draft essay "Shadows," for instance, shows how Haines collects, gathers, and expands material on a common theme, then decides that the material is best served by being separated into several essays and dispersed strategically within *The Stars, the Snow, the Fire*. In another way, the poems "Homestead" and "News from the Glacier" show how Haines gathers material and creates two very different sequences that embody a new poetry of the earth. "Homestead" is marked by narrative structures of departure, memory, and return, while "News from the Glacier" follows a spatial or cartographical organization. In these two sequences, in fact, we see some of the greatest potential for new directions in Haines's mature poetry.

In the 1980s, Haines explored the new directions in a series of collections, none of which is exactly like anything else he had ever produced before. The first, *News from the Glacier: Selected Poems, 1960–1980*, published by Wesleyan University Press in 1982, would seem at first to be a simple act of selection and summation. Haines suggests this reading of selection by using the title of the major sequence from *In a Dusty Light* to name the new volume. But while that is clearly one important aspect of a "selected poems," Haines does not limit himself to a summary selection. The eleven poems of *In a Dusty Light*, including the two major sequences, appear in the last section of *News from the Glacier*. In addition, Haines includes two poems from *Leaves and Ashes* not printed in *Cicada*: "The Ghost Hunter" and "On the Mountain." Moreover, the lead poem of the last section, "The Sun on Your Shoulder," dates from 1975 and was published by Graywolf Press in a pamphlet series. Three other interesting poems date from 1977 and are not included in either *Cicada* or *In a Dusty Light*: "Hunger," "The Fossil," and "Mothball Fleet: Benicia, California." The final poem, in the section and the volume, is "Harvest," dated 1962–1980; it serves as a retrospect over Haines's career, including the volume of selected poems itself. Haines in effect gives both a summarizing selection and a forecast of future possibilities. Thus the poems of Section V evoke the poetry of the earth developed in *In a Dusty Light*, and the theme of deep time functions significantly in "The Ghost Hunter," "Hunger," and "The Fossil," giving a capacious temporal frame to Haines's reflections, both on his place in the world and on the place of his poems in American literature. Haines delivers news from the glacier that is truly both ancient and fresh.

The potential of *News from the Glacier* is abundantly realized in Haines's next volume of poems, *New Poems: 1980–88* (Story Line Press, 1990). The book includes eight long poems composed of multiple parts, and six of these are sequences composed of from six to fifteen sections. The sequences clearly build on the earlier successful experiments of "Homestead" and "News from the Glacier." As a writer, Haines grows into the sequence as a form, and all eight of the long poems are major accomplishments by a mature poet. Three of the sequences explore new directions for Haines's poetry of the earth: "Rain Country" is set in Richardson and has close connections to Haines's prose memoirs, while "Water of Night" and "In the Forest Without Leaves" expand the scope and range of Haines's ecopoetry in several important ways. The relationship between nature and culture is the central focus of all three sequences. Further, that key relationship functions as the central idea in "Meditation on a Skull Carved in Crystal," "Death and the Miser," and "Days of Edward Hopper." But in these three sequences, Haines focuses explicitly on artworks and the life of the artist, making new statements on the art of poetry. Even in seven shorter poems—"Head of Sorrow, Head of Thought," "Of Michelangelo, His Question," "On a Certain Field in Auvers," "Paolo and Francesca," "Broken Mirrors," "The Owl in the Mask of the Dreamer," and "Ancestor of the Hunting Heart"—Haines develops intriguing new aspects of his theories of art and art history. Despite the seemingly prosaic title, *New Poems: 1980–88* is one of Haines's greatest poetic achievements, and the poems are decidedly new.

THE OWL IN THE MASK OF THE DREAMER

The short poem "The Owl in the Mask of the Dreamer" can serve as a synecdochic commentary on *New Poems* and on *The Owl in the Mask of the Dreamer: Collected Poems* (1993). In a note to the poem in the later collection, Haines calls it "a concentrated history of the art of sculpture, from early times to the present. The last three stanzas refer to a famous metal sculpture by Alberto Giacometti" (*The Owl in the Mask of the Dreamer* 245; hereafter cited as OMD). Perhaps it would be more accurate to call the poem a history of what we have lost in the history of art. The first four stanzas take us immediately to a landscape of loss:

> Nothing bestial or human remains
> in all the brass and tin
> that we strike and break and weld.
>
> Nothing of the hand-warmed stone
> made flesh, of the poured heat
> filling breast, belly, and thigh.
>
> The craft of an old affection
> that called by name the lion shape
> of night, gave rain its body
>
> and the wind its mouth—the owl
> in the mask of the dreamer,
> one of the animal stones asleep . . .

The underlying assumption that Haines makes here is that the source of art lies in the "old affection" of human beings for wild animals. In the terse metaphors of the poem, the owl is the true source of the mask that the dreamer fashions, even if the mask does not strictly imitate the form of the owl. In the first four stanzas, the poet laments the fact that "nothing bestial or human remains" because the human depends upon the bestial. We have forgotten, or have decided to ignore, our obligation to "the lion shape of night," the rain and the wind. The central figure of the poem thus recapitulates Haines's early idea of the "old spiritual vitality" that we derive from wild animals.

The art described in the poem is already abstract, modern, and divorced from the quasi-sexual "hand-warmed stone" and "poured heat" of past artists. Even though the last three stanzas describe Giacometti's "people of drawn wire" in specific terms, the whole poem seems to lament twentieth-century industrial techniques of "cutting torch," "grinding wheels," and "the lathe." From the very beginning of Haines's history, metals threaten the artistic imagination: brass and tin, a fist of slag, a knot of rust, a face of chrome, black dust, a sinewy metal shaving or curl, a swept square of bronze. The result of the history is most important in those three stanzas focusing on Giacometti's sculpture. The metallic people of drawn wire "stride toward each other," but they remain figures of severe isolation, so much so that it is difficult to say who the poet asks to speak on their behalf:

> Speak for these people of drawn wire
> striding toward each other
> over a swept square of bronze.
>
> For them the silence is loud
> and the sunlight is strong.
>
> No matter how far they walk
> they will never be closer.

The ambiguity of the unfinished sentence reveals the double distance of the "people of drawn wire." They will never be closer to one another, and they will never be closer to subtleties of sound and shadow. In tellingly unadorned language, Haines captures his history of art and suggests that it outlines deeper spiritual losses in the history of modern humankind.

By titling his collected poems *The Owl in the Mask of the Dreamer*, Haines indicates the central significance of nature, art, and artists to his mature poems. As "Owl in the Mask of the Dreamer" suggests, these poems are more than exercises in ekphrasis. In fact, the new poems of both *New Poems* and *The Owl in the Mask of the Dreamer* represent Haines's development of a new poetic vision. As we have seen in "The Hole in the Bucket," the vision is what Haines refers to as an "idea":

> By "idea" I mean, among other things, some kind of conviction about the world and the place of poetry in it. It is an insight, let's say, that makes of experience and perception a particular way of seeing: what we sometimes call the poet's "vision." The insight may come as a sudden revelation, but it is more likely to be achieved slowly as a result of

> simply living and responding to things in the world, of reading and thinking, and of the daily work of writing poems and thinking about writing poems. (*LOC* 65)

The language of this passage recalls the "place of conviction" that Haines describes in the earlier essay "Roots" (*LOC* 85–89). In that sense, the new "idea" of the 1980s and 1990s continues the work of earlier books like *The Stone Harp*, *Cicada*, and *In a Dusty Light*, for it is just as ambitious and all-encompassing as the poetry of the earth that emerges in the 1970s. But in another sense, the "idea" breaks new ground and fashions a new place of conviction for Haines's poetry.

FOREST WITHOUT LEAVES

Two unpublished typescripts from the 1980s provide key insights into Haines's developing idea, and together they usefully frame the major sequences in *New Poems, 1980–88*. The first, dated 1982–1983, is titled "A Provisional Draft of an Essay on 'Forest Without Leaves'" (JHP Box 25, no folder). In twelve pages, Haines details the origin of the sequence "In the Forest Without Leaves," his three-year collaboration with composer John Luther Adams to make a new artwork combining words and music. Moreover, the provisional draft elaborates on ideas that came to light for Haines during the collaboration. As I will argue, these ideas constitute Haines's "changed pastoral," a new poetic vision of the earth. The second unpublished typescript, dated August–November 1987, is a thirty-three-page transcript of an interview between Adams and Haines, revised several times by Haines during the four months. The interview, in fact, becomes a conversation between the two artists about their collaboration and about the role of art as a means of meditating deeply on the relations among nature, history, and culture. In several ways, the conversation echoes Haines's draft essay on "Forest Without Leaves" and suggests some of the key words in Haines's mature poetic vocabulary.

Haines seems overly modest in calling his essay a "provisional draft." In the three-page preamble to the essay, he notes that the original phrase "forest without leaves" occurred to him in 1976, while he was "driving through a particularly blighted part of southern Ontario—an area that had been drastically altered, made barren by mineral development and heavy industry." Furthermore, he suggests that the phrase might "contain an image that would stand for the modern world—to speak, as phrase and image, for a world spiritually blighted and physically threatened with destruction" ("Provisional Draft" 1). Haines drafted a few poems along these lines and outlined a sequence in his notebooks, and he thought that the phrase could become an "idea" that would "contain the whole, or at least a good portion, of the history of humankind. But this was not enough." Characteristically, Haines demands that the idea become "a conception that would hold, and stand up to any analysis. An idea like this starts out with an immediate handicap: ours is not a time in which successful poetry can be written to a theme or constructed around a conception—or so goes a notion currently popular" (1). Caught between his ambitions and the lack of a clear path forward, Haines stopped working on the sequence, but he continued to "consider the whole thing with the patience due a long term work" (2).

At this point, in the summer and fall of 1981, John Luther Adams entered the scene, becoming one of Haines's closest friends over the next thirty years. Not yet thirty years old, and not yet the accomplished, avant-garde composer of today, Adams proposed writing a cycle of songs or setting poems to music for solo voice and chorus. In effect, the young Adams reawakened Haines's sense of the possibilities in the poems of "In the Forest Without Leaves." As Haines describes the process, he rediscovered the "lyrical or melodic" (2) quality of the poems, and over the next three years the two artists developed more and more possibilities for the musical composition and the poetic sequence, as Haines's progress report makes clear: "The original arrangement of verses has been redefined, changed as circumstances have changed and the latent possibility in the poems became clearer, until finally a firm structure of eighteen poems was arrived at. As the various parts have been set to music, the original conception has been clarified" (3). Ultimately, Adams's cantata, "Forest Without Leaves," was first performed by the Arctic Chamber Orchestra in November 1984.[1]

After this preamble, Haines's discussion of "the latent form and content of 'Forest Without Leaves'" (4) becomes a wide-ranging essay on nature, language, and art. Throughout the essay, Haines consistently maintains a mimetic theory of art: the word "forest," for instance, stands for "the original home in nature," and the way in which nature is "perceived, absorbed, and acted upon" constitutes "a world and a way of life." Haines's theory emphasizes mimetic process: "The sounds, the colors, the motion, and the visual and aural imagery that came to stand in some way for these, formed a language, a code, intelligible and approximate to reality" (4). Ultimately, this language or code forms art—"poetry, music, or the plastic arts," in Haines's definition—and, over time, systems of art become "more and more complicated, sophisticated, and capable of abstract power and of infinite recall" (4). At the same time, the language of art becomes "a kind of solace, a consolation to the human creature ever more separated, distant from the natural home, the original hearth of all that had since come to replace the forest" (5).

In Haines's mimetic theory of art, the musical composition or poem is "an attempt to reconstruct the world" and to "approach in some degree a *natural* order that we understand, if at times only dimly, as existing somewhere" (5). Nature, in Haines's mimesis, is always the source to which the artist returns, not only for models of order but "for that confirmation of our existence, of our relatedness to the world—a relatedness otherwise threatened with dispersal into abstractions or, as in our own time and place, into rawly manipulated commercial images of reality" (6).

As the "craft of an old affection" in "The Owl in the Mask of the Dreamer" suggests, Haines figures the return to nature in terms of the hunter. For Haines, all art forms, social structures, and political actions manifest the human need for order, and all "take their initiative, their initial character, from the original alertness of the hunter, the man to whom the natural world is a text, an arrangement of significances." As if he were turning the essay "Snow" inside out, Haines asserts that "the words put down on paper—letters of the alphabet, cyphers, musical notes—are a mode of game-tracking, as the process of thought itself brings into play all the instinct and skill of the hunting mind" (6). Even the mind itself is mimetic, "a kind of imitation, or reflection, of the world" (8). Through aesthetic "game-tracking," according to Haines, we find our way to a playful, delight-filled sense of infinite variety and possibility in nature and, by extension, in ourselves.

If not for the dynamic role of play, human practices such as art become "fixed and incapable of further variation and development, so that often enough a kind of violence is required to change or reform them" (7–8). In fact, the tendency of art forms to become fixed and stale requires that "some reconstruction must take place—the form must be renewed, the understanding, the relation among the elements must be redefined and reestablished.

In that renewal it may be that subtlety assumes more and more the place of substance" (8). Given the close relationship between art and other social practices, moreover, Haines concludes that the artistic "renovation of values" extends to the revolutionary impulse in society at large, while at the same time it imitates the process of renewal in nature. For this reason, too, Haines draws the inference that art "at its fullest potential becomes representative of a harmony at rest somewhere between nature and society" (10). More than a simple one-way reflection, then, art becomes "a kind of mediation between us and the world" (10). Thus Haines forges a dynamic, socially active, mediating theory of mimesis.

Returning to the specific case of "Forest Without Leaves," Haines emphasizes the natural source of all knowledge: "That the Cumaean Sybil wrote her replies on leaves is in itself significant; that the leaves were scattered afterwards by the wind recreates that persistent image of a world whose particles and fibers must be continuously sorted out and recombined to create a sensible and living order" (12). If Haines's artist resembles the figure of the Cumaean Sybil, the figure is very different from the famous epigraph to T. S. Eliot's *The Waste Land* (1922). For Haines, the *leaves* take precedence and create significance. Haines makes a similar point in the opening of "Of Michelangelo, His Question," published in *New Poems.* "Sybil and prophet have spoken, / are fixed in their chairs," but, unlike the fixed sybil, Michelangelo remains open to the painful reconstructions of art:

> once more the whirlwind sweeps
> the dark-tongued leaves
> to the lap of a woman so old
> she is a child who cannot remember
> when her book of the marvelous
> came unthreaded
> and the pages were scattered.

Instead of a fixed and permanent truth, art creates a perpetual whirlwind of "sensible and living order." The artist is charged, in the poem, with gathering and ordering the scattered leaves, translating their dark tongues, and then beginning the process over again. But the most authoritative figure remains the sweeping whirlwind, so reminiscent of the wind in "The Stone Harp" and the poems of *In a Dusty Light.*

The 1987 conversation between Haines and Adams echoes the "Provisional Draft" in a number of topics and terms. Their discussion begins, as it must, with Alaska and the importance of place, but Haines insists on placing those terms in a larger context. For Haines, the homesteading experience can stand as "a late episode in the American romance with the frontier" (JHP Box 18, Folder 8, p. 4). But it is more deeply, and characteristically for Haines, a metaphor for "the human journey." Haines moves toward the old ways of deep time, just as he moves toward the figure of the ancient hunter in the "Provisional Draft." Here he notes that "the journey of human life begins right here, on this ground—in that old hunting and gathering existence. It goes from there into tribal life, into town life and civilization, and increasing complexity. And at periodic intervals it returns to something that is fairly simplified, even primitive" (4). For Haines, this recurring process is more than simply an experience of authenticity. The repeated journey allows him to "understand events and particulars, to sort them out so that they make a higher kind of sense—more or less as an historian or an anthropologist will do, in sifting the evidence, and consulting the texts, to find some useful pattern" (5). The larger historical and mythic context is significant for Haines personally, as well, for he admits to Adams that over the past ten to twelve years he has experienced "a real descent into the underworld," a "black depression and confusion of mind," and "periods of personal doubt and confusion" (5–6). On the other hand, "periods of clarification" come in the form of a sense of direction, along with a sense of being part of the larger human journey.

In addition to the trope of the journey, Haines dwells at some length on the critical usefulness of what he calls the "European tradition." He gladly acknowledges his debts to Chinese poetry and indigenous cultures (9), but he does not pretend to expertise in these areas. Instead, he sounds very much like a Modernist poet when he calls his aim in poetry "to bring the contemporary world and the past together in some sort of dialogue, or have them fuse together in such a way as to create a new reality" (13). That perspective also explains his defense of "the old, verifiable verse structures" and the careful dialogue he seeks to create with them. Finally, the conversation makes clear that Haines remains an active and rather conservative theorist of mimesis. When Adams expands on his own sense of inherited musical forms and structures as being in some sense "architectural" and expresses a desire to create new forms and structures, Haines responds by asking, "But don't you think that what you're describing in reference to inherited structures, once had its origin in nature, and that the whole sense of structure, in music, in art and language, does have its source there? Isn't there a sense in which we could speak of natural forms as architectural? Doesn't, perhaps, to take just one example, sonata form represent a refinement of some remote natural sequence?" (20).

The question of sources, whether natural or cultural, raises the issue of Haines's interest in visual art and artists. Once again, he is careful to explain that "sources" may not even be the right word to describe what he is attempting to do:

> My interest in painting, in art, has been a way of thinking back into history and culture, a kind of meditation. History as such is one thing; I can go to a text, read it, and think about what I've read. But what we call art is another text, I think we can say, and I'm drawn to that, not because I want to turn specific works into poems—that's all too easy, and many people have done it. To put it another way, art is itself a language, a way of telling; and what it tells is, in a sense, what I am trying to make clear to myself in the poems I write. I have gone back to it to see what, in certain individuals, works, and periods, I can find that will illuminate this moment in time. (22)

Clearly the ekphrastic poem, describing a specific artwork, is the least of Haines's concerns, even though he includes ekphrastic elements in several of his poems about art and artists. As in the "Provisional Draft," art is a means for Haines to meditate on large issues of history, language, culture, and nature; to see how humanity has arrived at its present situation; and to deliberate on possibly useful ways to see ourselves in the present moment. In another response to Adams, he says that he is "trying to go into what I see there, even if it's only one or two or three images in a given artist's work, and distill from them something that is apparent not only in the painted images, but in the unconscious material I sense is there behind the images" (22). The phrase "unconscious material" signals Haines's abiding interest in the psychological role of dreams in the artistic imagination, an interest that is embodied in the owl in the mask of the dreamer.

The search for a holistic vision or "idea" leads Haines to conclude that the artist must pursue more than material success or institutional sinecure.

As is often the case during the conversation, he begins with questions: "Whether you are concerned with a single creative act or a lifetime of effort: how do we reconcile these apparently unrelated elements of our present reality? How do we, in our lives, deal with them and the questions and the pseudo-answers they bring up? Is it enough, for example, to sit in the university, draw one's salary and save for retirement, on the assumption that one's position there, no matter what its title, is no different than it might be in any corporation or professional field?" (32). In response to his own questions, Haines offers an entirely different vision: "I attempt in one way or another to deal with [these questions] when I write, whether a poem or an essay; to find a place there for history, for nature, for art and poetry, to mingle and say something to each other and be in some way a revelation to us. I suspect that you in your own way attempt something like this in your music. And I think any serious and thoughtful person, in the arts and elsewhere, will be looking for ways to do this" (33).

Haines's deep journey to place becomes, finally, a recurring process of game-tracking history, nature, and art.

THE CHANGED PASTORAL

In the six major sequences in *New Poems*, Haines creates a place for nature and culture to mingle. Even though the mingling renders moot the question of topic or subject, it is still helpful to see "Rain Country," "Water of Night," and "In the Forest Without Leaves" as primarily focused on nature, developing Haines's new poetry of the earth. On the other hand, "Meditation on a Skull Carved in Crystal," "Death and the Miser," and "Days of Edward Hopper" focus on the role of art, especially the visual arts, in defining humanity's place in relation to nature and history. In addition, Part V of *New Poems* includes two shorter sequences on Vincent Van Gogh ("On a Certain Field in Auvers") and Pablo Picasso ("Broken Mirrors") as well as brief poems on works by Auguste Rodin and Michelangelo. Thus four of the seven parts in *New Poems* are devoted to art and artists. But the two longest sequences, "Water of Night" and "In the Forest Without Leaves," come last in the volume and make the greatest effort at integrating the "apparently unrelated elements" of twentieth-century reality into a new poetic place, a thoroughly modern pastoral vision. "Rain Country"

(1978–1983) is the most accessible of the three sequences of earth poetry. The six sections form a pastoral elegy, inspired by Haines's early homesteading years and his abiding admiration for the generation of old-timers who had mined, hunted, trapped, and fished the area surrounding Richardson from the first years of the twentieth century. The poem is structured both as a narrative and as a remembrance. Haines is once again practicing the art of memory that he perfected in *The Stars, the Snow, the Fire*. Indeed, "Rain Country" has much in common with the unpublished 1981 essay "The View from Buckeye Dome," for like that essay it uses a present narrative to frame the story of an earlier event, in this case a rainy autumn walk Haines and his first wife, Peg, took with Fred Campbell in 1952. Nothing remarkable takes place in the sequence, but Haines employs several of the conventional *topoi* of pastoral elegy. Thus Section II features the grieving landscape, but an earthquake is described simply as "a sound / the earth made that morning— / a heavy rumble in the grey / hills toward Fairbanks." Second, and more important, like every modern pastoral elegy from "Lycidas" to "In Memory of W. B. Yeats," the memory of the beloved dead becomes the occasion for political or social commentary on the present, as in this stanza from Section IV:

And all the stammering folly
aimed toward us
from the rigged pavilions—
malign dictations, insane
pride of the fox-eyed men
who align the earth
to a tax-bitten dream
of metal and smoke—

all drank of the silence
to which we turned.

Later in Section IV, Haines implicitly contrasts the "tax-bitten dream" with the "time-bitten earth," for the poet can accept the devouring losses of time much more readily than the contrived costs that align the earth with human greed. Ultimately, the poet helps heal the time-bitten earth by "remembering, fitting names / to a rain-soaked map" (Sec. V).

In Section VI the poet becomes a changing, deepening shadow of the Cumaean Sibyl. This figure combines imagination, dream, and memory. It occupies a specific geographical place but transforms it into a dream-place, an idealized place of conviction. And the sybilline poet embraces a world that is always in motion:

> I write this down
> in the brown ink of leaves,
> of the changed pastoral
> deepening to mist on my page.
>
> I see in the shadow-pool
> beneath my hand a mile
> and thirty years beyond
> this rain-driven autumn.
>
> All that we loved: a fire
> long dampened, the quenched
> whispering down of faded
> straw and yellowing leaves.
>
> The names, and the voices
> within them, speak now
> for the slow rust of things
> that are muttered in sleep.
>
> There is ice on the water
> I look through, the steep
> rain turning to snow.

The quatrains shift to a tercet at the end of the poem, marking closure at the same time that the imagery evokes the poet's acceptance of seasonal changes and the dreamlike utterance of the "slow rust of things." Haines also recognizes the need for a "changed pastoral" to deepen our connections to the earth. Part of the deepening change takes place by looking into the "shadow-pool" of the past, bringing those collective memories into the present and allowing them to speak now. Part of the deepening occurs because the poet brings memory into relation with dream. Another part depends on the poet's vision, the ability to look through the present and see how rain is always turning to snow. As in *The Stars, the Snow, the Fire*, Haines creates a richly elegiac shadow language, a language that allows him to "claim this clearing / in the one country I know" (Sec. V).

The three art sequences and Part V of *New Poems* in effect surround "Rain Country" with ideas of history and culture. Haines's approach develops a deepening, changed pastoral. The many forms of pastoral provide great amplitude for treating the relationships Haines defines as his "idea" in the essay on "Forest Without Leaves," and that pastoral idea organizes the three art sequences as well. We can see this clearly in an asterisked manuscript note that Haines wrote on a draft sheet of "Death and the Miser," in a folder of typescripts headed "Poems on Art":

> [The] secret of the poem, and of the paintings, is the revenge of nature and its denied forms on a humanity that has in the face of its gifts erected another world—of false values . . . and false securities.
>
> Into the confusion caused by this turning away from the given world come the nightmare creatures of that world, distorted, maimed, combined with wrenched human forms—this confusion is the content of Bosch's and Breughel's paintings of the period.
>
> One could say also that it is the content of surrealism—? (JHP Box 18, Folder 7)

Like the "Provisional Draft" and the 1987 interview with John Luther Adams, this brief passage provides a number of key insights into Haines's organizing pastoral idea for the art poems. First, he sees the paintings and poems as aligned with one another in outlining the crucial idea of "the revenge of nature." Second, in Haines's conservative theory of mimesis, nature is clearly the primary source of cultural values, and humanity has denied the forms of nature in its historical development of culture. Third, the denial of natural forms leads to "distorted, maimed" imaginative creations. Fourth, great artists like Bosch and Breughel expose this distorted development by making confusion the content of their work. Fifth, Haines conjectures that the same could be said of surrealism, but he does not specify whether he means the artistic movement of post-World War I Europe or the poetic movement of American writers like Robert Bly, James Wright, and himself. Finally, the passage provides a specific "game-tracking" commentary on the synecdochic poem "The Owl in the Mask of the Dreamer," and the tracks open up readings of the sequences as new versions of the changed pastoral that Haines recognizes in "Rain Country."

The lead sequence in *New Poems*, "Meditation on a Skull Carved in Crystal," takes as its ostensible subject a crystal skull, perhaps of pre-Columbian Mesoamerican origin.[2] Haines seems to take the skull at face value, since in Sections II and VI he alludes to Aztec or Mayan cultural developments like "the wheel of the calendar." But the real focus of the sequence, clear in the very beginning, is the skull as a metaphor for a specific thought: "To think that the world / lies wholly in this mind; / that this frozen water, / this clarity of quartz, / this ice, is all." The skull symbolizes not simply the mind but the all-containing mind. That thought erases the world and delivers nature to "the fate / of water sealed in a jar" (Sec. III). In Sections IV and V, however, the poet resists the fixedness of the crystal skull, calling for it to "return to water and mist" and to "go back to rain." In lines that could easily appear in "The Owl in the Mask of the Dreamer," Haines praises the predator's instinct for blood and laments the loss of the body in the fixed grin of the skull:

> Nothing of beast or man
> remains, of the stroked fur
> and the aroused flesh;
> but the filed teeth fixed
> in their glitter,
> a smile of ferocious peace. (Sec. V)

In Section VI, the poet calls for an art that will rejoin humanity and nature, even if the means of reunion is violent: "Break open the breast-cage, / let the creature-heart redden / in the light that remains." In the last four sections of the sequence, Haines uses direct address relentlessly, but the addressee is certainly both the reader and the poet, at least as much as the crystal skull or what it represents. In the "Provisional Draft," as we have seen, Haines conjectures that "the language of art would become in some way, and to a degree, a kind of solace, a consolation to the human creature ever more separated, distant from the natural home, the original hearth of all that had since come to replace the forest" (5). Even though the commanding voice of the "Meditation on a Skull Carved in Crystal" gives little solace or consolation, it achieves a sense of community in the plural pronoun of the final section: "Intelligence is what we find, / gazing into rock as into water / at the same depth shining." The skull does not absorb or contain the world. It is a mirror, or in the cold closing stanza, it is "a grain of ice in the stellar / blackness, lighted / by a sun, distant within." In that last tiny image of distance, Haines suggests that the abstractions of art both create and combat our distance from the "natural home."

The second art sequence, "Death and the Miser," is formally the most traditional in *New Poems*, even more so than "Rain Country." The six parts focus specifically on Hieronymus Bosch's painting of 1490, in the National Gallery of Art in Washington, DC. Section I is an exercise in ekphrasis, combined with a resolute direct address to the miser of the poem and painting. Rather than taunting the dying miser, the address includes the speaker and reader from the very beginning, so that the reflections on death weigh equally on us all. Words like "bitten" and "glittering" recall both "Rain Country" and "Meditation on a Skull Carved in Crystal," so that the resonant language begins to suggest a larger pastoral network, a sequence of pastoral sequences.

From the initial ekphrasis, "Death and the Miser" expands to enact the revenge of nature. Section II begins with "the dream within the acorn, / still green at the heart / of the forest," but Haines rapidly moves to the miser's separation from nature's fecundity, leading in Sections III and IV to the many guises of death. Though Section IV holds out some hope in the figure of "the angel beside you," Section V signals the turn to inwardness. Like the all-containing crystal skull, inwardness leads to a violent descent with its own "steep momentum." The dying become like "yoked and branded cattle, / stunned with the blood / of the killing floor," their companions hellishly distorted reminders of a world they disregarded and destroyed:

> Not creatures of your mind alone,
> neither men nor women
> nor angels—but stooped
> and pilfering
> they swarm about you
> with cold beaks and probing
> snouts—quarreling

rodents, insects
as large as yourself.

And their voices that are no voices,
but like the sounds of things
broken underfoot—crushed leaves
and littered shells—
thicken the air you breathe
with muddy whispers,
suppressed whines
and stifled barking.

As the manuscript note to the poem suggests, these stanzas present distorted and maimed nightmare creatures, avenging themselves upon any dying miser who ignores the gifts of the earth. The lines also recall the "slow rust of things / that are muttered in sleep" from Section VI of "Rain Country," but the creatures are not only imagined or dreamed. They are real, even if their voices are no voices but only the broken sounds of the earthly things we thought we had mastered.

"Days of Edward Hopper" follows, in two different versions. In *New Poems*, the sequence is in six parts, but in the later collected poems, *The Owl in the Mask of the Dreamer*, Haines adds two more parts, making eight, and dates the sequence 1981–1991. The two added parts emphasize the empty, sour commercialism and political lies of twentieth-century America (Sections II and VII in *OMD*). In both versions, Edward Hopper (1882–1967) is the imagined speaker and prophetic artist, commenting on a modern world of garages, motels, diners, and highways, a world marked by solitude, isolation, and glare. Like Haines, Hopper is a realist, practicing a conservative but supple mimesis and expressing a critical, personal vision of his contemporary scene. Many images recall paintings by Hopper, but specific allusions are not really the point of these poems. Instead, Haines figures Hopper as a visionary witness, commenting directly and indirectly on the destructive transformations of the twentieth century. For readers today, the voice of Haines/Hopper might even seem prophetic:

So much for this child
of amazed colonials,

deceived as to the shore
they claimed; so much
for the citizen who
with such passion swore
allegiance to tar sands. (Sec. III)

This is close to the critical vision Haines takes of the Alaska oil boom in the 1970s and 1980s. Then as now, he might say, "Smoke was the emblem for manhood, / then as now; and *Gasoline* / the name of our country— / high octane that fueled / a tribal frenzy in the music / we danced to, the manic / vacancies we took for joy" (Sec. IV). As in "Rain Country," Haines's changed pastoral holds the past and the present together, not in the service of nostalgia but for a future audience that now includes a new century's readers, who face the consequences of the tribal frenzy of the previous century.

The gentlest treatment of the days of Edward Hopper (as well as our own) comes in Section VI, in which Haines looks at the elderly citizens of a city, seated on park benches: "dry catarrhal crickets, / rustling their papers, / minding their dogs." The last stanza of the section enacts the revenge of nature and creates a new, urban form of changed pastoral, but it does so with a sad wisdom, strikingly different from the tone of "Death and the Miser":

The darkness reaches
toward them out of the trees
and flowering shrubs:
they do not see it,
not one of them understands
how soon, how swiftly,
the grass at their feet,
the paths by which they came,
the words on their lips
will vanish.

No less wise or sad is the speaker's self-knowledge, ending the sequence in three short stanzas. The speaker is both Haines and Hopper, personal and yet also representative, a figure of one moment who speaks beyond the limits of time:

And once for me also,
when quarreling whispers
were abroad, the damp wind
of an autumn night
blew the one sheer curtain
aside.

Light that signaled
the end of a game begun
by the earth's wise children
came with its slow red pulse
to the room where I lay
awake, dismantling night.

Long knives of the shadows
slit the walls. A news-throat
muttered interrogations
at the rain-frontier: names
of the still-to-be-missing,
the sold, the bloodied
and trampled—small peace
and unforgiven crime. (Sec. VIII)

This remarkably powerful passage holds us in Hopper's moment, on an anonymous autumn night before World War II, at the same time that it holds us in the "small peace" after and before other wars—Korea, Vietnam, Kuwait, Iraq, and Afghanistan, to name the most obvious examples from recent American history. Then as now, the wind blows "the one sheer curtain / aside," allowing the artificial light of a neon sign to enter the room. The sign shines ironic light on "earth's wise children," then as now. The descriptive language evokes such early Hopper works as "Evening Wind" (1921) and "Night Window" (1928), but the effect, as Haines explains in the interview with John Luther Adams, is one of meditative distillation rather than ekphrasis (JHP Box 18, Folder 8, p. 22).

The second nature sequence in *New Poems*, "Water of Night," follows the Section V poems about art and artists, and like most of the art poems and sequences, it creates an effect of distillation. Just as "The Owl in the Mask of the Dreamer" presents the history of the natural world that modern sculpture has left behind, "Water of Night" presents a rough narrative of humanity's journey away from nature. The epigraph, from Wordsworth's "Home at Grasmere" (Part I of *The Recluse*), has the "naked trees" and "icy brooks" ask us, "Whence came ye, to what end?" The entire sequence "Water of Night" provides a brooding answer in the form of a broad history. Section I reaches back into deep, prehistoric time to evoke the shamanistic augury of reading "feather of auk, beak of owl" in order to "work the shadows." But already in Section II the "night people," who call to the shadows and awaken them, give way to "the reader / solitary in his pages." In Haines's history, the imagination shifts from communal to individual, from spiritual to literary, and in both shifts there is an accompanying reduction in amplitude or scale. It is as if the imagination had a narrower ground on which to work. In the next two sections, agriculture and the production of grains appear ominous because of the "deep changes" they bring, but the "people of shadow" refuse to lie still in the farmer's furrows: "Each turn of his plow, / a swarm of ashes / rained upward from the ground" (Secs. III, IV). Haines suggests that nature magically combines with the past to warn the farmer of what he has lost in the ground he plows and cultivates.

If the first half of the sequence focuses on the early history of agriculture and implies a set of deep changes that are not historically inevitable, the second half becomes increasingly apocalyptic. Section V presents the battle-scarred industrial landscape as another version of how human beings scratch and dig at the earth, while Section VI connects deathly buildings of civilization with the hierarchical architecture of churches and monuments. In Section VII, Haines is most explicit about the role of fossil fuels in changing the landscape and transforming "an old fragrance of the forest" into "a sour reek and ash / blown down from chimneys."

Finally, Section VIII reflects on shadows, very much in the language Haines uses in the essay "Shadows." The imagery of "Shadows" begins with the "shadows over the land," focusing on the shadows cast by everyday things like clouds or stones or trees. But the shadows also come from "out of the past," evoking extinct animals like mastodons and triceratops, or "primitive birds with terrible beaks and claws" (*SSF* 167). These haunting shadows from the world "speak to the shadows within us, old ghosts that will not die" (167). And like "trapped, primordial birds," the shadows of past things break out from our imaginations and fly into "walls built long ago." In the poem, the most potent ghost or shadow is our recognition of death itself, "another self we carry / as long as we walk in the sunlight, / and a dead thing's shadow dies" (Sec. VIII). Like the shadows in the essay, the shadows in the poem lead to imaginative representations, as when "dry heads of thistles" make shadows in the shape of a man. But the most powerful shadows overwhelm us and our attempts at holding them back with our walls. Those shadows, echoing the language of the essay, give the final answer to the questions posed by the trees and brooks in Wordsworth's poem:

> Shadows into pools, and pools
> into lakes flood back,
> windlass ropes hauling darkness
> out of foaming wells:
>
> comes up with sound of frogs
> and the night cries of birds,
> strong blood of something
> killed in the earth.
>
> And these shadows are climbing,
> big hands on our walls,
> sticking and sucking . . .
>
> Over the drowned gullies,
> houses, fields of the earth,
> seething and rocking,
> water of night. (Sec. VIII)

In these last stanzas, a flood of shadows overwhelms the earth and its inhabitants, but the apocalypse is not necessarily a completely dark one. In a 1996 interview with Matthew Cooperman, Haines expounded on the idea that "humanity must periodically be returned to original sources, whether we do so willingly as individuals, conscious to some degree as to why we do it, or are driven to it by circumstances of nature and history—by the collapse of civilizations, or the breakdown of society, by warfare or pestilence, etc. But sooner or later that return to something like primal condition will occur."[3] In this interview, Haines is retelling the story of artistic abstraction and cultural destruction that informs his mimetic history of modern art in the "Provisional Draft" (7–8). The inevitable return to original sources also bears a strong resemblance to William Carlos Williams's idea of descent, as we have seen it in *Winter News* and *The Stone Harp*. One way of interpreting Haines's apocalypse in "Water of Night," then, is that the poem returns to us the power of shadows to spark our imagination, even if the shadows evoke death and our fear of death. In the interview with Matthew Cooperman, moreover, Haines suggests that the return of the shadows can lead to a new release of creative, artistic energy, such as he witnessed after World War II (134–35). In that case, the flood of shadows at the end of "Water of Night" could evoke a new creative period of history, a necessary washing away of the fixed walls and houses of culture. Thus Haines's changed pastoral, rather than a retreat into nature, argues for an ever-renewing relationship between culture and nature.

LANGUAGE AND THE FOREST

In a brief comment introducing his essay on *The Stars, the Snow, the Fire*, John Knott comments tellingly on the complications of Haines's "In the Forest Without Leaves," which he thinks "may be his best poem":

> Haines juxtaposes surreal images of an industrialized and constricted modern life that he imagines devastated by some future catastrophe to others that suggest the restoration of a simpler and more satisfying way of being in the world regulated by natural rhythms: "It is equinox, the time of old calendars, / when birds set out on their polar journeys, / whales turned north, / men thought of the plow and the net" (Sec. XIV). Details drawn from Haines's Alaskan experience become emblematic of older patterns of human experience that are not easily located in time or space. Throughout his work Haines shows an instinct for finding the archetypal beneath the surface of experience, often using dreams or a dreamlike atmosphere to dissolve the distance between present and past and suggest the universality of an experience.[4]

Knott emphasizes the contrasts between past and present, nature and culture, a universal, archetypal "dreamtime" and the temporalities of history.

All of these contrasts fit well within Haines's vision of a changed pastoral. One crucial question raised by "In the Forest Without Leaves" is whether the pastoral can lead toward a new integration of nature and culture. In other words, can a sequence of poems dissolve the distance between past and present, in effect restoring us to our original home in the forest? Better, can it offer us some new place to begin again?

Haines's "Provisional Draft" on the sequence supports Knott's reading and suggests several ways of understanding the paradoxes of his pastoral vision. First, a fundamental aspect of Haines's mimetic theory of nature and culture is his view of art as a "code or language that equaled or came to stand for the original work of nature " ("Provisional Draft" 4). Second, Haines asserts that the language of art inevitably becomes "more and more complicated, sophisticated, and capable of abstract power and of infinite recall" (4) Third, the language of art can become "a kind of solace, a consolation to the human creature ever more separated, distant from the natural home, the original hearth of all that had since come to replace the forest" (5). The paradox in these three points arises from the triple actions of language, which is the source of metaphorical substitution, existential distance, and spiritual consolation. Because these three actions are not necessarily in harmony with one another, it falls to the poet to find ways to integrate them into "a harmony at rest somewhere between nature and society," in which "art, poetry, become a kind of mediation between us and the world" (10).

The first three sections of "In the Forest Without Leaves" set the key terms for the mediations of the entire sequence. Section I introduces the physical landscape, "drastically altered, made barren by mineral development and heavy industry" ("Provisional Draft" 1), but it also introduces the central relationship of the sequence: "The seasons are of rust / and renewal, / or there are no seasons at all." The alliteration provides two alternatives for the seasons, but the final line reduces the alternatives to an absence. The rest of Section I insists on the metallic, industrial elements of the forest without leaves, where there are no seasons, "only shadows," and "not the shadows of leaves, / but shadows where the leaves might be." The word "shadows," of course, evokes the key metaphor for death in Haines's vocabulary. This strategy of reducing alternatives to insubstantial shadows continues in Section II, in which the sounds to be heard in the forest without leaves are not natural but those of "freezer-mutter" and "rubber-chatter," "gas-bark" and "chopper-bite," the "green chirp / of the dial-crickets." The compound words emphasize the juxtaposition of industrial and natural, evoking the substantial takeover of nature by industrial detritus.

In Section III, language itself becomes the focus of Haines's meditation on the relationship between nature and culture, and here the multiple possibilities of language rise up with a vengeance:

> This earth written over with words,
> with names, and the names
> come out of the ground,
> the words like spoken seeds.
>
> What field, what dust,
> what namesake for a stone
> that moves by inches
> and clears a path in the mud?
>
> Ice moved once, a river of stones,
> and the road it drove
> through the forest can still be walked.
> Look there—you will find
> for your house a standing boulder.
>
> Earth worn deep by its names,
> written over with words:
>
> there are spaces inside those words,
> and silence for the clearing
> where no house stands.

This terse poem presents the central dynamic relationship of the sequence. The earth acts as a kind of substrate for language, "written over with words, / with names," and, in the beginning, names and words can grow out of the ground itself, like "spoken seeds." The glacial landscape of the north presents a forbidding version of nature, as far from traditional pastoral poetry and its memorializing as one can imagine. Still, the glaciers clear a road for human beings, and a glacial erratic boulder can resemble a house. Even in such a vast land, Haines emphasizes the effects of human beings on the earth, "worn deep by its names" and "written over with words." But the final stanza holds out a flickering promise of renewal through language. The "spaces inside those words" open up to "silence" and "clearing," creating a place "where no house stands." Thus the poem creates a countermovement, in which language itself can combat the dominating tendencies of words and names.

Language appears in some form in nearly every section of the sequence, often in counterpoint to another important theme. For example, Sections IV, V, and VI focus on the development of agricultural technologies in eroding the surface of the earth, and in Haines's pastoral the "Earth speech" responds: "the furrow sighing / behind the plow, / the clods talk together" (Sec. V). The image of dust also prevails in the three sections: in Section V, "mobs of dust protest / in whispers, / pushed on by the wind," and in Section VI the windblown dust takes a number of shapes, though "you cannot say what name it had." In Sections VII–X, Haines shows how human beings have used mathematical language to partition and enclose the earth, making both space and time tractable to our purposes. In Section IX, in particular, Haines focuses on "those who write sorrow on the earth," and it is clear who he has in mind: "Agents and clerks, masters / of sprawl— / playful men who traffic in pain." Implicitly paired in Sections IV–X are the narrative of technological development that leads to a destructive, mercenary mastery of the earth and the poet's use of language as a counterforce to writing over the earth with words. For Haines, mimetic language is a means of investigating how art and poetry can mediate between us and the world, and the investigation has a distinctly ethical aspect.

In Sections XI–XII, Haines returns to the forest as a possibility of renewal. The pastoral imagery is both beautiful and austere. The sun comes to the forest, the rain speaks, and the "green branch" flowers, but unlike the traditional pastoral trope of cyclical seasons, in this poem the seasons always proceed in a singularly linear fashion: "Death made a space in the forest / where snow would come, // and silence, and night" (Sec. XI). Winter descends on the forest in Section XII, and the sybilline poet notes in ironic parentheses that "over the leaves is written: / how great the harvest, / how deep the plow." By contrast, Haines does not maintain the fixed view of the landscape taken by "those who write sorrow on the earth" (Sec. IX). Instead, he ends the section with a provisional statement of another kind of certainty:

I know one truth:

Nothing stains like blood,
Nothing whitens like snow.

Here the poet expresses the "one truth" as a kind of alertness. As Haines sees it, the possibility of artistic renewal resides in the "original alertness of the hunter, the man to whom the natural world is a text, an arrangement of significances" ("Provisional Draft" 6). The poet's game-tracking truth bespeaks violence, but it also expresses a kind of purity. Bloodstains on white snow seem to form an "arrangement of significances" or an especially intense kind of writing, countering the plow's deep, sorrowful inscriptions on the earth. The truth of nature implies that the deeper cycles of life and death extend to civilizations, too. We may fear destruction, but we must also yearn for renewal.

Haines devotes the final three sections to the possibility of a renewed and renewing forest. The three poems are grounded in concrete, physical images, but the forest also figures "the original home in nature" that constitutes "a world and a way of life" ("Provisional Draft" 4). In Section XIII, Haines makes the metaphor explicit and universal by addressing the "tree of life," asking what will be said of the tree after it has been stripped of all significance: "And no one left to tell / of your heartwood / peeled down to a seed of ash, / your crowned solitude / crushed to a smoldering knot." The deeper irony, of course, is that the loss of the tree also entails the loss of anyone left behind to tell of it. Thus Haines suggests the entwined fates of nature and humanity. The section ends with the apocalyptic fall of the tree, a prophecy that shadows the forest with potential loss: "The ages parted to let you fall, / and a tall star blazed."

The figure of a blazing star leads to the imagery of fire in Section XIV, in which Haines traces a new season of deepest winter. Each stanza portrays a desperate attempt to find some source of heat and light, but "a stillness in the sun" prevails. Again the fate of the earth is bound up with—determines—the fate of humanity, and even though Haines forecasts a persistent hope that "speaks of soil and spring," it does so "with frost-thickened tongue." Our thoughts turn with the spring equinox, a time of renewal, but those thoughts appear in an ancient past tense, as if the great migrations of birds and whales no longer take place:

> It is equinox, the time of old calendars,
> when birds set out on their polar journeys,
> whales turned north,
> men thought of the plow and the net.
>
> Snow is falling, the sun is late,
> and someone has gone with a lantern
> to search the roads.

The anonymous searcher recalls the hooded figure in "Richardson: The Dream," along with a number of Haines's other travelers and drifters, but here the tone is even less hopeful than it is in the essay. What calendar gives the date in such a place? What can we do now with our belief "in the decimal" (Sec. VII)? What has become of our original home? And what do we hope to find as we search the roads?

Section XV closes the sequence by returning to the first line and title, "In the forest without leaves," but now Haines focuses on a single birch tree, "slender and white." Like the tree of life, the birch tree is stripped to bareness. The first half of the poem describes what has been lost and how it has been lost:

> Only the paper bark stayed
> to weather and peel,
> be sunlight or tinder
> burned in the hunter's fire,
>
> and the wind took away all the rest.

The "paper bark" is both physical and symbolic, but it is most heartening in providing tinder for "the hunter's fire." That image evokes the warmth and light missing from Section XIV, and it also alludes to the game-tracking process of the hunter's imagination. The wind is always a powerful force in Haines's poems, even when it leaves behind a scoured landscape.

In the second half of Section XV, the speaker returns, echoing the truth-telling figure of Section XII, and while the vision he delivers is reductive, it is as powerful as the wind:

If and whenever we come again,
I will know that tree.

A birch leaf held fast
in limestone ten million years
still quietly burns,
though claimed by the darkness.

Let earth be this windfall
swept to a handful of seeds—
one tree, one leaf,
gives us plenty of light.

The birch leaf is both singular and plural. As an image of sole survivorship, it is as unitary as can be imagined. After the wholesale destruction Haines envisions, the "one tree, one leaf" seems a kind of miracle of light. Even if the final stanza is only a prayer, it balances the reductions to singularity with the image of plenty.

At the same time, the "one tree, one leaf" resonates deeply with other passages in *New Poems*. In "Of Michelangelo, His Question," for instance, Haines takes the reader to the end of the corridor to view Michelangelo's famous sculpture of David, only to discover much more than the artwork alone:

Here, at the end of the corridor,
where night and dawn,
dusk and noon, are gathered
in the one standing tree,
art and history
compose their towering image.

To this cloudlit stillness
the pilgrims come, reading
prayers from a guidebook—
to see, to question, and depart.

On its own terms, this passage figures the sculpture as "the one standing tree" and a "towering image" of art and history. In relation to "one tree, one leaf" and the close of Haines's masterful sequence of poems, earthly processes mingle with art and history. The light still burns, even though it may be "cloudlit" and finally claimed by darkness.

A second echo resonates with the image of the hunter's fire, coming from near the end of "Ancestor of the Hunting Heart." In "Ancestor," Haines traces the "distance in the heart," a distance that takes us back through settled landscapes toward "something wilder," associated only with fire and wind. As cold as the distance might be, it has the look of the truth that the speaker perceives in Sections XII and XV of "In the Forest Without Leaves":

> Trees that are black at morning
> are in the evening grey.
> The distance lies between them,
> a seed-strewn whiteness
> through which the hunter comes.

The spatial image of distance combines with the "ten million years" of deep time in Section XV, but even in the harshest reductions Haines finds a windfall. If earth is itself "this windfall / swept to a handful of seeds," moreover, the single word resonates in several figurative and semantic registers. The windfall is primarily the destruction of the single birch tree depicted in the first half of Section XV, but a windfall is also any fruit unexpectedly blown down by the wind to be harvested and eaten. The "handful of seeds" is a windfall. In economic terms, the windfall is usually an unexpected profit, though in John Maynard Keynes's first usages it could also describe a loss (*OED*). Thus the single word "windfall," equated figuratively with the earth, combines ideas of reduction and plenty, destruction and harvest.

As the closing image of "In the Forest Without Leaves" and of *New Poems: 1980–88*, the earthly windfall crystallizes Haines's changed pastoral. As Haines puts it in the provisional draft essay on "In the Forest Without Leaves," the double significance of the Cumaean Sybil is that she writes her replies on leaves and that the image of wind-scattered leaves "recreates that persistent image of a world whose particles and fibers must be continuously sorted out and recombined to create a sensible and living order" ("Provisional Draft" 12). Haines knows, ultimately, that there is no final pastoral place of conviction, that the poet never restores an ultimate retreat or haven for meaning. There are only the recurring, significant relationships of nature to human culture—art, poetry, history—expressed in languages and codes through deep time, stretching from prehistoric cave drawings to Rodin, Hopper, or Giacometti. The world and its places are never fixed and permanent, however much artists or writers may wish to make them so. For Haines, the expansive sequences of *New Poems* represent that persistent image of the changing world as a "tree of life" and the searching artist's persistent efforts to track the earthly windfall.

CHAPTER 5

THE PLACE OF CONVICTION AND THE PUBLIC VOICE

ANOTHER COUNTRY

In the preface to the 1996 collection of essays *Fables and Distances*, John Haines reveals that he had considered titling the book *Another Country* as a way of relating it to his first book of prose, *Living Off the Country* (1981). He also notes that the later work has "less of Alaska" in it because he has "gone beyond a particular locality," although he admits to returning to Alaska as a way of "checking" on himself (*Fables and Distances* xii; hereafter cited as FD). If the two collections differ in their specific focus on "country," they are alike in being hybrids, including critical essays on poetry, book reviews, personal essays on Alaska, and autobiographical sketches. In both collections, the hybrid form is particularly appropriate because Haines does not separate essays about poetry and poets from a larger, deeper sense of a writer's place and work. In that regard, he names Wendell Berry as an exemplary figure, "whose range of interest and competence includes literature, agriculture, and the necessary health of rural communities" (xi). Haines sees Berry as part of "that other community, scattered and not always apparent, of individuals who have sought in one way or another to further the effort in thought and art by which we may know ourselves in this world" (xii). Haines closely resembles Berry in criticizing our present country and pointing toward "another country" that we might still become.

Among these ideas of "another country," Haines does not mention the most obvious meaning, which reappears in the essay "Another Country." In this poetic, place-based meditation, Haines describes two different moose carcasses in order to evoke a deep and pervasive sense of death: "To be nothing and nowhere. Shreds, particles adrift, a little pallor spun in the dark" (*FD* 206). The specific theme of the essay casts light on the broader ideas of "another country" in the book, ideas about the country "as nation, as society, as spiritual home" (xii). In addition, death and the limits of earthly life always cast a deeply haunting shadow in Haines's country, giving him a way of "checking" on himself and his ideas of poetry, place, and community.

Even if there is somewhat less of Alaska in the book, *Fables and Distances* reaches back to *Living Off the Country* in significant ways by foregrounding the idea of the "place of conviction." In the 1971 essay "Roots," Haines reflects on place as more than a geographical center or region:

> The work, and the life, must have their origin in a place of conviction for the poet. It may be an entirely imaginary place invented for the poem, but it is nonetheless true. The poet believes in, or he is becoming a believer in, or he may be letting go of a belief in, a self, a way of being, a way of seeing and feeling. He occupies, or is in the process of occupying, an actual or imaginary ground, ground on which he sees himself with some inner clarity. It is a known place, full of meaning for the poet. What he is and does takes its vitality from that place, that certainty. The work itself may be a search for that place, an approach to it, or even an exit from it into or toward a more substantial reality. (*LOC* 85)

The essayist's voice in "Roots" gives a strong sense of searching for his place of conviction, a process that requires him to define his imaginary ground as well as himself so that he might speak with his own voice from that particular place. In *Fables and Distances*, on the other hand, the older Haines does not use the specific phrase "place of conviction," even though the idea of speaking from a place of conviction is a key to his later poetry and prose.

A second key idea for Haines at the turn of the twenty-first century is public voice. In the 1995 essay "What Are Poets For?" Haines develops the idea that poets express an "ethical passion" by turning to a "public rebuke of persons and policies" (*FD* 20).[1] Citing a long and varied tradition of poems from Dryden, Goldsmith, Blake, Wordsworth, Cummings, Williams, and Pound, he arrives at an answer to the question posed by his essay title:

> In order to write such poems [of ethical passion] you must have a certain conviction, and be willing to submit that conviction to scrutiny, to questioning and, if justified, to doubt. One assumes, in other words, a public voice and an audience, even if that audience must, to some extent, be imagined, as Yeats suggested; or projected into another time, as Robinson Jeffers felt was essential.
>
> That earlier poetry, together with its more modern counterpart, assumed a society and a place for literature within it, however estranged and at odds with society a poet might be. The poets assumed the possibility of a dialogue, however interrupted that might be. And where there is no true dialogue the art itself is in question, and the result will be a poetry of increasing isolation and narcissism, more or less what we have today in abundant measure. (*FD* 31)

The public voice of the poet speaks from the place of conviction, and part of that conviction is the certainty of an imagined audience. Further, the poet assumes that there is a place for literature within the world, a possibility of public dialogue between the poet and the world of "persons and policies." Those assumptions, in fact, ground Haines's dissatisfaction with contemporary American poetry, which he characterizes as resolutely avoiding such public engagement. Although the dissatisfaction becomes more pronounced at the end of the century, it has been present from the very beginning of Haines's writing career.

In a parenthetical paragraph, Haines adds another conviction to his sense of the poet's role in public discourse. "At the center of my argument," he asserts, "is that ancient, myth-dominated relation to the world that has been called magical. Words, thoughts, forms, and acts, once constructed and set in motion, might have an effect on the world—on nature, on the enemy, on the object of one's desire, and so forth—and often enough were intended to do just that. If poetry loses that conviction entirely, it loses the better part of its energy, and will lose as well its justification for existence" (32). If the poet speaks with an authentic public voice, the voice will be magical in its energy, convincing in its authority. Thus Haines confers special powers upon the public voice, and by doing so he places special demands on contemporary American poets. A bit later in the essay, he does name poets who write with "moral and ethical passion"—Hayden Carruth, Philip Levine, Denise Levertov, Louis Simpson, Elizabeth Bishop, Robert Bly, James Wright, John Logan, and Robert Duncan—and he echoes the preface by calling Wendell Berry "the most consistent voice of conscience and conviction in American letters of recent years" (34). Rather than ranking poets or praising poets of his own generation, however, Haines is concerned with defining the need for all poets to write from a place of conviction, most especially the conviction that their words have "an effect on the world" (32).

At the close of the twentieth century, Haines makes concerted efforts to create the public voice he describes in "What Are Poets For?" and to consolidate the series of convictions that had led him from *Winter News* to *New Poems, 1980–88*. These efforts appear in prose and in poetry, in memoir and in critical essay, in expansive sequence and brief lyric. The forms are miscellaneous, and for that reason it is difficult to claim a climactic achievement such as we have seen in previous chapters. Instead, persistence itself becomes a cumulative sign of Haines's convictions and a signal element of his public voice. By seeking to define the public voice, Haines creates his own.

In *Fables and Distances*, Haines's public voice appears in a variety of forms and contexts. Writing in the essay "Something for Our Poetry" (1983), for instance, Haines conducts what he calls "an interrupted rumination on poetry and politics" (68), sparked at first by an overheard conversation about political poetry and by Edwin Muir's evocation of "a constant invisible pressure" in Prague following World War II (68–69). The pressure described by Muir becomes a metaphor for social dread, the weighty tone of voice that Haines finds in writers like Czeslaw Milosz and Octavio Paz (71–75). For Haines, American poetry has not spoken loudly enough to oppose the forces of oppression, whatever economic and political form they take. Thus in answer both to the overheard conversation and to a certain uneasy blankness that arises from considering politics in poems, Haines praises Carolyn Forché's second book of poems, *The Country Between Us* (1981), especially for "the conviction of voice" (74). More pointedly, he deliberately echoes her controversial prose poem "The Colonel" with the title of his essay. In Forché's poem, the dictatorial colonel produces a grocery sack of human ears, spills them onto a table and the floor; losing patience with his foreign visitors, he tells the poet that her people can go "fuck themselves" and that the ears are "something for your poetry, no?"[2] Whatever his aesthetic reservations about politics in poetry might be, Haines agrees with Forché's forceful intervention through the surreal violence of her poem.

Many of the essays in *Fables and Distances* echo Haines's "Provisional Draft of an Essay on 'Forest Without Leaves'" and his interview with John Luther Adams. Indeed, the ideas in these two texts become a major component of Haines's public voice. In a lengthy hybrid piece, "Notes, Letters, and Reflections" (1975–1993), for example, Haines elaborates on at least seven key points that we have seen both in the earlier poems and in the two collaborations with Adams:

- The mimetic theory of art, not as reflection but as mediation
- The declinist interpretation of art history and literary history
- The belief in the primacy of sacred nature, especially what we call wilderness
- The attraction to mythic journeys and movements in poetry
- The figure of the haunted, displaced hunter-gatherer in modern landscapes
- The idea of animal images in dreams as expressing an ancient spiritual vitality
- The idea of reading texts as grounded in reading the world around us, as a matter of survival and a kind of game-tracking. (129–41)

In addition to being a compendium of the writer's major ideas, "Notes, Letters, and Reflections" shows that these ideas maintain a persistent presence in Haines's mature thinking. Taken together, the ideas form a somewhat conservative artistic vision, and they give Haines an independent position from which to critique mainstream American society, politics, and culture.

In "The Creative Spirit in Art and Literature" (1987–1994) and "On a Certain Attention to the World" (1994), Haines develops a fundamental tenet of mimesis, that culture finds its truest foundation in nature. As a corollary, in the latter essay he calls for a sense of wonder, even "*rapture*" (120), in art and literature. Rather than thinking of this emotional tone as mystical, Haines considers it a form of humility, distinct from "our own modern attitude and practice of reducing everything to its particular function and direct usefulness to us" (122). For Haines, nature and culture form "two separate and yet inseparable histories," and the task of the artist is to reconcile them (127). In "The Creative Spirit in Art and Literature," Haines once again argues that the artist or poet fills the role of the Cumaean Sybil, whose prophecies are written on leaves that blow away in the wind: "It may be that the creative impulse can be defined as an eternal search, both actual and symbolic, for those lost leaves and the answers written upon them" (165). The magical figure of the sybil first appears in the "Provisional Draft of an Essay on 'Forest Without Leaves,'" in which Haines emphasizes the dynamic, mediating role of nature: "That the Cumaean Sybil wrote her replies on leaves is in itself significant; that the leaves were scattered afterwards by the wind recreates that persistent image of a world whose particles and fibers must be continuously sorted out and recombined to create a sensible and living order" (12). In addition, the figure reappears in "Of Michelangelo, His Question," again as a metaphor for the scattering of unrelated materials and the creative impulse to order, unify, and harmonize them.

Place, the second major idea in *Fables and Distances*, signifies both the physical, geographical place and the imaginary place of conviction. In Part V, *Days in the Field*, seven essays dwell on ideas of place, and several of these essays are directly related to the "Shadows" essays of the memoir *The Stars, the Snow, the Fire*. "Notes from an Interrupted Journal," for example, is a partial version of "The View from Buckeye Dome," the 1981 manuscript essay that Haines drafted in conjunction with other pieces for *The Stars, the Snow, the Fire* but then did not include in the final version of the book.[3] The essay "Days in the Field" (1980–1994) is similar to the "Interrupted Journal," for it narrates a series of harvest memories set at the Richardson homestead without rigidly fixing the temporal framework. In both essays, past and present flow into and out of one another. "Shadows and Vistas" directly quotes from the "Shadows" essay in *The Stars, the Snow, the Fire*, using the earlier essay to frame Haines's reflections on the spirit of the land and the need for "an essential vista, a sheer sense of the land in its original presence" (201). First presented as an address to the Alaska Environmental Assembly in May 1982, "Shadows and Vistas" calls for an environmental ethic in relation to Alaska lands. In Haines's view, such an ethic would include self-restraint, "a fullness of spirit and being," and a "dimension of imagination, the instilled power to think and to visualize that poetry, for example, nourishes in us" (204). Without all of these elements, Haines clearly suggests in a quotation from "Shadows," we may find ourselves looking out on a cherished landscape to find "only the wind and the distance, the silence of a vast, creatureless earth" (205). As I noted earlier, the essay "Another Country" uses the physical landscape of Richardson (snow, soil, and blood) to ground the writer's imaginative perceptions of a moose's winter death, tying place to a deep sense of our common mortality. The essay is closely related, in language and theme, to longer manuscript versions of "Shadows" (JHP Box 27, Folder 3) and "Death Is a Meadowlark" (JHP Box 18, Folders 4 and 5; Box 25, Folder 2).

Finally, in "Leaving Alaska" (1991), Haines returns to the Richardson homestead a decade later, on August 4, 1991, in order to take his final leave of the place. But of course there is no leaving such a place of conviction. It always remains as a presence and a standard, a way of thinking and perceiving, and it becomes a means by which Haines attains his most persuasive public voice:

> There is something at once inevitable and foreboding in the changes that have taken place here in my lifetime, and the more so in recent years: this relentless filling up of open spaces, and the search for yet another space. And the question I have voiced many times repeats itself: What will happen when we at last understand that there is nowhere to go? No more Alaskas, and no more Yukons, no more open and unsettled places on the continent nor on the earth. Will we be able to face that and decide to make a suitable and habitable place where we are? Or, lacking that resolution, will we turn on each other in that ever more limited and constrictive space and destroy everything? No question seems to me more urgent and needing an answer. To face one's history with insight and courage, admit mistakes, and decide to make the best of what remains of time and place: Few things would seem easier to agree on, yet nothing has proved more difficult for humanity, as the history of civilizations demonstrates over and over. (*FD* 212)

Cumulatively, the seven essays of *Days in the Field* bring the concrete value of place and the Alaskan landscape to bear on Haines's sometimes general ideas concerning mimesis, poetry, the history of nature and culture, and the future of the planet. He can seem downright dreamy in discussing the role of animals in the unconscious, but in an essay like "Another Country" the bull moose and the moose calf become two strikingly evocative figures, both symbolic and actual. The idea of the spiritual presence of a landscape may seem a bit wooly, but not when it emerges from the writer's memory of standing near Maclaren Summit on an October afternoon, gazing down on the Maclaren River basin and the patchy, sunlit tundra ("Shadows and Vistas" 200). In "Leaving Alaska," rather than becoming nostalgic for some vague pastoral ideal, the older writer considers the impact of industrial civilization on the land and poses urgent, passionate questions. Because the questions arise from a concrete place of conviction, they effectively call for another country.

THE TIME OF EARTH CHANGES

The Owl in the Mask of the Dreamer: Collected Poems by John Haines exists in two different editions from Graywolf Press. The first, printed in 1993, is a hardbound collection of Haines's published poems, distributed in eight sections. Six sections are keyed to specific books. So, for example, Section I is "*from* WINTER NEWS (1966)," and Section II is "*from* THE STONE HARP (1971)." Section III is keyed to *Twenty Poems* (1971), Section V to *Cicada* (1977), Section VI to *News from the Glacier* (1982), and Section VII to *New Poems: 1980–88* (1990). While this is a relatively straightforward way of organizing the poems, Haines excludes titles like *Leaves and Ashes*, *In Five Years' Time*, and *In a Dusty Light*. Poems from the first two books are included in Section IV, titled "INTERIM: *Uncollected Poems from the 1970s*." The important poems of *In a Dusty Light* are subsumed within the section devoted to *News from the Glacier*. As in several previous collections, Haines uses the final section for recent work. Thus Section VIII is called "NEW AND UNCOLLECTED POEMS (1993)," and it includes fifteen poems that appear nowhere else in Haines's work.

The second, paperback edition of *The Owl in the Mask of the Dreamer*, printed in 1996, makes one major addition, including a new Section II, "*from* WHERE THE TWILIGHT NEVER ENDS: *Uncollected Poems from the 1960s*." This section reprints nineteen poems from the collection Haines had published with Limberlost Press in 1994. Haines had rediscovered these poems after the first edition of *The Owl in the Mask of the Dreamer* was in press. Many of the poems follow the models of classical Chinese poetry, and all of these poems are worthy additions to Haines's collected works. The new section makes the paperback edition of *The Owl in the Mask of the Dreamer* a better representation of Haines's development as a poet. The final section of the paperback edition adds two poems, "The Glutton" and "Rodin: The Gates of Hell." The first is a decidedly minor work. The second is a welcome addition to poems like "The Burghers of Calais" and "Age of Bronze."

The new and uncollected poems in the final section of *The Owl in the Mask of the Dreamer* resonate deeply with the poems of art and artists in *New Poems*. Haines provides extensive notes on several of the texts, pointing out the specific artwork to which a poem refers or from which he draws inspiration. The technique recalls Haines's conversation with John Luther Adams, in which the poet is careful to define his poems as "a way of thinking back into history and culture, a kind of meditation," rather than ekphrastic descriptions: "To put it another way, art is itself a language, a way of telling; and what it tells is, in a sense, what I am trying to make clear to myself in the poems I write. I have gone back to it to see what, in certain individuals, works, and periods, I can find that will illuminate this moment in time" (JHP Box 18, Folder 8, p. 22). For Haines, the usefulness of art is that it brings the past and its insights to bear on the present and its problems.

The later works of Francisco Goya figure prominently in the final section of *The Owl in the Mask of the Dreamer*. First, "In the Sleep of Reason" refers to the etching "The Sleep of Reason Brings Forth Monsters" from a series of eighty satirical etchings called *Los Caprichos*, or *Caprices*. Second, "The Fates" is, according to Haines's note, "in part an interpretation of one of Goya's etchings in the series called *Los Disparates*," or *Follies* (*OMD* 246). Finally, "Stalled Colossus" points to two of Goya's "Black Paintings" and to the etchings in the series *The Disasters of War*. In all three poems, Goya is a painter with a public voice, speaking out by portraying the follies of Spanish society and the atrocities of Napoleon's Peninsular War. Goya's late works also feature nightmarish imagery of great psychological and emotional power, so that for Haines he is also clearly a model figure of the visionary artist.[4]

In "Stalled Colossus," Haines makes a particularly significant attempt at fashioning a short sequence of seven poems, bringing several of Goya's artworks together. The poet speaks in a public voice that brings modern readers into a close relationship with Goya's works. The two most clearly described "Black Paintings" in the poem are "Fight with Cudgels" and

"Witches' Sabbath (The Great He-Goat)." The first painting gives a frame for the sequence. In Sections I–III, Haines directly addresses the two figures in the foreground of the painting. Sunk to their knees in mud, two giants are battering each other with clubs. In Sections VI and VII, the poet again uses direct address, but now the "you" becomes the reader, or the poet himself, or some anonymous other. "You" are the surviving combatant, but what do you win? The final stanza provides an implied answer:

> You rise, alone with your welts
> and bruises—your blood,
> your steep and violent night;
> you stand alone, facing
> the stone forehead of heaven,
> like a mountain
> no one can hope to climb. (Sec. VII)

Section IV presents images and titles from the "Disasters of War" and "Follies" etchings, temporarily brightening the palate of the poem in order to enforce a harshly ironic contrast between the images and the well-known atrocities depicted in Goya's etchings "Courage—Against Corpses" and "And It Can't Be Helped."

Section V differs from the "Fight with Cudgels" sections and the mordant ironies of Section IV. Here the famous "Witches' Sabbath" occupies the center of Haines's attention, and he uses the "Black Painting" in order to meditate on audience. In three stanzas, the poet envisions humanity as a war-torn multitude of refugees, a whirlwind of forms who seek to escape but find they cannot budge from their place:

> And a thing that is stranger,
> more terrible still:
> as if to say that earth
> does not contain its fugitives,
> but that they multiply
> and break into virulent forms . . .
>
> So now the twilight sings:
> a wind-struck moaning

> from the goat-mouths of people
> transfixed in a circle—
> a bundled and buffeted mass
> who sway as if they would flee;
>
> and yet they stay, instructed
> by a creature that brays
> as it tries to read
> from a book held upside down;
> the pages stick and tear
> like leaves from a tree
> stripped in the flooding darkness. (Sec. V)

If this depicts a place of conviction, the occupants are surely the convicted rather than the convinced. Their immobility recalls the gigantic figures in "Fight with Cudgels," while the satanic figure of the "He-Goat" reduces them to a mass of unreasoning, damned fools. The "He-Goat" cannot read, and if the book he holds upside down somehow recalls the Cumaean Sybil's leaves, here the "pages stick and tear." Despite the flooding darkness, the tone is neither accusing nor self-righteous. Indeed, in Section VI the poet includes himself in the multitude: "you, driven to your knees, / a thing shattered earth-bitten— / you that are you, myself, / and so many others—cry out."

The unstated allusion in "Stalled Colossus" is to the painting "The Colossus," also known as "The Giant." Haines suggests the allusion in the epigraph to the poem: "*El Gigante*—Goya." The painting itself, in the Museo del Prado in Madrid, is traditionally attributed to Goya, though in recent years some scholars have argued that it was painted by a friend or follower. It depicts a huge, hairy male nude standing against a black, cloud-filled horizon, his left arm raised, his legs visible only to his thighs, and his muscled back turned toward the viewer. In the foreground, fleeing in gross panic, are tiny civilians in covered wagons and carts, surrounded by their livestock. The painting suggests that the giant represents an impending disaster such as the Peninsular War, while the fleeing multitude represents the Spanish victims of the French invasion.

In the poem, Haines presents a multitude of paralyzed figures. Thus the giant is "stalled," and the two gigantic fighters with cudgels are standing "to your waist / in a painted cloud at evening" (Sec. I). Likewise, the people in Section V are "transfixed in a circle," forced to receive instruction from the braying "He-Goat." Finally, the lone survivor at the end of the poem stands "facing / the stone forehead of heaven, / like a mountain / no one can hope to climb." The persistent imagery of fixedness and immobility runs counter to Haines's favorite tropes of journeys and movements, as if he were presenting a poetic version of a "Black Painting" to contemporary readers. Given the dates of composition (1986–1991), moreover, it is reasonable to connect the poem to Haines's view of America, the stalled colossus, as it stumbled toward the first Persian Gulf War of 1990–1991. From our present day, furthermore, the poem is prophetic in its vision of continuing military quagmires like the twenty-first-century American wars in Iraq and Afghanistan.

Other poems of art and artists recur to figures from *New Poems*. Prominent in "Head of Sorrow, Head of Thought" and "Paolo and Francesca," Auguste Rodin's work appears in three successful poems in *The Owl in the Mask of the Dreamer*: "The Burghers of Calais," "Age of Bronze," and, in the paperback edition, "Rodin: The Gates of Hell." Rodin's muscular realism seems to appeal to Haines's mimetic imagination: "Flesh that is iron, stone / that is flesh" ("Burghers of Calais"). Rodin's subjects are certainly appropriate for creating a poetic version of the artist's public voice. "The Burghers of Calais" is a political statement, in bronze or in words, and in his note, rather than focusing on the actual historical event depicted in Rodin's sculpture, Haines asserts that the group symbolizes "a universal condition, common to exiles and refugees throughout history" (*OMD* 246). Haines calls "Age of Bronze" a "condensed history of Western art" (*OMD* 246), but in addition to the formal echoes of Michelangelo's "Dying Slave," the sculpture and poem also suggest the relationship of art and poetry to political events such as wars and the resulting plight of exiles and refugees. Rodin's sculpture "Age of Bronze" was originally titled "The Vanquished," evoking the French defeat in the Franco-Prussian War of 1870–1871. For Haines, however, a defeat in war may not be as severe as the modern reduction of the human figure to "a great spider of tin" he depicts in Section III. In Haines's condensed history, the loss of figuration in art is directly related to the ensuing decimation of artworks and ecclesiastical architecture in World War II. The Holocaust is also aesthetic, and that loss might prove even more costly than the horrors of the war. That is the implication of the closing lines of "Age of Bronze": "When the age of bronze is over, / the day of smoke begins."[5] "Rodin: The

Gates of Hell" could be a reflection on the solitary artist's never-completed masterpiece, but it also functions as a meditation on the inherent incompletions of all artists' grand projects.

Perhaps the most interesting figure of the artist in the 1993 poems is Michelangelo, who plays a major role in "Night," the final poem of *The Owl in the Mask of the Dreamer*. The speaker of "Night" also recurs to "Of Michelangelo, His Question," from *New Poems*. Haines avoids simple ekphrasis in "Night," but he associates the speaker of the poem with a sybil and notes that the figure is "represented by Michelangelo's immense reclining female figure of *Night* in the Medici Chapel in Florence" (*OMD* 246). In addition, Haines writes that the sculpture includes "a tragic mask and the figure of an owl," both of which appear in the poem as well as in the title of the collected poems. Of course, the phrase "the owl in the mask of the dreamer" recalls the poem of that title in *New Poems*, which narrates the loss of mimesis in the history of sculpture. These layered associations enrich "Night" greatly, but it is already a highly layered text if taken on its own terms.

"Night" is composed of three segments. Haines employs tercets as the basic stanza form through the poem, punctuating the end of a segment with a single line or doublet. In the first tercet, the sibyl frames the poem with the command "Do not wake me, for I am not ready / to speak, to break the spell / fixed in these sleeping stones." The signal irony is that the speaker claims not to be ready to speak, but the six stanzas of the first segment effectively embody the public voice of the poet. The sibyl speaks with authority, commanding the reader, "Go quietly here," and the authoritative words of the public voice establish a sacred place of hushed significance. Outside that place, "it is the time of earth-changes," of potentially apocalyptic events or merely ominous signs. Haines links the "earth-changes" with those who would "harness the wind and drive the water," and the sibyl addresses "you that govern, / who yoke and stride the world," commanding them to "be still." This is the one moment in which the poem is clearly political, though the environmental apocalypse overwhelms any specific political context. The political aspect resembles that of "The Night that Ryder Knew" or "To the Wall," both of which suggest that our rulers are responsible for our much-reduced possibilities, and that the "night is coming" that will hold them accountable.

In the second segment of "Night," Haines shifts to eight stanzas of description, but he does not focus on Michelangelo's sibylline sculpture.

Instead, he recurs to the image of "one standing tree," last seen in Section XV of "Forest Without Leaves":

> Leaves of the one standing tree
> fall through the twilight;
> the nightborn images rise, the owl
>
> in the mask of the dreamer wakes:
> Who is the guest?
> Who is it who knocks and whispers?
>
> As one calmed in his death-dream
> would never return
> to this hunted world—
>
> one more key to the clockwork
> that drives the stunned machine,
> another cry under the wheel . . .
>
> But calmed and stationed aloft,
> delight in his distance,
> to see on the star-pavilions
>
> the bright, imperial creatures rise,
> ascend their thrones, rule
> and prosper. The thrones darken,
>
> earth in the moon-shadow fails,
> and he alone in that cold
> and drifting waste keeps alight
>
> memorial constellations . . .

Haines connects the tree and its falling leaves to rising dreams, the "nightborn images," and the awakening of "the owl / in the mask of the dreamer." The dreamer (whom, in the note to the poem, Haines connects to C. G. Jung and his dream of interstellar space) is "as one calmed in his death-dream," and he moves, "calmed and stationed aloft," among "memorial constellations." The only threat appears to be that the dreamer might awaken from his dream of transcendence. For if the dreamer awakens, he will discover that he is alone in his bright imaginings. The thrones darken, the earth fails in the deathly moon shadow, and the dreamer drifts along with drifting waste. Haines notes that in Jung's case, the awakening "return to life and consciousness plunged him into a deep depression" (*OMD* 246).

In the third segment, composed of two tercets and a final couplet, the sibyl returns to the center of the poem. Speaking from "this quiet sleep of stone," the sibyl once again commands the reader to leave to her "this one sustaining solace": night, with "more night / to come." The poem ends with the kind of paradox that Michelangelo's androgynous *Night* evokes. The sibyl is "mute in [her] transformation," but she can still command the reader, "Do not wake me." Like the poems inspired by Goya and Rodin, this Michelangelo poem is powerful in its visionary, public voice, even if the authoritative commands of the sibyl do not point us in a clear direction. We are caught in apocalyptic visions of chaos, death, and cosmic destruction, and the only escape seems to be a return to "the owl / in the mask of the dreamer." But what would such a return do for us or for the world? Question without answer. For, after all, that is how the sibyl always speaks.

THE PLACE OF CONVICTION IN *FOR THE CENTURY'S END*

If the poems about art and artists in *The Owl in the Mask of the Dreamer* are oblique in their political angles, Haines takes sharp steps in developing the public voice in his last book of poetry, *For the Century's End: Poems, 1990–1999*.[6] In fact, many of the poems in *For the Century's End* are quite pointed in their politics. As in all of Haines's books of poetry, the poems are grouped in significant sections. After an introductory "Poem for the End of the Century," Part I presents a sweeping panorama of deep time and cosmic space, from dinosaurs, *Gilgamesh*, and prehistoric cave paintings to contemporary explorations by NASA. Part II presents the ambitious, twelve-section sequence "In the House of Wax," Haines's most successful attempt at creating a public voice in his late poetry. Part III features nine poems focusing on democratic politics and the economics of capitalism. Part IV focuses on forms of human love, joining the sequence "A Guide to the Four-Chambered Heart" with four short, personal poems. Part V is a miscellany of nine short poems, several focusing on the characteristic theme of the journey or movement. Many of these poems, however, could have appeared in other sections. "Star Struck," "The Ice Child," and "Eclipse" all resonate strongly with the poems of Part I, while "For a Young Student" would fit well in Part IV. "Days of Slaughter" could easily appear in Part III, while "The Ghost Towns" and "Roadside Weeds" could deepen the economic context of that section, too.

In the preface to the book, Haines notes the prominence of the political content in some of the poems, which he considers "inevitable, an element not to be refused" (*For the Century's End* ix; hereafter cited as FCE). In his political vision, as we have seen in the poems about Goya, Rodin, and Michelangelo, Haines is concerned with aesthetics as much as issues of governance or justice. As he puts it in the preface, "I have always sought a poetry that, as in the classical past and in the case of many of our prominent modernists, can include the public events of our time and do so in a way that makes them at once contemporary and unavoidably linked with humanity's long and troubled history" (ix). The terms of Haines's politics, in fact, evoke the public voice of the poet, speaking from an imaginative place of conviction to a possible audience of listeners or readers. The poems of *For the Century's End* present compelling examples of the public voice, and in several cases they represent significant additions to Haines's poetic achievement.

The three long sequences in *For the Century's End* are the most telling additions to Haines's poems, especially "In the House of Wax." Haines began working on all three of the sequences in the 1970s, so they reach back to the sequences of *New Poems*, specifically to "Meditation on a Skull Carved in Crystal," "Rain Country," "Water of Night," and "In the Forest Without Leaves." In chronology they even reach back to the two sequences of *In a Dusty Light*—"Homestead" and "News from the Glacier"—both of which date from 1975.

The first of the three sequences in *For the Century's End*, "In a Cave at Lone Tree Meadow," is a six-section meditation on deep time, the culture of hunter-gatherer ancestors, and the fundamental relationship between wild animals and the human imagination. The second sequence, "In the House of Wax," in twelve sections, is the most ambitious and successful poem Haines wrote after "In the Forest Without Leaves." Like that earlier sequence, it dives profoundly into "humanity's long and troubled history"

(*FCE* ix). Like the art sequences "Death and the Miser" and "Days of Edward Hopper," it employs an aesthetic context—in this case, the wax museum and its figures—in order to consider larger issues of "what art, wax, and history / have made of the dead" (Sec. II). The third sequence, "A Guide to the Four-Chambered Heart," is close to Part V of *New Poems*, with its epigraph by Paul Klee, "Somewhat closer to the heart . . . but far from close enough." Here Haines attempts to negotiate a passage from the personal, emotional history of his third marriage to a larger sense of relationships and meaning. The attempt recalls Haines's 1989 letter to the *AWP Chronicle*, in which he laments "a qualitative loss of relation and fellowship, of that spontaneous flow of feeling for, of delight in, another person or another creature. The disappearance of the love poem alone should have warned us" (*FD* 93).

In all three sequences, the personal and public flow into one another. The six sections of "In the Cave at Lone Tree Meadow" figure the speaker as a singular individual who finds that his "home is in the rock, / in the fire-thicket, at rest / with fleeting bird shadows" (Sec. I). Just as in the essays of *The Stars, the Snow, the Fire*, Haines creates a shadow language, for the cave reveals the fundamental relationship between hunter and hunted:

> A long time gone, a quiet hunter
> carved in this smoky wall
> an image of the thing he followed.
>
> Companion or shadow, changing
> its shape or its name:
> it was fish or reptile, bird,
> or something marked like a man. (Sec. II)

The speaker participates in the hunt by reading the shadow language of cave paintings, following the tracks left behind by the ancient inhabitants of Lone Tree Meadow. The participation gains power through the poet's memory of actual hunts. Thus Haines begins Section III with the painted image of the bear print, which leads to his memory of seeing, thirty years before, an actual bear print—and then the actual bear. The memory merges the figure of the bear with a more abstract image of "Fear," which "stood up and turned toward me / its face, ferocious and blind." Instead of concluding the memory of an actual hunt, the poet focuses on the hunter's timeless tracking of the shadowy bear, and the hunt concludes only when the poet returns to the cave at Lone Tree Meadow: "I find my quarry here, / in the sand of an old sea-bed, / uplifted and changed to stone" (Sec. III).

In the second half of the poem, Haines meditates on larger patterns of movement and journey. Thus Section IV moves from the hunter's tracking of the bear to the poet's lifelong following "the stone track of things, / the snail-trace and watermark / of our troubled passage." This search leads to "the red cave of my heart" and to "an old companion," closely linked to the personification of Fear in Section III. In Section V, Haines describes the companion as a hybrid, "man-headed beast or beast-headed man," who joins the poet in a hybrid place of dream and actuality:

> Whisper of names, fever of old mythologies,
> stale causes and coupling priests.
> Who made fire and who made shadow,
> the blood move and the flesh walk?
>
> Was it dream or actual man I saw?
> A forehead puckered with thought,
> a wind-truth that furrowed the grass—
> no more than a shrugged mattress
> that loomed and seemed to speak.
>
> I ask once more in this late hour
> where nothing is forgotten
> and nothing forgiven, but now
> as in the first light of a first dawn,
> this one clear face in the darkness.
>
> And like a slow, damaged figure of sleep
> he left me, parting dry leaves,
> a step in the great silence beyond. (Sec. V)

The first two stanzas in this passage construct a place of conviction, even though Haines mixes skeptical language with what he calls, in "What Are Poets For," "that ancient, myth-dominated relation to the world that has been called magical" (*FD* 32). The section narrates a kind of visitation, reminiscent of T. S. Eliot's "Little Gidding," a poem Haines admired greatly. In "Notes, Letters, and Reflections," for example, Haines defines "the impression of physical movement, of journey and action," as the "key to narrative in poetry," and he cites Eliot as a great recent example, especially "the wonderful passage in which he is walking the streets at dawn and meets his compound ghost: once again the theme is that of movement" (*FD* 136). In Section V, the visitant compound figure is "man-headed beast or beast-headed man," and the narrative seems to take place in the poet's dream. In the final stanza, the figure is "a slow, damaged figure of sleep," but it is still moving, "parting dry leaves, / a step in the great silence beyond." Even though the figure does not deliver a clear message, it imparts a sense of clarity and insight: "as in the first light of a first dawn, / this one clear face in the darkness." That certainly suggests that the image functions as Haines often says about animal images in dreams, which "can be read as expressions of a fuller, more intense, life" (*FD* 136).

In the final section of "In the Cave at Lone Tree Meadow," the hunter becomes the hunted. The poet waits in the cave for a sound he will recognize: "the slow, climbing tread / that has followed me all my life / and will track me down." The companion, bearlike, will return as the poet's killer, "his stone feet forcing me down," and the poet will become "dust and scattered, / my bones dry as dust, on the floor / of a cave in this mountain." Haines repeats the key words "follow," "track," and "stone," echoing similar diction in Sections I–IV. In Section V, during the visitation, the key words do not appear, and in Section VI they effect the reversal of hunter and hunted. As Haines remarks in "Notes, Letters, and Reflections," the appearance of animal images in dreams "can be fearful and threatening, but only from the point of view of the person disposed to see them that way: i.e., the conventional person. The open and creative individual will see them for what they are: friendly and encouraging images" (*FD* 134). Thus, even though the intensity of the dream is allied with the individual's fear of death, it transforms the cave into a place of imaginative conviction.

THE PLURAL WITNESS OF "IN THE HOUSE OF WAX"

"In the House of Wax" creates an even more elaborately conceived place of conviction. In twelve sections, Haines's meditation on "what art, wax, and history / have made of the dead" embodies a particularly moving example of the poet's public voice. If the setting of the sequence recalls the poems of art and artists from *New Poems* and *The Owl in the Mask of the Dreamer*, it differs from the earlier aesthetic poems by placing the poet and reader in the position of visitors, walking through a wax museum and viewing a popularized version of history with a measure of detached and knowing irony. Yet there is no hint of condescension in the sequence. Instead, the idea of the sequence resembles that of "In the Forest Without Leaves," and the poems are earnestly thoughtful in tone. In Section I, for instance, Haines introduces the house of wax in three stanzas describing the rulers of yesterday, their judicial deputies, and their victims. The "presidents and kings" are creatures of "charters and speeches," and their power makes them "masters of unconscious evil." The deputies, "judges, robed executioners," are "steely and triumphant," but like the rulers they remain anonymous. Finally, "the beheaded, the betrayed" lie "stunned at their feet," but they are "healed and hallowed now / in this grave sorrow of wax" (Sec. I). Only in the last two lines does Haines reveal his clear sympathies for the victims of history.

The public voice of "In the House of Wax" emerges as a plural witness, a concretely realized "we," who visits the wax museum and describes the place in sharp physical detail. In some passages the "we" seems to be an individualized speaker, as when "we think to ourselves, murmur / to the one standing beside us" (Sec. II). In other passages, the "we" encompasses all of us:

> These are the people whose names
> we learned, whose lives we studied,
> whose thoughts we have become. (Sec. II)

At the same time that the "we" moves from singular to plural and back again, this collective speaker comments on the wax figures and on the relationship between them and us, often in rather general, summarizing terms. The result is what Haines calls, at the end of Section II, "something more than a mirror, / less than a telling likeness; / an ideality slick with blood." Like the speaker, the wax figures are a compound, a complex: they are both mimetic and expressive, grounded in ideality, and yet, in that ambiguous phrase combining birth and death, "slick with blood."

Sections III–VI narrate a roughly chronological passage through history, focusing on scenes of violence, torture, and war. In Section V, however, Haines shifts from European history to American history, from outright war to the “rigged transactions” by which “our wigged colonials” pilfered land and acquired power. The second half of Section V shifts again, to our contemporary moment, “our late arrival,” and to the “slick banality” of contemporary American presidents:

> To Ike, to Kennedy and Ford,
> golfers and temporizers;
> to perennial candidate Nixon,
> whose cheek was never turned.
>
> Out of his sleek arrest
> he steps toward us,
> as if to greet a voter—
>
> a fixed, ferocious smile
> on the blue jowls
> brushed with powder.

Modern America is no less violent than the Old World; its manners have changed, a stylistic accommodation to our late arrival. As the poet asserts in Section IX, “In all these wax memorials / only appearance changes.” The names may change, but the mask hides the same face.

While political and military history dominates the sequence, Haines includes interesting material relating to dreams and fairy tales. Section VII, for instance, presents a collage of fairy-tale figures: the queen in the Snow White tale; Sleeping Beauty; Hansel and Gretel and the witch; Rumpelstiltskin. Haines even finds a place for Walt Disney films in the history of the imagination, evoking our modern fairy tales in “the crafty Queen / and her players, / the musical mice.” If Disney provides another escape, a “scampering rush” to find “the nearest exit,” it actually returns us to the dark truths of both history and fantasy. Of course, history itself is the house of wax, and we all live within its walls, “sharing these murderous spaces, / this blood-haunted silence” (Sec. X). If fantasy provides us with moments of escape, Haines is determined to speak us back into reality:

> And once we started from sleep,
> terrorized and whimpering,

to see in the luminous,
sunken light, the head
of a long-forgotten agent:

a face like a father,
one who might have comforted,
but cannot see or hear us:
bald, vacant, and amused. (Sec. X)

This is a perfect nightmare, both particular to Haines and common to all of us. The disembodied head is the image of an uncanny, terrorizing Big Other, most frightening because it appears to ignore us at the same time that it calls us into being.[7]

In only two passages does Haines clearly shift from the collective to a singular speaker. In Section VI, the plural "we" describes "these iron centuries" and their ability to confine and torture all of us in one form or another. In the last two stanzas, Haines takes the power of the iron centuries to the most intimate level, fittingly evoked as a personal memory:

As once in a stone embrasure
I saw a belt for virgins,
a hinged and rusted clasp,
with a lock, and a slit
for functions—all but one.

Imagine with what shocked
dismay a man might grope
for his sweetness there,
and all too soon awaken,
clamped in his ecstasy. (Sec. VI)

If the stanzas somehow feel like an invasion of our privacy, that could be a measure of their expressive power. Memory of a museum visit is transformed into carceral castration fantasy.

The second instance of the singular speaker occurs in Section XI. The poem is set as "here at the story's end," and the plural "we" controls the first five stanzas, meditating on the walk through the museum and the "painted fiction" of history that we have witnessed. Then the speaker commands us to "see how they bring toward us / the old, sustaining gestures," only to reveal the false, Nixonian appearance when "the furrows in the smiles / deepen, and the red lips smear." As if called forth by the end of the story, the "I" reemerges:

> Great captains command, obedient
> ranks go down. In all these propped
> assemblies I know a substance
> neither wax nor wholly flesh—
> a tried and mortal nature,
> familiar as the warmth in my hand.

Here at the story's end, the insight of the poet provides a substantial knowledge of loss, recalling the compound ambiguities of Section II. The insight also recalls the final section of "In the Cave at Lone Tree Meadow," for the generous tone of the stanza depends on the poet's strong sense of mortality, "familiar as the warmth in my hand."

Though reassuring, this is not the end of the story—not yet. In Section XII, Haines once again performs a kind of double act, evoking the strongest version of his public voice and yet remaining tied to the composite audience who occupy the house of wax. The poem opens in the conditional mood, locating the speaker as part of the audience, but that composite speaker then imagines a singular public voice speaking out of the crowd:

> Were we not lost, condemned
> to repeat these names
> and to honor their crimes,
> a voice among us might cry out,
> speak to those who are
> stopped here:
> Whose faces are these
> that melt and run?
>
> Children and guardians, giants
> and dwarfs—
> Oh, people, people . . .

Who are these heroes
and where are their victims?

These jagged stanzas match the figure of the public voice, crying out amid the lost and subservient audience in the house of wax. The questions jostle between rhetorical and actual, just as the voice shifts back and forth between accusation and lamentation. The underlying question is where hope might lie in such a place, and the implied answer seems to be that it lies in the act of speaking out to "those who are / stopped here." Hope lies in the idea that this audience might respond to the public voice crying out to them—to us—and that we might ask after the fates of the children, the dwarfs, and the victims, since the Big Others will no doubt take care of themselves.

In the second half of Section XII, Haines reestablishes the perspective of the composite audience, emphasizing the physical stance of those who are "standing here / with our guidebooks suddenly closed / and all the exits darkened. . . . " The fixedness of the audience, standing without guidance or direction in the darkness, makes a hell of the wax museum. And the last lines are only a partial redemption:

Until another gallery opens,
or the sun through that skylight
strikes us all—
souls in torment,
pilgrims and doting fathers . . .

As fixed and constricted as the audience appears to be, these last lines open up to a certain largeness of expression and conception. Without absolutely redeeming the souls in torment or giving the pilgrims an easy journey, the last images of "In the House of Wax" suggest that the sun shines outside the walls and can reach inside them to illuminate the darkness. Tellingly, Haines does not use the conditional mood in the stanza, so that the projected opening is figured more as an eventual reality than as a distant possibility. Meanwhile, faced with the questions posed by the authoritative public voice, we remain who we are, standing where we must stand, and feeling everything that we ought to feel. Without the public voice and its actions, we could not say even that much.

RETURNS

Haines attains a high level of mature public expression in the two sequences "In the Cave at Lone Tree Meadow" and "In the House of Wax." As he remarks in the essay "Formal Objections," there is a kind of "sequential intelligence," evident in long poems from Dante's *Divine Comedy* to Eliot's *Four Quartets*, that displays "an ability to incorporate, to combine and articulate, a number of modes of expression, narrative as well as dramatic, verse paragraph as well as lyric stanza, and all within a thematic, musical structure for which no adequate prose equivalent seems to exist" (*FD* 66). That definition sets a demanding standard for what we can consider a major work. In "Guide to the Four-Chambered Heart," there are moments of emotional and expressive depth, but the four sections do not seem to express a public voice or speak from a deep place of conviction. The other four poems in Part IV, especially "Orpheus" and "Another Country," combine with "Guide to the Four-Chambered Heart" to create an elegiac sense of lost love. The elegy is perhaps most beautiful in "Another Country," for the poem evokes the speaker's own love of the northern landscape of Richardson. In the speaker's song, we hear the voice of the young John Haines, singing his way toward *Winter News* and the poetry of the earth:

> *Come to me in the shape*
> *of a lynx or a wolf . . .*
> *Come in your frost-fur*
> *on enormous, silent feet . . .*
>
> Into that fabulous woodland
> its hunting lairs and icy springs,
>
> *For I would follow you there . . .*

Part III includes nine poems that specifically address political events in contemporary America. All of the poems bring public events into a context at once contemporary and representative of "humanity's long and troubled history" (Preface ix). Given the successes of "In the Cave at Lone Tree Meadow" and "In the House of Wax," however, the short poems seem like afterthoughts. What marks them as accomplished poems in their own right is Haines's decision to employ traditional stanzas, as if the regularity of the form could somehow help to contain the dark, dangerous content. In "Kent State, May 1970," "Politics and the Dead," and "The Unemployed, Disabled, and Insane," for instance, Haines employs the quatrain as a balancing counterpoint to the "fraying / voices of distracted candidates." Indeed, voice is a recurring trope in the nine poems, and the formal voice of the poet creates an authentic alternative to the "distracted voices / astray in the thrumming wires" ("Blood"). "It Could Happen Again" and "The Last Election" use regular five-line stanzas as a formal counterpoint to political apocalypse, and the formality of Haines's public voice is the most important aspect of the poems.

Like the final gatherings in earlier books, Part V of *For the Century's End* appears to be a miscellany of recent poems, some of which might fit perfectly well in earlier parts of the volume. In particular, "The Ice Child" would fit nicely alongside "In the Cave at Lone Tree Meadow," while "Eclipse" and "Star Struck" could appear with the other lyrics of outer-space exploration in Part I. "For a Young Student" is a memory of lost love, much in keeping with the lyrics of Part IV. "The Ghost Towns," "Roadside Weeds," and "Days of Slaughter" would broaden and deepen the economic and political critique of American progress in Part III.

Finally, "To the End" is a good poem to place at the end of the book, even though the "end" it contemplates is "the end of one's life" rather than the end of a century or a civilization. Haines creates a kind of figurative boomerang in the poem, opening with the idea of the end of life in order to move back as nearly as possible to the beginning of life. Memory and imagination blend, as they often do in Haines's best poems and essays, to create a delicate tone of loss and retrieval:

> It was all there in that moment,
> both distance and welcome, stillness
> and departure . . . The clouds moved
> in once more, and the sun darkened.
>
> All that remains of a childhood,
> restored in a faded album:
> the fleeting image of a vacant house,
> a dust of snow on the steps—
>
> All that was and would be. ("To the End")

The balancing quatrains parallel the imagery of past and future caught in a present moment. The moment is complex, moreover—much more complex than simple oppositions. Thus "distance and welcome" give a kind of emotional tension to the memory, and "stillness / and departure" offer alternative futures somehow grasped by a child sitting in a carriage. The complications develop further when the clouds move and the sun darkens. In the second quatrain, the imagery shifts to a photo album, but the restored images are actually "fleeting," the house "vacant," the snow an ephemeral "dust . . . on the steps." The final, isolated line reaches back and forth across the speaker's life, from end to beginning, and matches that span with the century. It is the image of an old man, finding his way back "into that place where / all was uncertain expectation." And the place remains one of uncertain expectation, now and always.

The last poem of *For the Century's End* does not really conclude the volume; instead, it continues the complex relationships of "all that was and would be." One way of responding to that final line is to return to the beginning of the book. The synecdochic first poem of the book, "Poem for the End of the Century," employs a first-person singular speaker, but the "I" projects a public voice. The speaker is "the dreamer who remains / when all the dreams are gone," speaking in a post-apocalyptic landscape in which "millennial winds" scatter the remains of a world. We have been in this place before, and when the speaker says, "I leave my house to the creditor wind," we hear strong echoes of poems like "The Stone Harp," "'It Must All Be Done Over,'" and "Missoula in a Dusty Light." In the closing lines of self-admonition, moreover, we hear the bracing close of such poems as "In the House of Wax":

> I am the one who touches fire,
> who rakes the leaves to watch them burn,
> and who says once more to himself
> on this calm evening of earth:
>
> Awake! The stars are out,
> mist is on the water,
> and tomorrow the sun will return. ("Poem for the End of the
> Century")

In the alternating quatrains and tercets, as in the imagery of renewal and awakening, Haines balances dark prophecies and earthly hopes. And the shift from mundane yardwork to rapt statement shows how effectively Haines's sybilline public voice can emerge from any gathering of scattered leaves.

A final major expression of Haines's public voice comes in the three-part poem "The Legend," which opens Part I of *For the Century's End* and immediately precedes "In the Cave at Lone Tree Meadow." Like the longer sequences, "The Legend" is a composition that Haines labored over for a long period, from 1981 to 1996. As Haines tells the story in the essay "The Theme of Loss, of Sorrow and Redemption in *Gilgamesh*," he first read the ancient Sumerian epic when he returned to live at the Richardson homestead in the early 1980s, and his response to the epic was intensely personal, connected to his own experiences as a hunter and trapper in Interior Alaska.[8] Like the art poems in *New Poems* and *The Owl in the Mask of the Dreamer*, "The Legend" is inspired by an artwork, though this is the rare instance in which a literary text lies behind Haines's poem. Not surprisingly, the public voice of "The Legend" is closely allied to "In the Cave at Lone Tree Meadow" and "In the House of Wax." Finally, Haines focuses especially on the theme of "that eternal, still modern story of offense to Nature, and for which we pay a lasting penalty. The story and its meaning for us takes on a contemporary importance in the light of our ongoing argument between the forces of economic expansion, and the conservation of resources, of wilderness management, and so forth, to make use of accepted terms that by no means adequately express the significance of the story for us now" (*Descent* 13). Thus "The Legend" returns us to several of Haines's most important themes and strategies.

Section I of "The Legend" features the poet's direct, personal response to the story of Gilgamesh and Enkidu, framed in the repeated phrasing "I understand" and "I know." The response is much like Haines's decision to avoid simple ekphrastic poems about famous artworks. Rather than repeat the episodes of the epic, he uses a particular aspect of the ancient poem to bring alive a contemporary parallel. In Section I, he evokes Enkidu's loss of kinship with wild animals in order to relate that loss to our own present "exile, / the form that it takes within us: / the parting and breaking of things, / the distance and anguish." The search for knowledge itself leads to estrangement, and that is the particular interpretation Haines gives to the story of Enkidu's transformation:

I know, too, in its utter strangeness,
that whoever asks of the sun its rising,
of the night its moonstruck depths,
stirs the envy of God in his lofty cabin.

And when Enkidu awoke, called
from his changed, companionless sleep
—singly, in glittering pairs,
the beasts vanished from the spring.

The restrained formality of the quatrains forecasts the technique that Haines employs at greater length in Parts III and V of *For the Century's End*. And the formal restraint seems especially appropriate to a mythic story of loss and alienation. Here, the poet's public voice brings the ancient epic to bear on our modern exile from the earth.

Section II opens in a timeless present that could describe Enkidu but seems just as fitting as a description of our own situation:

The forest bond is broken,
and the tongued leaves no longer
speak for the dumb soul lost
in the wilderness of his own flesh.

The rest of the section portrays the exile's journey, "to try the roads" and "become that wasted pilgrim." The imagery evokes several journeys from the *Gilgamesh* texts: Enkidu's journey to the walled city of Uruk to combat Gilgamesh; the two heroes' journey to the Cedar Forest to slay the monster guardian Humbaba; Gilgamesh's journey to the garden of the gods, in search of wisdom concerning Enkidu's death and his own mortality; and the often-omitted story of Gilgamesh's descent to the netherworld. Haines is most interested in the descent to hell and the questioning of the dead, merging that mythic journey with the descent "deep into rootland," which alludes to the large-scale technological shift from hunting and gathering to agriculture. Thus Enkidu, the central figure of Section II, comes to stand for a number of "grieving and lost" travelers.

Section III is framed by a stanza summarizing tragic actions from *Gilgamesh*, and the parallelism suggests that stealth, language, and the killing of animals are equally responsible for the breaking of the forest bond. Then the loss becomes ours: "Rain only speaks / there now on the pelted leaves." It is as if the scattered leaves of the Cumaean Sibyl were transferred to the forests of Babylon and then blown into our present day. In a supple play of verse paragraphs, ending with a quatrain, Haines creates one of his finest meditations on our earthly life:

> Overheard through the downpour,
> in the stillness of my own
> late-learned solace, I understand
> through what repeated error
> we were driven from Paradise.
> The nailed gate and the fiery angel
> are true.
>
> Could we ask them,
> speaking their wind-language
> of cries, of indecipherable song,
> it may be that the swallows
> who thread the water at evening
> could tell us; or that the sparrows
> who flock after rain would write
> in the coarse yellow meal
> we have strewn at the threshold,
> why God gave death to men,
> keeping life for himself.
>
> For the strong man driven to question,
> and for him who, equally strong,
> believes without asking,
> sleep follows like a lasting shadow.

The four-stress lines in the first verse paragraph lead to three-stress lines in the second verse paragraph; then they tighten into the more formal metrical verse of the quatrain. The prosody is a masterful counterpart to Haines's public voice, which translates the downpour into words of solace. Haines also echoes the masterful imagery of *Paradise Lost*, but he wisely chooses to show us a reduced, minimalist contrast to Milton's blank verse.

The second verse paragraph moves to the animating language of birds, both in songs and in footprints. Reading those signs, the poet becomes a composite speaker, for it is "we" who ask the swallows and sparrows to answer our question. It is tempting to read this passage as an evocation of Romantic poetry, the lyric questioning of "Ode to a Nightingale" or the pastoral grieving of "When Lilacs Last in the Dooryard Bloom'd." But even if there is an echo of such poems, the passage finds its own powerful voice in the double conditional: if we *could* ask the swallows to tell us, it *may be* that they *could* tell us; it *may be* that the sparrows *would* write an answer for us in the meal we have strewn at the threshold.

The question is the same one that Gilgamesh asks of the immortal Utnapishtim. As Haines phrases it, "why God gave death to men, / keeping life for himself." The answer echoes the epic once again. Utnapishtim teaches Gilgamesh to accept his mortality by showing him that he cannot even stay awake and aware for six days without falling asleep. If you cannot overcome sleep, how can you overcome death? Whether or not we question our mortality, "sleep follows like a lasting shadow." For Haines and his readers, that last image is especially resonant. The shadow recalls the animals who leave tracks behind, like a shadow language, in the essays of *The Stars, the Snow, the Fire*. It also suggests that despite our separation from nature, we remain tied to the earth in more ways than we can count. Birdsongs are indecipherable, but we recognize them as a kind of "wind-language." We see the footprints of sparrows on the threshold and think of cuneiform tablets. We listen to the pouring rain and recall Book 9 of *Paradise Lost*:

> Earth trembl'd from her entrails, as again
> In pangs, and Nature gave a second groan,
> Skie lowr'd, and muttering Thunder, som sad drops
> Wept at compleating of the mortal Sin
> Original. (9.1000–04)

For Haines, this iconic moment parallels the awakening of Enkidu, an awakening that we all recognize and acknowledge. Cutting across thousands of years and cultural artifacts, Haines fastens on a moment of transgression and loss, but it is equally a moment that leads to self-knowledge and partial redemption. The redemption, Haines tells us in the essay on *Gilgamesh*, "can never be complete, but only partial, and for some of us, never permanent. It is, however, a quest we may never entirely abandon, for in it lies our best hope of salvation" (*Descent* 19). If we cannot find salvation itself, then perhaps we can find a form of wisdom, recognizing "a profound need in our nature, for belief in and love of the world we inhabit" (*Descent* 14). That is wisdom for the end of the century, and it is also wisdom to take with us into the new one.

CHAPTER 6

SOMEBODY THERE

A Career In Correspondence

On April 4, 1960, in one of his first letters to Robert Bly from the Richardson homestead, John Haines gave his new correspondent a sidelong compliment: "I like to write letters to intelligent people—that is, I like the feeling of somebody THERE at the other end to whom I can say what I want with some assurance that it will be understood."[1] Many of the letters to Bly in the late 1950s and 1960s are tinged with this mixed tone of defiant need. On February 11, 1960, for instance, Haines ended a long letter about Bly's poems with this jaunty send-off: "So, all I can say is good luck, and keep on with it. I think that when you've assimilated your influences (Lorca is the one I see most here) you're going to do some really fine things" (Robert Bly Papers, Box 4, Folder 1). Here Haines temporarily takes on the role played by William Carlos Williams in his letters to Haines in the 1950s. That is, Haines assumes the role of poetic mentor to Bly, but in this case the role is unearned, to say the least. Even though Bly was not by any means a celebrity in 1960, he was already an accomplished writer and editor, while Haines was unknown and largely unpublished. Still, the posturing reveals Haines's isolation and his desire to communicate with someone who could understand what he is attempting to achieve. That Bly maintained a healthy relationship and steady correspondence with the Alaska poet through the publication of *Winter News* suggests that Haines enjoyed as much good luck as did Bly.

Letters—to and from students, friends, family, editors, and fellow artists—proved to be a necessary lifeline for Haines through his entire career. They gave him contact with the world outside Richardson and placed him as a member of a larger community, and at the same time they allowed him to maintain a degree of independence and solitude that he found vital to his identity as a writer. His generation of literary figures was perhaps one of the very last to write letters in such copious quantities. The poet and editor Hayden Carruth, for example, remarked to Haines in a letter of January 15, 2000, that he had written 964 letters on his computer during 1999, to which he could add another hundred handwritten notes.[2] Haines would not be far behind in such numbers.

The thousands of letters that form Haines's correspondence reveal a host of relationships. In the 1950s and 1960s, there are the filial letters to Mrs. Arthur DeWar, or "Madre," answered by Haines's mother with gifts of small checks and postage stamps. There are love letters to his first two wives, sent from the Richardson homestead and intended to woo the young women to join him there. Haines writes charming "family" letters to Robert and Carol Bly and to Orrin and Kathryn Bly, Robert Bly's brother and sister-in-law. He writes respectful, professional letters to George Hitchcock at *Kayak* magazine, to Alberta Turner at Oberlin College, to Alan Brilliant and Teo Savoy at Unicorn Press. He is intimate and persuasive in a number of letters to young women, mostly former students. He is admirable and generous in letters to fellow writers like Sheila Nickerson, Nancy Lord, Cheryl Morse, Carolyn Kremers, Annie Dillard, and Louise Glück. There are interesting surprises, too, such as a steady if sporadic correspondence, as intimate as it is professional, with American literature scholar Sacvan Bercovitch. As part of the last generation of real letter writers in our literature, Haines maintained a rich, varied correspondence with hundreds of men and women.

Among Haines's many correspondents, six men played an especially crucial role as a combination of advisor, colleague, and friend. In the early years, Robert Bly was the most influential and helpful of Haines's artistic mentors, and he helped the Alaska poet shape his work leading to the publication of *Winter News* in 1966. From the 1970s to the mid-1990s, Scott Walker of Graywolf Press served as one of Haines's principal readers, encouraging him to write both poems and essays, and shepherding through the publishing process four major works: *In a Dusty Light*, *The*

Owl in the Mask of the Dreamer, *The Stars, the Snow, the Fire*, and *Fables and Distances*. As Haines reached his sixth decade, the younger artists Dana Gioia and John Luther Adams engaged him in ongoing conversations that led to some of Haines's best work in the 1980s and 1990s, especially the volume *New Poems*. And from first to last, the contemporaries Hayden Carruth and Wendell Berry wrote constantly and demandingly to Haines in terms of poetic form, aesthetic language, and the social role of the writer. These six correspondents are in some ways a select, even elite group, and they do not represent the full range of Haines's many relationships. Taken together, however, the letters form an inside narrative of Haines's career as a poet and essayist.

FLOATING HOMEWARD: ROBERT BLY AS MENTOR

The letters between Robert Bly and John Haines waver a good deal in frequency and tone over the years. On July 8, 1959, Haines began writing to Bly in his role as the editor of *The Fifties*. In a number of letters from 1959 and 1960, Haines was intent on proving himself as a poet, defending the poems he sent to Bly, citing William Carlos Williams and Ezra Pound as his authorities, and mentioning the two letters from Williams that he had received. Bly was the first editor to accept a poem by Haines and pay him for it. On August 28, 1960, Haines thanked Bly for the ten dollars he had received for "If the Owl Calls Again," and after that professional success their letters became more and more personal and friendly. As a comparatively young writer, Haines saw himself as essentially in agreement with Bly's Deep Image surrealism. On January 21, 1961, for instance, he wrote, "I'm with you, or at least bringing up the rear somewhere. Or to put it another way—we're on the same road, going the same direction, only maybe we're just driving slightly different cars" (Robert Bly Papers, Box 5, Folder 4). In another letter from June 14, 1961, Haines confided the intimate fact that "every year we run out of grub about the first of May, and from then until the garden begins to grow we have nothing much but fish and a few wild greens, though we were lucky to find a few canned goods in an old cabin to help us over the bad time, this year. Sounds like we're a couple of tramps"

(Robert Bly Papers, Box 5, Folder 4). Even though Bly often disappointed Haines by not accepting his poems for publication, Haines seems to have accepted Bly's editorial judgments, and at first the poetic disagreements did not harm their growing friendship.

From his side, Bly saw his role as that of a mentor to Haines. On March 17, 1963, Haines sent Bly a typescript of a first book, "such as it is." He suggested trial titles, "This Dark Water" and "Poems for a Cold Journey," neither one of which Bly would accept. Haines did not know what to do with the typescript, but he expressed a strong interest in Wesleyan University Press, since they had recently published Bly's first book, *Silence in the Snowy Fields* (1962). The Robert Bly papers at the University of Minnesota contain Haines's typescript and Bly's notes on it, along with an offprint of an essay, "A New Nature Poetry," which Haines had published in *Snowy Egret*.[3] Bly's notes are far-ranging and deep. Several concern the order of the poems, and many of the typescript poems bear Bly's manuscript revisions. The typescript includes, moreover, at least a dozen poems that Haines never published, as if Bly had decided they were not strong enough for the book. In one note, Bly writes that Haines's poems are noteworthy for three reasons: they are "not provincial"; they feature "wilderness"; and they exhibit "delicacy," especially because of "a great gift for language, a sensibility, but also because the sounds listened for are faint, delicate ones, unheard by other people" (Robert Bly Papers Box 278, Folder 1). By August 22, 1963, Bly had returned the typescript with his commentary, new arrangements, and a new title, *Floating Homeward*. Haines accepted most of Bly's revisions, but the revised typescript was rejected by Wesleyan University Press in October 1963.

Despite the lack of success with *Floating Homeward*, Bly played an important role in shaping *Winter News*. As we have seen in chapter 1, Bly sent Haines's later typescript to Donald Hall in August 1964, and Hall sent Haines a helpful, encouraging letter on September 4, 1964, giving him advice on cutting clichés and dead metaphors from the poems. In addition, Bly went through the later typescript with great care, as it appears from the Robert Bly papers. In one typescript of *Winter News*, Bly lists three section titles: "In Alaska," "Dreams," and "Preparing for Winter" (Robert Bly Papers Box 278, Folder 1). These would become three of the four section titles in the final version of the book, as Haines's complete typescript of *Winter News* shows (JHP Box 8, Folder 6).

Perhaps even more important, a poem like "The House of the Injured" reveals Bly's careful attention to Haines's language in specific poems. In a typescript of the poem, Haines concludes with these two stanzas:

> And from deep within me
> came a voice: "This is Life!
> It is beautiful! Ravenous,
> wounded, inexhaustible Life!"
>
> I sank to my knees with a heart
> full of terror and love, like
> a man shown the face of God.

Bly cuts the two stanzas, replacing them with the two lines: "I sank to my knees like / a man shown the face of God." Following Bly's recommendations, Haines takes the condensation and directness yet further, fashioning the following lines as the end of the poem: "I sank to my knees— / a man shown the face of God."

The deletion of "like" might seem to make the poem end on a literal note, but in fact it simplifies and clarifies the final metaphor. Through a kind of reciprocal condensation, Bly deletes Haines's early rhetorical posturings, and ultimately Haines doubles down by reducing Bly's doubling of metaphor and simile. No wonder, then, that in preparing the final version of *Winter News* for publication Haines would draft (and delete) his acknowledgment of "a special debt of gratitude" to Bly for his "encouragement in preparing the manuscript of this book" (JHP Box 8, Folder 6).

After the publication of *Winter News* in 1966, the correspondence between Haines and Bly became less frequent and more acrimonious. By July 8, 1966, Bly was complaining to Haines about his tone, which he described as "condescending and touched with malice. It is the tone of a man working off a grudge, not of a man trying to help another man with his poetry" (JHP Box 1, Folder 18). In a letter of April 24, 1972, Haines wrote in somewhat vulgar language about the poems he had read *The Seventies* #1. On May 15, 1972, Haines apologized for his blunt attack, but then he hedged his apology: "You know, I am damned serious, and don't know how, at least yet, to temper my seriousness when I come to judge the work of others" (JHP Box

1, Folder 18). As the letter continued, Haines waxed more and more vehement, criticizing the work of W. S. Merwin, Charles Simic, and James Wright in harsh terms. Finally, however, he relented, saying that "one reason I'm so apt to stomp on others is that I'm insecure in myself." One letter, even one like this, was not enough to cause a rupture between the two writers. Both Bly and Haines made several attempts to reconcile their differences, but ultimately their correspondence became more and more sporadic, as if it were easier not to communicate at all rather than to argue. Except for an occasional postcard, the conversation dwindled to a trickle and effectively ended by 1975. In the poetic discoveries that led to *Winter News*, however, no correspondent was more crucially helpful and encouraging than Robert Bly.

SCOTT WALKER AS EDITOR AND AGENT

Scott Walker founded Graywolf Press at Port Townsend, Washington, in 1974. He started a correspondence with Haines in October 1973, when he was working for the journals *Skywriting* and *Twelve Poems*. Walker was inspired by his reading of Haines's *Twenty Poems*, the short book that Unicorn Press had brought out in 1971. In fact, Walker reviewed the book enthusiastically in *Skywriting* and enclosed the review in a November 6, 1973, letter to Haines. Two lines from "Sleep" struck Walker as emblematic of Haines's work: "we become at last like trees / who stand within themselves, thinking." Walker's enthusiasm for Haines's poetry led him to suggest a special issue of *Skywriting* devoted to Haines's work, and in January 1974 he asked to interview Haines as well. The two became close friends when Haines was teaching nearby at the University of Washington in 1974.

Walker and Haines corresponded with each other consistently from 1974 to around 1995, when Walker stepped down as director of Graywolf Press. During those twenty-one years, Walker served as a combination of editor, agent, and friend to Haines, and from the very beginning the two shared a deep passion for contemporary poetry. Like Bly, Walker was a perceptive reader of Haines's poems, and he always offered solid editorial advice about arranging poems and essays into collections to be published by Graywolf. Indeed, Scott Walker's Graywolf Press was the most prestigious publisher Haines ever had, with Wesleyan University Press a close second.

Haines's first Graywolf book, *In a Dusty Light*, appeared in 1977, and the archival evidence suggests that Walker was instrumental in the selection and arrangement of the eleven poems.[4] In addition to announcing a new poetry of the earth, *In a Dusty Light* was physically the most beautiful book Haines ever published. By 1979, Walker was urging Haines to publish a collection of prose. From the outset, Walker was working both with critical essays, which would eventually become the core of *Living Off the Country* (1981), and with a selection of personal memoirs, which would become *The Stars, the Snow, the Fire* (1989). Although he struggled with the tone and content of Haines's essays on poetry, Walker was from the very beginning much taken with the homestead essays. In a letter of October 18, 1979, Walker suggested, as an interim idea, a limited edition of the prose memoirs, to be called *Other Days: Selections from a Work-in-Progress*. He even drafted a trial table of contents, including the essays "Snow," "Other Days," "On Wolves," "Lost," "Spring," and "Richardson: The Dream" (JHP Box 21, Folder 6).

Over the next several months, Haines and Walker worked closely on the prose projects, and more than once Walker showed Haines remarkable generosity. On December 20, 1979, for instance, Walker wrote that he had sent Donald Hall some copies of Haines's critical essays on poetry, because Tess Gallagher (an active Graywolf poet at the time) had told him that Hall was publishing critical books about poetry with the University of Michigan Press. In the meantime, Walker labored over Haines's typescript, which he was calling *From the Beginning: Essays, 1969–1979*. Walker's reading notes on the typescript, contained in the Graywolf Press Archives, show that he was a thorough, intelligent reader who worked to edit the typescript in terms of organization, impact, and needless repetition. He tended to read in two different ways, with one set of notes called "Placement and Selection" and the other called simply "Notes," focusing on specific passages and essays. In a third kind of reading, he made production notes as well, even for books he helped place with other presses (Graywolf Press Archives, Box 117; Box 10 Editorial, Folder 3). Eventually Haines would place the first book of criticism with Hall's series at Michigan, and at the same time Walker pursued the editing and publishing of *Other Days*, the first significant gathering of essays about the homestead years at Richardson. The two books appeared within a year of one another—*Living Off the Country* in 1981 and *Other Days* in 1982.

Perhaps one could fault Scott Walker for a lack of business acumen, but in all of his letters to Haines he acted more as a friend than as a publisher seeking to sell books for profit. In the fall of 1980, for instance, Walker was urging Haines to publish *From the Beginning* with the University of Michigan series. In addition, he agreed to give Wesleyan University Press permission to reprint the poems of *In a Dusty Light*, without any payment, as part of Haines's *News from the Glacier: Selected Poems, 1960–1980*. It was, of course, obvious that the inclusion of the poems in *News from the Glacier* would hurt the sales of the paperback edition of *In a Dusty Light*. But despite Walker's qualms, in a letter of August 11, 1982, he advised Haines to ask Wesleyan for 7.5 percent for paperback royalties, which Haines immediately did in a September 16, 1982, exchange with Jeannette Hopkins (JHP Box 26, Folder 3). In this case, Walker gave his friend excellent financial advice. No wonder, then, that Haines asked Walker to be his literary executor, which Walker agreed to do in a letter of November 4, 1982 (JHP Box 25 loose correspondence).

As Graywolf Press grew and expanded, Walker continued to promote Haines's publishing interests. Even though *Other Days* did not produce huge sales (only 292 copies sold in 1984–1985), Walker urged Haines to produce an expanded memoir of the homestead years, and he somehow managed not to express anger at Haines for finding a rival to publish a small-press edition of seven homestead essays as *Stories We Listened To* (The Bench Press, 1986). Indeed, in 1986 Walker published *The Graywolf Annual Three: Essays, Memoirs & Reflections*, which he had himself edited, and he included the previously unpublished version of Haines's essay "Shadows," which would eventually occupy an important place in *The Stars, the Snow, the Fire*.

The correspondence between Walker and Haines continued through a series of major publications. Without Walker, it is doubtful that Haines could have finished *The Stars, the Snow, the Fire*. Walker was a constant source of encouragement and criticism from the first unpublished drafts of the essays to the publication of the book in 1989. Walker discussed every aspect of the book, from the title to offers for the paperback rights, and Tree Swenson of Copper Canyon Press also consulted on the design of the book.[5]

Until his resignation from Graywolf Press in March 1994, Walker worked with Haines on two more significant projects. The first was the collected poems *The Owl in the Mask of the Dreamer*, published in 1993 and, in the enlarged paperback edition, in 1996. The second was *Fables and Distances: New and Selected Essays*, published in 1996. In effect, Walker's

Graywolf Press was responsible for bringing out Haines's collected works, essays, and poems that he had been writing and revising at least since the 1970s, and in some cases even earlier. As in the early books *In a Dusty Light* and *Other Days*, Walker made a host of reading notes on Haines's typescripts, focusing especially on the intricate details of selecting and arranging the essays in *Fables and Distances*. At one point, in a letter of February 14, 1994, Walker considered dividing the material into two separate collections, one containing essays about nature and the other containing literary essays. But as Haines, Walker, and editor Anne Czarniecki worked on the book through a series of stages in 1994 and 1995, it took on a hybrid shape, similar to that of *Living Off the Country* (Graywolf Press Archives, Box 051, Folders 1–14). This was Haines's wish the entire time, and as we have seen he deliberately echoed the earlier book in the working title for the collection, *Another Country*.

After Walker left Graywolf Press in 1994, Haines continued to correspond with Fiona Macrae, the new director of the press, and with Anne Czarniecki, as well as with other members of the Graywolf staff. His relations with Macrae and Czarniecki were cordial, and he respected Czarniecki's work very highly. Still, Haines's deepest connection to Graywolf had really been through Scott Walker. In the early days of the twenty-first century, Haines repeatedly proposed the idea of an omnibus volume, *The John Haines Reader*, even though Macrae explained quite reasonably that the paperback editions of *The Owl in the Mask of the Dreamer* (1996) and *The Stars, the Snow, the Fire* (2000) made such a venture unwise (Graywolf Press Archives, Box 09 Editorial, Folder D). By the end of 2000, Haines's relationship with Graywolf Press was effectively over. His correspondence with Scott Walker also became sporadic, and even though the two remained friends until Haines's death in 2011, Walker was no longer Haines's literary executor.[6]

NEW GENERATION: DANA GIOIA AND JOHN LUTHER ADAMS

It would make conventional sense to interpret the relationship of Haines to poet Dana Gioia and composer John Luther Adams as that of an elder and mentor. But as with other aspects of Haines's career, the conventional expectation does not match the facts. In both cases, the younger artist became a close personal friend of the poet, offering support and advice that proved crucial to Haines's development as a mature writer. In both cases, the relationship grew into a friendship between artistic equals.

Dana Gioia and John Haines shared a number of perspectives that made their friendship seem inevitable. Both were active poets who also wrote literary criticism; both wrote initially from outside the academy, insisting on the civic role of poetry in American culture; both were critical of the prevailing fashions in American poetry in the decades of the 1980s and 1990s, especially those fostered by proliferating creative writing programs in universities; both were interested in the public performance of poetry and music together. Gioia's most famous statement of these positions came in a seminal essay first published in the May 1991 issue of the *Atlantic*, "Can Poetry Matter?"[7] As part of the analysis of the present situation of poetry, Gioia describes American poetry in 1940 as engaged with a broad audience of the American intelligentsia, readily available in magazines and journals, and providing diverse forms of reading to the American public. In the 1990s, by contrast, Gioia sees poetry as an alienated subculture, badly needing to reconnect with American readers by offering a more diverse poetry and criticism in an accessible public idiom.

A shared appreciation for the poetry of Robinson Jeffers is perhaps the most telling connection between Gioia and Haines. In "On Robinson Jeffers," originally published in 1989 in *The Gettysburg Review*, Haines focuses especially on the relationship of the poet to the landscape of Big Sur, which Haines first visited in 1952:

> In the situation in which I lived and wrote then, an older poet whom I admired was to me like a spring in the desert. I wanted very much to meet the man and talk with him; but as a still young and unformed poet I never had the courage to attempt to visit him, and I do not know what I would have found to say to him had I by some chance met him. I respected his solitude. At the same time, his spirit was everywhere in that countryside, so much so that already it was unthinkable that I, or anyone, should attempt to write anything about that coast, its ranges and valleys, so fully had the man and his poetry seized upon it and changed it forever. (*FD* 53)

For Haines as a young poet, Jeffers is preeminently a poet of place, so much so that his spirit inhabits every corner of the physical place itself. Haines even recalls imagining that such a power could be his, that he could find such a place at Richardson "and there live out my life, separate and perceiving":

> This was not, I was to discover, an entirely true conception, and I had much to learn about myself. In spite of the intensity of my attachment to that given place, I have since come to understand that there is more than one way to growth; a man is not a tree, however much he admires in trees and stones their immobility. The life of our time is not necessarily to be lived at its most intense in a single place. But in season and out, coping with the difficulties of weather and isolation, I dreamed the country and filled it with spirits and voices of my own. (*FD* 55)

However much Jeffers is the direct source or model for these ideas, Haines certainly connects Jeffers to the idea that "to live deeply in a certain place and, through voice and imagery and story, make it a permanent part of our heritage, is a thing most admirable" (55). Jeffers remained a constant presence for Haines, from the early visit to Big Sur to a late tribute presented at a Jeffers conference in Carmel in 2000 and reprinted in *Descent* (23–33).

Gioia's review of *Rock and Hawk*, Robert Hass's edition of Jeffers's shorter poems, appeared in the January 16, 1988, issue of the *Nation* and has been reprinted in *Can Poetry Matter?* The essay begins with the provocative line "No major American poet has been treated worse by posterity than Robinson Jeffers" and then traces Jeffers's remarkably rapid "rise to literary fame and his plunge to critical dismissal" (*Can Poetry Matter?* 48). According to Gioia's narrative, a major part of Jeffers's plunge came as a result of his staying in California (52). Thus the very spirit of place that attracted Haines in 1952 is paradoxically a reason for Jeffers's lack of renown. Gioia maintains, in fact, that Jeffers "remains invisible to critics."[8] In both essays, Jeffers emerges clearly as a major poet and an exemplary literary outsider—a position both Gioia and Haines admire.

Gioia's excellent introduction to Haines's *New Poems: 1980–88* opens with the image of Robinson Jeffers discovering the landscape around Carmel in the fall of 1914, and he contends that Jeffers identified so deeply with "the spirit of the place" that he was "spiritually reborn" (*New Poems* xi). According to Gioia, the identification with place is the key to Jeffers's achievement as the West Coast's first great poet: "Rooted in one specific landscape as deeply as any poet in American literature, Jeffers managed to create work which was both distinctly regional and unequivocally universal" (xi). The clear implication is that Alaska functioned in the same way for John Haines. The term "spirit of the place," from D. H. Lawrence's *Studies in Classic American Literature*, takes on particular resonance, for Gioia argues that Richardson becomes for Haines "a world of meditation" and that Haines's writings are "suffused with a sense of the sacred" (xiii). Later in the essay, Gioia specifies Haines's spirituality as "not so much personal as tribal," sparked by an imagination that is "frequently mythic" and given to ideas "revealed in bare narrative terms like ancient legends, half obscured by time" (xv).

As for the spirit of a specific place, Gioia treats the idea of regionalism at some length. He makes a sharp distinction between prose and poetry, finding Haines the essayist "a determined regionalist" and the mature poet one who can write "as convincingly about Albert Pinkham Ryder or Arlington Cemetery as he did about glaciers and wolf packs" (xiv). Gioia notes quite pointedly that "there is little sense of regionalism in Haines's *New Poems*. Only one sequence refers directly to Alaska. If one views Haines's poetic development as a journey from the specific geography of the Alaskan wilderness to the uncharted places of the spirit, then that journey is now complete" (xviii). *New Poems* is certainly a departure for Haines, both in geographic and in artistic terms, though some of these terms are already apparent in *In a Dusty Light*. The poet's formal experimentation with longer sequences is joined to a focus on artistic identity and a willingness to display his considerable erudition. But in addition, Gioia insists, *New Poems* is a book that repays solitary, deep meditation: "These unusual poems make the reader work, but they repay labor with spiritual refreshment" (xx).

Haines had no direct role in shaping Gioia's introduction, but he did read it and make minor corrections to it in January 1990. In letters to Gioia from the end of 1989 and the beginning of 1990, Haines emphasized that the art poems in *New Poems* were not merely ekphrastic. Taking the case of "Head of Sorrow, Head of Thought," Haines wrote in a letter of November 13, 1989, "The sculptures were simply a departure point, from which I tried to suggest a form of meditation, or how in thinking a certain passion or turmoil might be resolved, particularly in the case of a woman, someone I might have known or perhaps only imagined."[9] As if he were following up on the case (poem or woman), Haines wrote again on December 9, detailing his major love relationships in frank terms but asking Gioia not to talk about his private life in the introduction. Haines quoted Wendell Berry, whom he had visited recently: "The work should be enough" (Ohio JHC, Series 1.2, Box 1, Folder 10). Haines was so happy with Gioia's introduction that in a letter of January 28, 1990, he asked him if he would be interested in editing his papers in the future (Ohio JHC, Series 1.2, Box 1, Folder 10).[10]

Gioia's second contribution to Haines's career was his critical reading of the typescript of *Fables and Distances*. This appears to have been an arrangement made by Scott Walker, who needed Gioia's help in persuading Haines to cut parts of the typescript. Walker also enlisted Donald Hall's services as a reader in this regard, thirty years after Hall had helped Haines with the typescript of *Winter News*. Haines sent the typescript to Gioia on January 28, 1994, and Gioia responded immediately with his criticisms in a letter of January 31, 1994. The most important point Gioia made in his reading of the typescript was that Haines had included "far too many letters . . . and far too many of them don't have much import to a non-Alaskan" (Ohio JHP II, Box 2, Folder 14). Here the assertion is that the local can be merely local, not universal. For Gioia, the place-based essayist must reach beyond the physical and temporal boundaries of geographical and historical contingencies. In a way, then, the critique follows up on Gioia's characterization of Haines the essayist as a "determined regionalist." Gioia was asking Haines to expand the boundaries of his prose and at the same time delete extraneous, overly topical material.

As a mature writer, addressing themes of art and nature in his poems and essays, Haines appreciated Gioia's ideas. In a February 9, 1994, letter to Scott Walker, he agreed with most of Gioia's suggestions for reducing and revising the typescript (Graywolf Press Archives, Box 051, Folder 1). Indeed, the editing arrangement was so successful that Haines acknowledged his "debt to Dana Gioia, to Scott Walker, and to Donald Hall, all of whom at one time or another read through a draft of these essays and offered both criticism and encouragement. My lasting thanks goes to these friends and editors" (*FD* xiii–xiv). Hayden Carruth noted, in a comment on the back cover of *Fables and Distances*, that "this book, in effect his collected essays, reveals more: a range of intelligence and affection such that I cannot imagine any reader being unmoved by them. It is a great and splendid book." Without the help of friends and editors, the book might not have expanded beyond the borders of Alaska.

It would be overly simple, however, to see Haines as easily persuaded by a forceful, intelligent critic like Dana Gioia. In the essay "Formal Objections," first published in the summer 1990 issue of the *Hudson Review*, Haines reviews the critical collection *Expansive Poetry: Essays on the New Narrative & the New Formalism* and finds several reasons to object. The most prominent reason seems to be the self-promoting tone and grandiose claims made by some writers, with little concrete evidence to support them. On the other hand, Haines praises Gioia's essay "Notes on the New Formalism," even though he questions Gioia's abiding "concern with an audience" and argues for the American poet's "resuming a rigorous criticism of society" (*FD* 64). In addition, Haines defends the poetic sequence against the attacks of the New Formalists, finding it a "ruminative form" that evokes "thought that moves in considered periods, through one formal variation to another, and which says that we do not always nor necessarily think in a straight line" (65). The essay effectively creates a tone of reasonable, often impassioned conversation, and Haines is certainly less vehement in his arguments than he was in his letters to Robert Bly in the 1960s. In effect the essay "Formal Objections" summarizes a mature friendship between two respectful, admiring artists, more conversational than controversial.

The same tone of respectful friendship pervades the correspondence of Haines and composer John Luther Adams, though in this case the two were often quite playful in their letters and postcards. Adams first met Haines in Fairbanks in spring 1980.[11] The correspondence between Adams and Haines began as early as January 1981 (JHP Box 17, Folder 6), and it would continue for over thirty years. The young composer's role in the writing and revising of "In the Forest Without Leaves" was vital. Adams first broached the idea of composing a secular cantata based on "In the Forest Without Leaves" in a letter of July 16, 1981 (JHP Box 33, loose correspondence). By the time the cantata was first performed, on November 11, 1984, the two had become close friends and artistic partners. Adams in effect reawakened Haines's sense of possibility in the sequence of poems, which had lain largely untouched for five years. Even more deeply, the dialogue between the two on the relationship between poetry and music sparked Haines's continuing meditations on mimesis, art history, nature, and culture. These meditations, as we have seen, emerge most strongly in the "Provisional Draft" of the essay on "Forest Without Leaves" and the unpublished "conversation" between Haines and Adams, which Haines wrote and revised through letters with Adams in 1987. Moreover, the central ideas sparked by the dialogue with Adams play a major role in the essays "On a Certain Attention to the World" and "Notes, Letters, and Reflections" (*FD* 119–41). Perhaps most important of all, the continuing meditations resulted in the major poetic sequences of *New Poems* and *For the Century's End.*

The correspondence does not always reveal the dialogue between Adams and Haines as clearly as the typescripts and published poems, probably because much of their dialogue took place in person rather than through letters. From 1995 through 1997, for example, and again from 2000 until his death in 2011, Haines lived for the most part in Fairbanks, able to see Adams on a daily basis. Adams also visited Haines several times in 1991–1992, while Haines was teaching at George Washington University, and the two began a joking exchange of postcards and letters referring to "stew dogs, pie pugs, and mulligan mutts." Along with the jokes, however, Adams would write this kind of message to Haines on November 29, 1995: "Carruth is right. Alienation is our home. But from that alienation grows our other, true home: our work. Increasingly, this is where we must live. And this is the one last wilderness that the bastards in Washington and the Big Oil companies can't rape and pillage" (Ohio JHP, Series II, Box 1, Folder 2). Adams's reference to Hayden Carruth is immediate and direct. Carruth had written to Haines on November 7, 1995: "As for the sense of loss and displacement, if my experience is a guide you will never lose it, you shouldn't expect to, probably you shouldn't even want to. Exile is the condition of our lives. Alienation is the house we live in. Yet we both have made something valuable out of this, something wryly affirmative, and I suspect it isn't altogether contrary to our 'natures'" (Ohio JHP, Series II, Box 1, Folder 39). As Adams's response makes clear, Haines had shared Carruth's letter with him; it is as if the three artists were holding a colloquy. The topic is the alienated artist, and Adams gives the theme an environmental, place-based turn with "the one last wilderness."

Adams's perspective on what he gained from the ongoing conversation with Haines comes through in an unpublished essay, "Other Voices."[12] The short meditation begins, "Music and poetry are separable only to our loss," and then Adams turns to the figures of the poet and the composer: "The composer and poet as separate individuals are relative upstarts. From the beginning of history, the two were of one voice. It is only recently that we have come to regard them as distinct. But reunited, they can embody still other voices, more powerful than the sum of their parts; voices which can transform individuals and even entire cultures; voices which speak perhaps more urgently to our time than to any other" (Ohio JHC, Series 2, Box 3, Folder 7). In addition to crossing the boundary between music and poetry, Adams extends the power of voice to "other voices" in nature: "The 'other voices' we discover by listening and responding to birds and rain, wolves and wind, whales and the sea, strike deep resonances within us. This is the music of nature, in the most universal sense; a music which encompasses not only mountain stillness, but the internal rhythms of human nature and our synthetic environments, as well. In the desert or the city, the source is the same. We need only listen with care and compassion to hear the unity of it all" ("Other Voices").

This passage synthesizes the ideas of John Haines, John Luther Adams, and Dana Gioia, bringing the aspect of spirituality to bear on the environmental soundscapes of contemporary music. The younger correspondents had struck "deep resonances" within Haines, and those universal resonances echoed strongly in the essays and poems of the 1990s and early 2000s.

LISTENING WITH CARE: HAYDEN CARRUTH AND WENDELL BERRY

The two steadiest influences on Haines's writing life were Hayden Carruth and Wendell Berry, and their letters called forth some of Haines's most important work, from the 1970s until the end of his life. The three writers were good friends to one another, and they maintained a long line of communication among themselves for the greater part of forty years. This is by no means to say they did not disagree with one another; however, in some instances disagreement was the means to a deep trust and fast friendship.

Hayden Carruth (1921–2008) was an award-winning poet, essayist, and longtime editor at major literary publications such as *Poetry* and *Harper's*. He was also a highly regarded teacher of literature and creative writing, both at Bucknell University and Syracuse University. His anthology of American poetry, *The Voice That Is Great Within Us*, was a mainstay among budding writers in the 1970s. In short, Carruth was a true man of letters of the old school, a highly successful and visible presence on the American literary scene from the publication of his first book of poems in 1959 until his death.

Carruth's correspondence with Haines began on August 9, 1971, after Carruth had published a review of *The Stone Harp* in the *Hudson Review*. Haines wrote to Carruth, asking him to explain the distinction between prosody and technique and registering his surprise that Carruth had printed one of Haines's poems in prose. Haines included several passages from well-known poems, written out as prose, to show that one could not detect line breaks within the prose. Still, he asserted, in poetry "there is a different rhythm operating compared with prose" (JHP Box 1, Folder 28). Carruth ultimately responded with a long letter, but he did not send it till December 15, 1971. By that time Haines had decided that Carruth was an unfriendly critic who was disparaging his poems as prosaic. Carruth argues in the letter that "my point was simply that poetry printed as poetry needs functionally vigorous line-structure, and if it doesn't have it then it will actually read better as prose. I may be mistaken about your poem—I hope I am—but I did feel, and still do, that that particular poem has very weak line structure, and that it reads better as prose—more smoothly, fluently, rhythmically, and with a better pointing of emphases. More meaningfully."[13] Somewhat placated, Haines responded on December 21: "I have been on the point more than once of writing you another letter, this one inviting you to a duel of some kind, filled with insults, and much other abuse. I was told by someone who seemed to know that I would never hear from you again, that you planted your daggers and then slunk off into an unreachable distance and silence. But your letter of yesterday has redeemed you" (Hayden Carruth Papers Carton 8, Folder 34). Interestingly, in his later teaching of creative writing, Haines used the very technique that Carruth had employed, having his students write out their poems as prose and having them read famous poems in prose formatting.

The younger poet David Budbill, a friend and neighbor of Carruth's in Vermont, became one of Haines's most faithful correspondents in the late 1960s and continued the communications until about 1983. The two read each other's work and reviewed each other's books in print. Budbill urged Haines to remain in Alaska, and Haines's letters to Budbill from 1970 to 1971 are some of his most detailed accounts of his reasons for leaving Alaska and divorcing his second wife, Jo Ellen Hussey.[14] On February 13, 1972, Haines wrote to Budbill, clearly still angry at Carruth for the review of *The Stone*

Harp and making his poem "seem less than it was." Over the next several years, Budbill sought to reconcile the two older writers. In a letter of May 23, 1976, for instance, Budbill offered to reintroduce Haines and Carruth to one another (JHP Box 19, Folder 2).

Thanks in large part to Budbill's unstinting efforts, Carruth began corresponding with Haines in 1977, and almost immediately he generously offered to send essays by Haines to *Harper's*; as poetry editor, he accepted several of Haines's poems for the magazine as well. In his omnibus review in the June 1978 *Harper's*, moreover, Carruth praised Haines's *Cicada* and *In a Dusty Light* as "the mature work of one of our best nature poets, or for that matter one of our best nature writers of any kind, best because he is so much more than a naturalist. Haines knows the ecological crisis as well as anyone, and he knows it is more than that. It is a crisis of consciousness, the human mind in ultimate confrontation with itself."[15]

Carruth's praise for the two books from 1977 seems to have led to the steady correspondence that the two writers maintained over the next thirty years. Carruth's letters were often long, literary, and typed; he loved to think out loud about his love relationships; his career moves; the effects of aging; his mental and physical health; his own writing as well as that of many others; his love of gardening, animals, and automobiles; and a host of other topics. Most important for Haines's career, Carruth was an incisive, constructive critic of Haines's prose and poetry. Like Scott Walker, he acted as both editor and agent, and often he was able to make specific suggestions for revisions, suggestions that Haines seems always to have taken very seriously.

Haines consistently enlisted Carruth's critical acumen in reading the poetic sequences that he was writing in the late 1970s. Two of these appeared in *In a Dusty Light*: "Homestead" and "News from the Glacier." Many more were to appear in *New Poems*, *The Owl in the Mask of the Dreamer*, and *For the Century's End*. Already in 1977, Haines sent Carruth some of the first sections of "In the Forest Without Leaves," and in 1978 and 1979, he was sending Carruth sections of "In the House of Wax," which would not be published in its final version until 2000. Even then, Haines noted in the preface to *For the Century's End* that the sequence was "slow to clarify" and that "a few of the poems meant to complete the sequence remain unfinished" (*FCE* x). Perhaps even at that late date Haines was echoing Carruth, who wrote the following in a letter of December 12, 1978:

> The sequence is the poem of our time partly because knowledge has become so intricate that we can't deal with it in separate bits and pieces. I don't know if Pound recognized this, but certainly in the *Cantos* it was a central problem, how not only to make it new but to say everything—everything relevant to his expansive view. . . . [T]he most moving and significant poem is one which is more than the sum of its parts, and you can't have the sum if you don't have the parts. The connections, unstated, between parts are what make the increment . . . . The work of art which is closest to telling the facts of our time is the unfinished work. Kafka's *Castle* is the perfect novel for me, because it doesn't end and it cannot end—it vanishes into the unspeakable. A poetic sequence, even if it breaks off at some sort of concluding point, gives the same sense; its spontaneity and innate evolutionism—meaning the way it makes itself up as it goes along—convey inevitably the quality of unfinishability. (JHP Box 19, Folder 13)

The problem with "unfinishability" is that the quality could prevent the poet from ending a sequence at all. Haines seems to have faced that problem, taking long years to bring a sequence like "In the House of Wax" to a provisional ending. As a correspondent, Carruth was superb at encouraging Haines when he seemed stalled or balked by a sequence in process. So, for instance, he wrote on September 19, 1980, that Haines should write more poems: "I thought the sections of the sequence you sent me a year or so ago were among the very best poems of yours I have read. I'm not trying to solace your feelings of age (or mine). You are in the midst of your strongest poetic vision and technique right now; I'm convinced of that" (JHP Box 19, Folder 12).

Carruth appreciated Haines's emphasis on the visual arts, singling out the "art poems" for special praise. In a letter of June 7, 1981, he responded to the sequence "Death and the Miser," based on the painting by Hieronymous Bosch: "Aside from the quality of the writing in your poems, which is superb, the quality of perception is so much clearer and different, and you don't *use* the painting. You make your poem workable in itself, and your feeling is human and practical (i.e., moral). It is a fine poem. If you are doing work of this quality I don't think you need worry much about the quantity" (JHP Box 28, Folder 2). As we have seen in chapters 4 and 5, the poetic sequence based on artworks or an artist's life is a hallmark of Haines's last two books. Without doubt, Hayden Carruth was instrumental in encouraging Haines to pursue these themes and techniques in the later poems. Carruth's encouragement was constant and often repeated, so that one can find him praising Haines's "graphic arts" poems and sequences throughout the 1980s and 1990s.

A characteristic letter from Carruth, written on March 24, 1986, shows how thoroughly he responded to Haines's poems. He begins with the kind of accurate praise that perhaps only the sharpest fellow writer can bring to a work: "Reading all your 'picture poems' together has given me the sense of pleasure combined with awe that I always get from poems that are truly original. I haven't seen any new poetry for quite a while that affects me this way. Your turns of phrasing and imagery are completely your own, and not just thrown out in the rote fashion of poets who have learned their own style too well (which is what I feel I do), but *worked*. The sense of your digging in and making an effort, that's what I get from these poems, but not at all the kind of effort that seems awkward: this makes the reading more worthwhile, the feeling more intense. I admire this in your work very much indeed, and I wish I could write as slowly as you do. . . . Taken altogether these poems are your best work, I believe" (Ohio JHC, Series 2, Box 3, Folder 3).

Even if this were all that Carruth said about the art poems, it would be vitally encouraging for Haines as he worked toward publishing *New Poems*. But Carruth followed the encouragement with detailed commentary on "Days of Edward Hopper," "Paolo and Francesca," and "On a Certain Field in Auvers." In the case of the last poem, Carruth returned the typescript with his marginal comments and suggested revisions. He made several notes for changes in diction, rhythm, and lineation, and he asked intelligent questions about obscurities in the three sections of the poem. Tellingly, Haines made only one specific change recommended by Carruth. In Section II, he changed "his hand" and "his thirst" to "my hand" and "my thirst," clarifying the relationship to the speaker.

The friends could also manage some retrospective humor in the midst of high literary seriousness. In a lengthy letter of January 25, 1986, Carruth summarized his admiration for Haines's "work as a whole, which I believe to be substantially original, genuine, damned interesting, relevant, intellectually attractive, and important. Your language, similarly, is genuine and your own. Twenty years ago I thought you had slackened up too much;

that's when I wrote the review which offended you and inaugurated this correspondence. (How do you feel about that now? I wonder if, unconsciously, you were influenced a little by Rexroth and especially his followers.) Anyway, it doesn't matter, because all of the recent poetry of yours that I've read, going back ten years or longer, is strong, the language is strong, syntax and rhythm quite different from the common mode" (JHP Box 25, loose correspondence). Haines replied by denying Rexroth's influence, causing Carruth to backpedal and explain the joke. This kind of continuing encouragement and guidance led Haines to dedicate *For the Century's End* to Carruth, "Poet and Friend."

Through a similar balance of precise criticism and insightful praise, Carruth acted as an excellent reader of Haines's prose. Even more than Scott Walker, Carruth used his position as poetry editor for the *Hudson Review* and *Harper's* to recommend Haines's essays for publication, and he was often successful. On July 22, 1977, for example, Carruth offered to send poems and essays to *Harper's*, and a month later he sent the magazine the essay "Spring." Within a matter of three weeks the essay was accepted for publication, earning Haines $500 (JHP Box 19, Folder 13). Later that year, Carruth sent *Harper's* the essay "Lost," which again was accepted in January 1978 and paid $500. Even though Carruth did not feel qualified to comment in depth on Haines's prose style, he clearly appreciated both the critical essays and memoirs. In a letter of July 6, 1980, he commented on "With Axe and Auger" as a "prose poem," though he also asked for more context and more elaboration of potential stories within the essay. In other letters, he found himself in complete agreement with Haines's more polemical arguments in "What Are Poets For?" (March 24, 1985), the review of John Ashbery titled "In and Out of the Loop" (July 2, 1993), and an essay on California poet Weldon Kees (October 22, 1996).[16]

In addition to these professional, writerly matters, Carruth and Haines connected regularly on a personal level. That was especially the case as the two writers entered old age. Haines felt able to complain about his loneliness in Athens, Ohio, and the "grip of profound melancholy" he could not seem to escape after having visited Fairbanks and the Richardson homestead (April 28, 1990). Carruth, too, regularly experienced depression and sought help through various medications. His constant advice to Haines in the 1990s was to put the homestead behind him and get out of Fairbanks for good. Haines's concerns for the property in Richardson and for his literary position at the University of Alaska Fairbanks were the trigger for Carruth's comment, "Alienation is the house we live in" (November 7, 1995), and another, "The artist's job is to respond to what's new, even if the response is negative" (December 13, 1995). Sometimes Carruth could be cranky and curmudgeonly, but most often his sense of his own aging body and mind was full of biting humor: "I wish I had a set of teeth like those in your crystal skull. Jesus!" (November 4, 1996); "I'd like to buy one of those neat little conversion vans and drive across the country to Alaska before I croak" (May 22, 1997); "Get a flu shot" (September 21, 1997); "My new book is out but I have only one copy so far. I like the cover a lot. As for the rest of it, who cares?" (August 28, 1998); "After the firecracker goes off it sputters for a while" (December 3, 1998).

Wendell Berry (b. 1934) is the link joining Haines and Hayden Carruth. Ten years younger than Haines and thirteen years younger than Carruth, Berry maintained a friendship with both writers that stretched over forty years. Berry was able, in fact, to memorialize both of his friends in the pages of the *Sewanee Review*, a culminating gesture of friendship in a lifelong relationship. In Berry's recent collection of essays, *Imagination in Place*, the two memorial essays appear side by side. In the tribute to Haines, "Speech After Long Silence," Berry recalls hearing Haines read his poems at Stanford University in 1969, and the primary memory is arresting: "His lines were qualified unremittingly by a silence that they came from and were going toward, that they for a moment broke."[17] Berry uses Haines's poems and essays to define the voice that breaks the silence, and he arrives at this formulation by Haines, from the end of "The Writer as Alaskan": "What counts finally in a work are not novel and interesting things, though these can be important, but the absolutely authentic. I think that there *is* a spirit of place, a presence asking to be expressed; and sometimes when we are lucky as writers, and quiet in a way few of us want to be anymore, a voice enters our own" (Berry 52). The idea of place, for Berry as for Haines, is central to the poet's voice, and Berry ends his tribute by recommending Haines's work to "the increasingly competent minority who long for an authentic settlement of our country" (53).

The tribute to Hayden Carruth, "My Friend Hayden," is longer, more personal, and quite humorous (*Imagination in Place* 55–72). Berry traces his first reading of Carruth's poems to the time "when I was in college and had become certain that Anonymous was not the name of a prolific medieval poet" (55), and he also recalls how nervous he was when Denise Levertov handed him a sheaf of Carruth's poems, the sequence *North Winter*, in May of 1964. As he describes the poems and what they meant to him at a crucial juncture in his own life and career, Berry once again connects the writer to the idea of place. In Carruth's case, the place was Johnson, Vermont, "a place not central to the culture even of Vermont, and yet a place obviously central to the consciousness and imagination of a fine poet. It was a place that, on the scale of grandeur, might have been any place, except that by the use of his senses, his wits, and his art, the poet had given standing to its unique life, first in his own imagination, then in Denise's, then in mine, and eventually in the imaginations of many others" (57). As in the essay on Haines, Berry uses Carruth's essays and poems to develop particular aspects of the poet's voice, in this case affection and reverence, and to tie those qualities to an authentic sense of place. Carruth's poem "Marshall Washer," from *Brothers, I Loved You All* (1978), is the proof text for Berry's account, connecting the "cowshit farmer" of the title to the "manure" that "is the link eternal, binding man and beast / and earth" (65). The linkage leads Berry to conclude with the image of "a cowshit sodality making places for reverence, still faithful to the old linkage, its knowledge and its work" (69).[18]

The correspondence between Berry and Haines began in 1969 and continued until Haines's death in 2011. Berry read all of Haines's books, both poetry and prose, as they came out, and in his letters he registered his appreciation for the writer's language and style as well as for his ideas. Ideas definitely dominate the correspondence, from first to last, and the two writers found that they had much in common. In a letter of November 6, 1981, for example, Berry wrote that the essays of *Living Off the Country* "will make it easier for me to live and say what I have to say" (JHP Box 33, loose correspondence). A couple of weeks later, in response to the typescript essay "The View from Buckeye Dome," Berry noted the effect of "companionship" and forecast his essay of twenty-five years later: "The number of people who have known a place for a long time is dwindling fast, and so, therefore, is the number of people who have any real experience or understanding of change" (JHP Box 26, Folder 4).

The friendship was not without its rough patches, but in general the two correspondents were respectful and fair to one another, even when they did not find themselves wholly in agreement. In a typed, six-page letter written over several days in December 1985, for example, Berry responded at length to the ideas in Haines's provocative essay "Something for Our Poetry," especially focusing on the idea of suffering in the modern world, whether suffering is something we need for good poetry, and whether we Americans have been "willfully innocent" of the kind of suffering that writers like Czeslaw Milosz and Octavio Paz underwent as part of their countries' histories (JHP Box 25, loose correspondence.). Haines's essay, first published in the *Northwest Review* in 1983 and reprinted in *Fables and Distances*, struck a nerve with Berry. Haines had sent the essay to Berry by letter, and Berry's response was delayed by travel, lack of time, and the need to answer properly. Writing on December 28 and 30, Berry agreed with Haines's assertions that "the artist takes up the more or less imposed position" (*FD* 71) and that "there is nothing attractive or excusable about 'a willful innocence,' and I am familiar enough with the guilt that one feels about the sufferings of people in the totalitarian countries." But then Berry drew a line. Not all guilt, he argued, is useful or helpful; not all does good. In fact, there are ills and sufferings aplenty in our own country, namely the 15.2 million people who left farms between 1950 and 1977, and the continuing displacement of people from their land and the means to support themselves. While Berry acknowledged the horrors of the modern history of Poland and sympathized with Milosz, he found more pressing the question of what is to be done for the dying rural communities of which he was a part.

On December 31, Berry took up questions Haines had asked about the ethical position of university professors and poets in the face of political evils like those portrayed by Carolyn Forché in *The Country Between Us*. But for Berry the position should not prevent "a commitment to belief and practice," and so he shifted the topic to the question of suffering. For Berry, Haines's essay drew an invidious distinction between American poets and poets who have suffered under totalitarian oppression. In response, Berry's sense of universal suffering made such a distinction less than persuasive, and he disagreed with the idea of comparing sufferings, finding it irresponsible and potentially dishonest: "I don't think American poets ought to be held responsible for other people's experience. I think that, in general, recent American poetry has been very poorly responsible for American experience, and that is what troubles me" (JHP Box 25).

Letters end, but the conversation continues, changing as it goes. As the two friends continued to debate the social responsibilities of the American poet, they also could exchange more personal messages. Just a few months after the discussion of suffering, Berry wrote on June 23, 1986, that he had read *Stories We Listened To* "with much pleasure and with admiration. It is spare and clear and beautiful, and evokes far more than it says. It speaks of animals with an authority that comes—that I guess can only come—from familiarity and affection. I'm very glad you're going on with this work, which I think has great value as testimony, in addition to its other values." As Haines proceeded slowly toward the publication of *The Stars, the Snow, the Fire*, Berry was a constant admirer of the essays and stories that eventually made up the volume. Finally, Berry could read the book, and he registered his deep delight in a letter of July 4, 1993: "I'm reading *The Stars, the Snow, the Fire* slowly and with great interest and pleasure. The prose is wonderful and what you say with it is wonderful too. That book sent me back to the poems again. The first time I heard you read was 23 or 24 years ago and the reading made a deep impression on me. I have remembered particularly 'The Traveler' and the man walking alone on the frozen road" (Ohio JHP II, Box 1, Folder 23). That memory, along with Haines's response on July 15, 1993, would eventually appear in Berry's tribute, "Speech After Long Silence." There, Berry would connect Haines's reading with his own sense of "The Traveler," lines from "In the Forest Without Leaves," and the ending of "Richardson: The Dream."[19]

A few years later, Berry found much to admire in the critical essays of *Fables and Distances*. In a letter of February 4, 1996, he declared that already in the first hundred pages of the book he had found the arguments "careful and sensible and fair-minded," and the book as a whole he called "full of sentences & paragraphs that seem to me to light up whole landscapes. Because I share so many of your convictions & concerns, I get from it a very comforting sense of companionship." But by "comfort" Berry did not mean "the folly & uselessness of the comforts usually offered by industrial society" but rather the comfort of seeing another person's "refusal to be fooled." The essay "Something for Our Poetry," which had prompted Berry's stem-winding, three-day letter on suffering a decade earlier, now seemed to him to be "an inspiring essay because of its willingness to confront some of the most disturbing facts of our world." As in the earlier letter, Berry insisted that our awareness of distant horrors should not blind us to the horrors around us that we need to recognize, and that "routine outrage" would always be a problem. For his own part, he was involved in several efforts having to do with the local economy (Ohio JHP II, Box 1, Folder 23).

As the "American century" drew to a close, the goal of bearing authentic testimony to passing experience was a constant topic for both writers. In a letter from September 9, 1986, for example, Berry reflected honestly on the Port William stories he had sent to Haines, sharing his correspondent's questions about the community depicted there:

> I'm glad you like the stories. I have some questions about them too. There is more consciousness of membership in those people than in any group of people I have actually known. And the gentleness and compassion is more realized in the stories than in the world as I have known it. But these things *exist* in the world as I have known it, so the stories seem to me to have been authentically suggested by the world. Behind some of the more compassionate and conscious moments of the stories real moments do exist. And yet I worry endlessly about the relation between imagination and reality. "Realism" seems to offer almost no help in this because so resistant to what I think of as imagination. (JHP Box 25, loose correspondence)

This self-reflective honesty is part of the ongoing conversation, and one can find the two writers discussing topics like community across the years, sometimes prompted by current events or by works they have read or themselves written.

One of the current events of most importance to both writers was the *Exxon Valdez* oil spill of March 1989. In a letter of June 6, 1989, Haines had thanked Berry for a pamphlet printing of "The Work of Local Culture," which he kept with him during the weeks as the damages of the oil spill became more and more apparent: "The recent oil spill demonstrated just how much at the mercy of these far-off corporations people are in many remote communities, and I use the word 'community' with caution when speaking of a place like Fairbanks" (WBC Box 5, Folder 3).[20] Despite his caution, Haines spoke out boldly in a letter to the editor of the Fairbanks *News-Miner*, a copy of which he sent to Berry in a letter of April 20, 1990. In the letter to the editor, Haines found the trial of Captain Hazelwood of the *Exxon Valdez* to be a farce because the responsibility for the oil spill could not be assigned to one person. As he proceeds with his argument, it is as if Haines were writing with the combined force of his own pen and Berry's:

> But even more important is the placing of the whole affair in some useful context. We have, for example and as usual, left out *Nature*. Nature not only in the shape of a hidden reef in Prince William Sound, but Nature in the form of human error. The writer Wendell Berry is certainly correct in commenting on this and similar recent accidents: that if we insist on placing the fate of communities, territorial waters, and natural systems, within the hull of a single tanker, within the metal skin of a thousand-mile pipeline, or in a nuclear plant, then sooner or later Nature will furnish the flaw and the rust, the fool, the drunk, the vandal or the terrorist, to bring on the necessary accident. We hear reports now of the possibility of new safeguards and watchdogs. These will not be enough; they will never be enough. If we have not learned from the casualties of *Exxon Valdez*, we can be certain that another and greater disaster is waiting and will without fail take place at some point. (WBC Box 7, Folder 5)

Haines's warning is prescient, and so is the way in which he uses Berry to set up his argument. Berry's name evokes authority, and Haines uses it to give a yet more exalted authority to Nature, figured as an omnipotent judge of human foolishness.

Berry's influence on Haines was deep, and it deepened considerably over the last twenty-five years of Haines's life. Beyond the occasional mention of Berry's name in an interview or letter, Haines seems to have grasped profoundly Berry's perspective on America at the turn of the new century—as a social world marked by modern industrial capitalism and global militarism, seemingly unstoppable regimes of specialization and an accompanying fragmentation of knowledge, inexorable processes of displacement from the land and the ruination of rural communities. In the letters to Berry over the last twenty years of his life, Haines continually sent his own typescripts as well as articles and newspaper clippings that he thought would be of interest to Berry. In July 1994, Haines was evicted from the homestead, where he had been living off and on for several years, and he registered his confusion and loss in several letters to Berry, who responded kindly over the next several months. Through all his sojourns—back and forth, in Fairbanks and Anchorage, Alaska; in Missoula and Helena, Montana; in Athens, Ohio; Clarksville, Tennessee; Washington, DC; and Lenox, Massachusetts—the correspondence was a kind of homecoming for Haines. By 2000, Haines admitted that his energies were low, that he was trying to be "as persistent as I need to be" (January 9, 2000). Still, he found the energy to write letters to Berry, on average one a month. Many veered into accounts of physical ailments and chronic pain, but Haines always found a place to reminisce about William Carlos Williams, George Hitchcock's *Kayak*, or their mutual friend Hayden. In one of the last letters, from May 2, 2009, Haines responded warmly to Berry's request that he be allowed to dedicate his new book of poems to Haines. This would be the book *Leavings*, which includes two poems of special importance.

The first, "A Letter (to Hayden Carruth)," begins with the poet's joy at reading "of your hatred of *Alice in Wonderland*." The humor persists through Berry's questioning, "But who the hell wants to go / down a rabbit hole?" Oh, he decides, to burrow like a mole or fly like a bird would be fine:

> Otherwise,
> my stratum of choice is the surface.
> I prefer skin to anatomy, green grass
> to buried rocks, terra firma to the view
> from anywhere higher than a tree.
> "Long live superficiality!" say I,
> as one foot fares waywardly graveward.

The tongue-in-cheek irony becomes more than droll in the last line's musical phrasing and roughened metrics. It is just the kind of precision of voice that Carruth would appreciate.

The second, "Sabbath Poem III" of 2005, could be addressed to Haines, though that requires a bit of imagination here at the end:

> "Are you back to normal?" asks
> my old friend, ill himself, after I,
> who have been ill, am well. "Yes,
> the gradient of normality now
> being downward." For when I walk
> now from rock to rock in the tumble
> of Camp Branch, under the trees,
> the singing stream, the stream
> of light that all my life

has drawn me as it has drawn
the ever-renewing waters, I clamber
where I used to leap, where once I could
have been a ghost for all the care
I paid to flesh and bone until
some hunger turned me home.

Self-deprecating humor is still at work in this poem, but the downward gradient is steeper than in the letter-poem addressed to Carruth. Even so, there is also great joy in the description of the "singing stream" and the "stream / of light," the "ever-renewing waters" of Camp Branch. And even though the poet claims to have been wandering past the boundaries of flesh and bone till "some hunger turned me home," the entire poem registers a strong sense of being at home in the flesh. It is as if the Sabbath poem were an answer or response to the letter-poem to Carruth, as if the two senses of walking along the surface of the earth were connected. Graveward or homeward, somebody could be there at the other end, listening—someone who might understand what the walker wishes to say.

CONCLUSION

JOHN HAINES'S PLACE AS ECOPOET

FACED WITH THE PROBLEM OF DEFINITION IN JANUARY 1842, Emerson addressed a curious audience at the Masonic Temple in Boston. "The first thing we have to say respecting what are called *new views* here in New England," he said, "is that they are not new, but the very oldest of thoughts cast into the mould of these new times." Then he went on to specify the *new views*: "What is popularly called Transcendentalism among us, is Idealism; Idealism as it appears in 1842."[1] The same might be said of what we are now calling ecopoetry, ecopoetics, and ecopoets. They are all a recent development of nature poetry, but nature poetry cast into the mold of our new times. As Emerson knew well, of course, the casting does create a new view, fitting the mold of new times.

As I write at this very moment, the online *Oxford English Dictionary* does not recognize the terms "ecopoetry," "ecopoetics," or "ecopoets." That simply means that the ideas are still flowing, not fixed, and that fact itself may be cause for celebration, not concern. Meanwhile, Scott Bryson offered a good working definition of "ecopoetry" over a decade ago:

> Ecopoetry is a subset of nature poetry that, while adhering to certain conventions of romanticism, also advances beyond that tradition and takes on distinctly contemporary problems and issues, thus resulting

> in a version of nature poetry generally marked by three primary characteristics. The first is an emphasis on maintaining an ecocentric perspective that recognizes the interdependent nature of the world; such a perspective leads to a devotion to specific places and to the land itself, along with those creatures that share it with humankind. . . . This awareness of the world as a community tends to produce the second attribute of ecopoetry: an imperative toward humility in relationships with both human and nonhuman nature. . . . Related to this humility is the third attribute of ecopoetry: an intense skepticism concerning hyperrationality, a skepticism that usually leads to an indictment of an overtechnologized modern world and a warning concerning the very real potential for ecological catastrophe.[2]

These three characteristics can stand for principal ideas of what we call ecopoetry in the English-speaking world of the early-twenty-first century. Bryson's clear definition suggests, moreover, both the continuities and the changes within the longer tradition of nature poetry.

John Haines belongs within the canon of American ecopoetry, and he belongs as a major ecopoet. Haines's career recapitulates many developments in contemporary American nature poetry, and in the 1970s and 1980s he developed a new poetry of the earth that constitutes a significant body of ecopoetry. Haines was closely connected to several figures we now recognize as major American ecopoets, especially Robert Bly and Wendell Berry. He worked slowly and deliberately throughout his writing career, and he was not by any means prolific. But Marianne Moore and Elizabeth Bishop wrote deliberately, too, and both of them have been accorded major status as modernist and contemporary poets, even major ecopoets. Like those two predecessors, Haines worked on poems for decades, and he only published his poems when he deemed them worthy of public reading. That should not be a deterrent to appreciating Haines as an ecopoet. Instead, they mark him as a poet of humility and healthy skepticism. Haines's career fits into four distinct phases. Because Haines wrote recursively, constantly revisiting and revising essays and poems for decades at a time, there is considerable chronological overlap between the phases, especially in the middle of Haines's career. For that reason, I have given each phase a formal or thematic title rather than a chronological one.

THE FIRST PHASE: POEMS OF THE FORGOTTEN

In the first phase, running roughly from 1948 to 1966, Haines works through his apprentice poems, discovering the voice and technique that leads to his first book of poems, *Winter News* (1966). William Carlos Williams exercises a major influence on the young writer, but the most significant influence in this first period is Robert Bly. Bly's Deep Image surrealism provides Haines with a model for writing about the subsistence life he leads at Richardson, Alaska, from 1947 to 1969. Like Bly, moreover, Haines's attraction to oneiric, psychological imagism involving wild animals mixes fruitfully with his disenchanted view of American political and military adventures in the 1960s and 1970s.

Bernard Quetchenbach's 2000 study of contemporary American nature poetry establishes important historical contexts for reading writers like Theodore Roethke, Robert Bly, Gary Snyder, and Wendell Berry. Through careful close readings and scholarship, Quetchenbach grounds theoretical discussions of ecopoetry, outlining some of the same characteristics offered by Scott Bryson and others. Quetchenbach uses the historical arguments of James Breslin's *From Modern to Contemporary* to show that American nature poetry makes a similar shift toward personal, idiosyncratic imagery, open forms, and the location of poetic authority in the individual voice. We find some of the tensions between modern and contemporary, public and private, in the careers of Roethke and Bly, and Quetchenbach uses the distinction to contrast the modern style of Robinson Jeffers to the contemporary style of Roethke. Perhaps most interesting of all, Quetchenbach's discussions of Bly, Snyder, and Berry continually raise questions about how the contemporary American ecopoet can speak with a public voice.[3]

These discussions, and the questions they raise, are of equal interest in reading John Haines as an ecopoet. In the first phase of his career, Haines recapitulates some of the movements in Robert Bly's early career, including the writing of political poetry during the 1960s and early 1970s. Like the early Bly, Haines is initially a poet of silence and snow, attracted to the northern landscape of Alaska for many of the same reasons Bly returns to his home country in Minnesota. Haines's years at the Richardson homestead give him a sense of both place and space, what we might call a provisional home. In "Poem of the Forgotten," for example, the speaker is "a young man green and lonely" (2), who is nevertheless "well quit of the world" (3). He lives in a house "of moss and timber" that he has framed himself, and he calls it "a home" (4–5). The speaker sings, but it is "singing to myself as a man sings / when he knows there is no one to hear" (7–8). As autumn shades into winter, the speaker awakes "in the first snow of autumn, / filled with silence" (11–12). The ambiguity of the last two lines of the poem perfectly balances between the silence of the speaker and the silence of first snowfall.

As realistic as "Poem of the Forgotten" may be, it also edges toward the surrealism of Deep Image poetry. Another poem from *Winter News*, "Snowy Night," evokes a similar merging, a barren richness of landscape and place:

> This is like a place
> we used to know,
> but stranger
> and filled with the cold
> imagination of a frozen
> sea, in which
> the moon is anchored
> like a ghost
> in heavy chains.

The title defines the scene as physical, but in the poem the place immediately becomes uncanny, familiar and yet estranged. It is a cold place, but the cold applies to the imagination rather than to the physical landscape. The moon, though it might be the actual moon, is anchored in an imagined "frozen sea," and it is further transformed into a ghost in heavy chains. In one sentence of nine lines, Haines creates a dream of the northern landscape. It is an emotionally powerful landscape, but Haines insists on the power of the place to resist our attempts at knowing and understanding it. In both poems, we may call nature a home, but it is stranger than any home we have ever known.

THE SECOND PHASE: THE PLACE OF CONVICTION

In the second phase of his career, Haines's search for what he calls "a place of conviction" leads him to explore political poetry, even though he criticizes Robert Bly's political poetry in the 1978 review of Bly's work from *Silence in the Snowy Fields* (1962) to *This Body Is Made of Camphor and Gopherwood* (1977) (*LOC* 113–19). There are many political poems in *The Stone Harp* (1971), *Leaves and Ashes* (1975), and *Cicada* (1977). The political theme is not always environmental, but Haines's critical detachment resembles the stance we find in Robert Bly, Gary Snyder, Wendell Berry, and W. S. Merwin. This detachment may depend upon a kind of pastoralism or, as Terry Gifford calls it, a "post-pastoral" undercutting of idealized pastoral places.[4] By consistently bringing nature and culture together, especially in ways that imply the critique of American culture occurs from an ecocentric perspective, Haines definitely creates a form of political ecopoetry.

Haines is so thoroughly a poet of place that landscapes tend to dominate his political poems. A poem like "Guevara," for instance, from *The Stone Harp*, locates "a country named / Guevara" in the body of the poet, "perhaps under my left shoulder" (2–4). The poem explores the landscape of that country, and the poet emerges "like a man / who has marched for years / under an enemy flag" (19–21). The poet climbs a steep hill, slippery with blood, and he climbs back down, restless and unsure of what he has suffered, what he has learned, or whether the landscape might be finally "the red slope of my heart" (29). For Haines, nature and culture constantly mirror each other. Thus a poem like "In Nature" can assert, "Here too, neighborhoods / in revolt, revengeful columns; / evenings at the broken wall, / black armies in flight . . . " (17–20). In *Cicada* (1977), poems from the late 1960s and early 1970s strike a broadly critical tone about the political and social state of American culture. "Poem about Birch Trees" (1971), "Men against the Sky" (1969), and "Dusk of the Revolutionaries" (1969) all use physical landscapes to launch figurative investigations into the hollowness of consumer capitalism in the late twentieth century. Even in a restrained elegy like "Arlington" (1972), Haines imagines transforming the strangely calm cemetery, where his father and grandfather lie buried, into a profoundly truthful landscape:

> The soil should be thick
> with shrapnel
> and splinters of bone;
> for a shrine, a lamp
> fueled with blood,
> if blood would burn.

The poems of *In a Dusty Light* (1977) consolidate Haines's new poetry of the earth and develop his broadly political critique of American society. The politics are less direct and topical than in the earlier poems, many of which focus resolutely on the Vietnam War. In "The Blood Lake," for example, we may hear echoes of "Arlington," but the landscape remains that of rural America, though no less bloody for all that. Indeed, the Montana landscapes of poems like "Alive in the World" and "Missoula in a Dusty Light" make the tone all the more ominous and foreboding. We stand "still in the middle of the world, / let it be Missoula," but it could just as well be "any crossroad in the west" ("Alive in the World" 1–3). Here, "the west" is deliberately and deeply imbricated as a figurative place.

THE MAJOR PHASE: POETIC SEQUENCES

Major poetic sequences mark the third phase of Haines's poetic career and give him amplitude to maneuver among a host of themes and perspectives, creating narratives, clusters, and constellations of poems in multiple sections. The sequences define Haines's changed pastoral, occupying the central core achievement of the mature ecopoet. They give Haines a breadth and depth that he was unable to develop in the short poems of the 1960s and early 1970s. Within multiple sections of a single poem, Haines can move from political, social, and aesthetic concerns to nature, environmental degradation, care of the earth, and the role of human beings in landscapes. The sequences give aesthetic pattern and shape to a writer's most intensely emotional material, allowing him to transform the personal into the visionary.

From the 1977 publication of *In a Dusty Light* to the 2001 publication of *For the Century's End*, poetic sequences mark the major achievements of Haines's ecopoetry. The central works adumbrate this third phase of Haines's career. According to the dates given in *The Owl in the Mask of the Dreamer*, Haines wrote both "Homestead" and "News from the Glacier," the two sequences in *In a Dusty Light*, in 1975. In the six major sequences of *New Poems*, on the other hand, the dates form a testament to sustained, disciplined composition and revision. "Meditation on a Skull Carved in Crystal" is dated 1977–1986; "Rain Country," 1978–1983; "Death and the Miser," 1980–1984; "Days of Edward Hopper," 1981–1991; "Water of Night," 1977–1982; and "In the Forest without Leaves," 1977–1984. The overlapping dates suggest that Haines kept developing these projects more or less simultaneously for nearly fifteen years. During those same years, moreover, Haines wrote the sequence "Stalled Colossus" (1986–1991), which appears in the last section, "New and Uncollected Poems" (1996), of the paperback edition of *The Owl in the Mask of the Dreamer*. Finally, the two major sequences of *For the Century's End*, "In a Cave at Lone Tree Meadow" and "In the House of Wax," reach back as far as 1974, the same period as the earlier sequences, and bring the major phase of Haines's career to a close.

Haines published ten major poetic sequences, in addition to many poems in multiple sections. Three of the sequences in *New Poems* focus on art and the artist: "Meditation on a Skull Carved in Crystal," "Death and the Miser," and "Days of Edward Hopper." The late sequence "In the House of Wax," from *For the Century's End*, uses a similar focus to meditate on political figures and their victims. The six other major sequences—"Homestead," "News from the Glacier," "Rain Country," "Water of Night," "In the Forest without Leaves," and "In the Cave at Lone Tree Meadow"—use nature as a basis for meditating on the place human beings occupy on the earth. As I have argued in earlier chapters, however, in some ways this distinction between topics obscures the connections among all ten sequences. In all of the sequences, Haines investigates the role of nature as the fundamental reality that underlies all art. In many of the poems, nature takes on sacred qualities, especially if it is wilderness, and therefore distant from human manipulation and transformation. These qualities combine in Haines's mimetic theory of art and culture, and they are also closely allied to his abiding interest in mythic journeys and heroic legends of animals and hunters. Haines also recognizes the distance between culture and nature, especially in the representations of language, but he still holds to the parallel between reading texts and reading the world around us.

Haines's abiding interest in poetic sequences from 1975 until his death in 2011 may also help to account for his disciplined work, during this same period, on critical essays, autobiographical essays, and memoirs. His greatest prose achievement is certainly the collection of lyric essays, *The Stars, the Snow, the Fire: Twenty-Five Years in the Northern Wilderness* (1989). In addition, the prose collections *Living Off the Country* (1981), *Fables and Distances* (1996), and *Descent* (2010) represent Haines's attempt to cross boundaries of genre, combining literary and social criticism, personal narratives, interviews, omnibus reviews, and poems. These volumes are important for gaining a complete view of Haines's career, but *The Stars, the Snow, the Fire* is indispensable. The essays in that collection could be considered prose poems: they powerfully evoke the landscapes of Interior Alaska in all their seasons, and they always place human beings as figures within the northern landscapes. From the very beginning of his homestead years at Richardson, Haines was trying to capture the experience in both poetry and prose.

THE FINAL PHASE: DESCENT

In the last phase of his career, Haines partly retreats from the concerns of contemporary ecopoetry, embracing modern writers of nature poetry from the early twentieth century. The last fifteen years of his life, in fact, constitute a period of reflection and summation, marked in part by the two editions of the collected poems *The Owl in the Mask of the Dreamer* (1993, 1996). Robinson Jeffers becomes a significant figure for Haines because Jeffers is the ideal example of a public poet who speaks beyond his own life and times. For similar reasons, T. S. Eliot of *Four Quartets* and the Orkney poet Edwin Muir (1887–1959) also loom in Haines's thinking about the role of poetry in a changing world. In his critical work from earlier in his career, Haines had demanded that American poetry become a public forum of significant ideas. That demand becomes all the more rigorous in the essays of *Fable and Distances* and *Descent*. In his admiration for writers who act as public intellectuals and artists, Haines resembles most closely his friends Hayden Carruth, Wendell Berry, and Dana Gioia.

The continuities between the major poetic sequences and the poet's critical stance suggest that Haines never completely accepted the private, individual, and quotidian aspects of contemporary American poetry. He seems to have sought the public, civic perspective of the modern writers from the first half of the twentieth century. The movement accords with Haines's declinist history of art and culture, and it might also mark him as a figure of some pastoral nostalgia. But even if that describes Haines's vision of American poetry, it should not obscure the fact that he produced major works of ecopoetry. The sequences do not lend themselves to easy inclusion in large anthologies, but readers and scholars can find most of the major poems in *The Owl in the Mask of the Dreamer*. John Haines became a significant poet in the American scene after the publication of *Winter News* and *The Stone Harp*. But the sequences of 1975 to 1999 are truly his most significant contribution to American poetry. In the tensions those works develop between private and public, between nature and culture, Haines occupies a place in keeping with the major ecopoets of his generation—Bly, Snyder, Merwin, and Berry.

BIBLIOGRAPHY

MANUSCRIPT REPOSITORIES

Kentucky Historical Society. Wendell Berry Collection. Correspondence.

New York Public Library. Henry W. and Albert A. Berg Collection of English and American Literature.

Ohio University. John Meade Haines Collection. Series 1.2: Outgoing Correspondence.

Ohio University. John Meade Haines Papers MSS 145.

University of Alaska, Fairbanks. Elmer E. Rasmuson Library, Alaska and Polar Regions Archives. John Haines Papers.

University of Minnesota. Graywolf Press Archives.

University of Minnesota. Robert Bly Papers. Correspondence.

University of Vermont Special Collections. David Budbill Papers.

University of Vermont Special Collections. Hayden Carruth Papers.

BOOKS BY JOHN HAINES

Winter News. Middletown, CT: Wesleyan University Press, 1966; revised, 1983.

The Stone Harp. Middletown, CT: Wesleyan University Press, 1971.

Twenty Poems. Santa Barbara, CA: Unicorn Press, 1971.

Leaves and Ashes. Santa Cruz, CA: Kayak Books, 1974.

In Five Years' Time. Missoula, MT: Smokeroot Press, 1976.

Cicada. Middletown, CT: Wesleyan University Press, 1977.

In a Dusty Light. Port Townsend, WA: Graywolf Press, 1977.

Living Off the Country: Essays on Poetry and Place. Ann Arbor, MI: University of Michigan Press, 1981.

Of Traps and Snares. Delta Junction, AK: Dragon Press, 1981.

News from the Glacier: Selected Poems, 1960–1980. Middletown, CT: Wesleyan University Press, 1982.

Other Days. Port Townsend, WA: Graywolf Press, 1982.

Stories We Listened To. Swarthmore, PA: Bench Press, 1986.
The Stars, the Snow, the Fire: Twenty-five Years in the Northern Wilderness: A Memoir. St. Paul, MN: Graywolf Press, 1989.
New Poems: 1980–88. Brownsville, OR: Story Line Press, 1990.
The Owl in the Mask of the Dreamer: Collected Poems. St. Paul, MN: Graywolf Press, 1993; revised paperback, 1996.
Where the Twilight Never Ends. Boise, ID: Limberlost Press, 1994.
Fables and Distances: New and Selected Essays. St. Paul, MN: Graywolf Press, 1996.
At the End of this Summer: Poems, 1948–1954. Port Townsend, WA: Copper Canyon Press, 1997.
For the Century's End: Poems, 1990–1999. Seattle, WA: University of Washington Press, 2001.
Descent: Selected Essays, Reviews, and Letters. Fort Lee, NJ: CavanKerry Press, 2010.

OTHER WORKS BY JOHN HAINES

"At Slim's River." *50 Contemporary Poets: The Creative Process*, ed. Alberta T. Turner. New York, NY: David McKay Co., 1977, 115–25.
"The Eye in the Rock." *45 Contemporary Poems: The Creative Process*, ed. Alberta T. Turner. London: Longman, 1985. Reprinted in *Fables and Distances*, 231–38.
"The Great Barrier Reef." *Michigan Quarterly Review* 11 (Summer 1972): 159–60.
"Richardson: The Dream." *permafrost* 1 (October 1977): 8–9.
"Shadows." *Alaska Fish and Game* 17 (November–December 1985): 18–19; *Alaska Fish and Game* 18 (January–February 1986): 18–19.

OTHER SOURCES

Abram, David. *Becoming Animal: An Earthly Cosmology*. New York, NY: Pantheon, 2010.
———. *The Spell of the Sensuous: Language and Perception in a More-than-Human World*. New York, NY: Pantheon, 1996.
Adams, John Luther. "I Do Not Expect to See His Kind Again." Unpublished TS.
———. "They Were My People." *Alaska Quarterly Review* 32 (Fall–Winter 2015): 5–82.
———. *Winter Music: Composing the North*. Middletown, CT: Wesleyan University Press, 2004.

Allen, Carolyn J. "Death and Dreams in John Haines's *Winter News*." *Alaska Review* 12 (Fall–Winter 1969): 28–36; rpt. in Bezner, Kevin, and Kevin Walzner, eds. *The Wilderness of Vision: On the Poetry of John Haines* (Brownsville, OR: Story Line Press, 1994), 145–54.

Berry, Wendell. *Imagination in Place*. Berkeley, CA: Counterpoint, 2010.

Bezner, Kevin, and Kevin Walzner, eds. *The Wilderness of Vision: On the Poetry of John Haines*. Brownsville, OR: Story Line Press, 1994.

Bowen, Claire. "Frames of Reference: Paterson in 'In the Waiting Room.'" *Twentieth Century Literature* 54, no. 4 (2008): 472+. *Literature Resource Center*, Web. 14 May 2014. <http://go.galegroup.com/ps/i.do?id=GALE%7CA203955356&v=2.1&u=vic_wlu&it=r&p=LitRC&sw=w&asid=3be2adfda6e64de1a1dc6eb47d6e27c8>.

Bryson, J. Scott, ed. *Ecopoetry: A Critical Introduction*. Salt Lake City, UT: University of Utah Press, 2002.

Carruth, Hayden. "Books." *Harper's* 256 (June 1978): 86–87.

———. "Here Today: A Poetry Chronicle." *Hudson Review* 24 (Summer 1971): 320–36.

Clarke, Bruce. "Posthumanism." *Johns Hopkins Guide to Literary Theory and Criticism*, 2nd ed. Baltimore, MD: Johns Hopkins University Press, 2005.

Cooperman, Matthew. "Wilderness and Witness: An Interview with John Haines." In *A Gradual Twilight*, edited by Steven B. Rogers, 127–45. Fort Lee, NJ: CavanKerry Press, 2003.

DeMott, Robert. "'Close to Religious Aspirations': Notes on John Haines's Poetry." In *A Gradual Twilight*, edited by Steven B. Rogers, 81–101. Fort Lee, NJ: CavanKerry Press, 2003.

Emerson, Ralph Waldo. *Essays and Lectures*. New York, NY: Library of America, 1983.

George, Andrew R. *The Babylonian Gilgamesh Epic: Critical Edition and Cuneiform Texts*, 2 vols. Oxford, UK: Oxford University Press, 2003.

Gifford, Terry. "Gary Snyder and the Post-Pastoral." In *Ecopoetry: A Critical Introduction*, edited by J. Scott Bryson, 77–87. Salt Lake City, UT: University of Utah Press, 2002.

———. *Pastoral*. New York, NY: Routledge, 1999.

Gioia, Dana. *Can Poetry Matter?* St. Paul, MN: Graywolf Press, 1992.

Greene, Roland, Stephen Cushman, et al., eds. *Princeton Encyclopedia of Poetry and Poetics*, 4th ed. Princeton, NJ: Princeton University Press, 2012.

Guthrie, Mary Lee. *Blue Babe: The Story of a Steppe Bison Mummy from Ice Age Alaska*. Fairbanks, AK: White Mammoth, 1988.

Guthrie, R. Dale. *Frozen Fauna of the Mammoth Steppe: The Story of Blue Babe.* Chicago, IL: University of Chicago Press, 1990.

Henry, Peter. "'The beautiful white ruins / of America': Surrealist Poetry and the Cold War." PhD diss., University of Virginia, 2013.

Knott, John. "The Dreamtime of John Haines." *Interdisciplinary Studies in Literature and Environment* 13, no. 1 (Winter 2006): 147–65.

McAninch, Jerry B. "John (Meade) Haines." In *American Poets Since World War II, Dictionary of Literary Biography*, vol. 5, edited by Donald J. Greiner. Detroit, MI: Gale, 1980. <http://go.galegroup.com/ps/i.do?id=GALE%7CH1200001290&v=2.1&u=vic_wlu&it=r&p=LitRC&sw=w&asid=1213d97f98c4dca524461a6630572082>.

McFarland, Ron. "John (Meade) Haines." In *Twentieth-Century American Western Writers: Second Series, Dictionary of Literary Biography*, vol. 212., edited by Richard H. Cracroft. Detroit, MI: Gale, 1999. <http://go.galegroup.com/ps/i.do?id=GALE%7CH1200008765&v=2.1&u=vic_wlu&it=r&p=LitRC&sw=w&asid=3da627e2aa53bdf5a62691a99d546b3b>.

The Milepost 2014. Anchorage, AK: Morris Communications Company, 2014.

Mitchell, Stephen. *Gilgamesh: A New English Version*. New York, NY: Free Press, 2004.

Quetchenbach, Bernard. *Back from the Far Field: American Nature Poetry in the Late Twentieth Century*. Charlottesville, VA: University of Virginia Press, 2000.

Rogers, Steven B. *A Gradual Twilight: An Appreciation of John Haines*. Fort Lee, NJ: CavanKerry Press, 2003.

Selby, Nick. "Ecopoetries in America." In *The Cambridge Companion to American Poetry since 1945*, edited by Jennifer Ashton, 127–42. Cambridge, UK: Cambridge University Press, 2013.

Taylor, Henry. "A Form of Patience: The Poems of John Haines." *The Hollins Critic* 35 (December 1998): 1–16; rpt. in Rogers, Steven B. *A Gradual Twilight*. Fort Lee, NJ: CavanKerry Press, 2003.

NOTES

INTRODUCTION

1. Ron McFarland, "John (Meade) Haines," in *Twentieth-Century American Western Writers: Second Series, Dictionary of Literary Biography*, vol. 212, ed. Richard H. Cracroft (Detroit, MI: Gale, 1999). *Literature Resource Center*, Web. 7 May 2015. <http://go.galegroup.com/ps/i.do?id=GALE%7CH1200008765&v=2.1&u=vic_wlu&it=r&p=LitRC&sw=w&asid=3da627e2aa53bdf5a62691a99d546b3b>. Other helpful biographical information can be found in "John Meade Haines," *Contemporary Authors Online* (Detroit, MI: Gale, 2011). *Literature Resource Center*. Web. 7 May 2015. <http://go.galegroup.com/ps/i.do?id=GALE%7CH1200001290&v=2.1&u=vic_wlu&it=r&p=LitRC&sw=w&asid=1213d97f98c4dca524461a6630572082>. See also Steven B. Rogers's chronology in *A Gradual Twilight: An Appreciation of John Haines*, ed. Steven B. Rogers (Fort Lee, NJ: CavanKerry Press, 2003), 277–81.

CHAPTER 1

1. University of Alaska Fairbanks, Elmer E. Rasmuson Library, Alaska and Polar Regions Archives, John Haines Papers, Box 5, Folder 20; all manuscript materials in this archive are cited as JHP with box number and folder number. The April 21, 1953, letter is reprinted in *A Gradual Twilight: An Appreciation of John Haines*, ed. Steven B. Rogers (Fort Lee, NJ: CavanKerry Press, 2003), 147–48.
2. In a one-page preface, Haines notes, along with these influences, that the poems "have been rescued from old notebooks and from files in the Rasmuson Library at the University of Alaska." *Where the Twilight Never Ends* (Boise, ID: Limberlost Press, 1994). Many of the manuscripts are still housed in the John Haines Papers.

3. *At the End of This Summer: Poems, 1948–1954* (Port Townsend, WA: Copper Canyon Press, 1997), x.
4. *Of Your Passage, O Summer: Uncollected Poems from the 1960s* (Boise, ID: Limberlost Press, 2004).
5. For a full discussion of the essay and its role in the making of Haines's great memoir, see chapter 3, "Shadow Language."
6. I wish to acknowledge helpful comments on this image by my friends Eric Heyne and John Knott, two very fine readers of Haines's poems.
7. The correspondence of the early years is contained in the John Haines Papers, Boxes 1–5. The more voluminous letters from 1970 to the late 1980s are contained in Boxes 17–26, 31. Most of these thousands of items are addressed to Haines, and only a few copies of the poet's outgoing letters are in the John Haines Papers. For an unvarnished and sympathetic view of the difficult conditions of homesteading, see Jo Haines's diary (Box 6, Folders 1 and 2).
8. Carolyn J. Allen, "Death and Dreams in John Haines's *Winter News*," *Alaska Review* 12 (Fall–Winter 1969): 28–36; rpt. in Kevin Bezner and Kevin Walzner, eds., *The Wilderness of Vision: On the Poetry of John Haines* (Brownsville, OR: Story Line Press, 1994), 145–46. Another fine commentary on the poem, as well as on Haines's work in general, is Henry Taylor, "A Form of Patience: The Poems of John Haines," *The Hollins Critic* 35 (December 1998): 1–16; rpt. in *A Gradual Twilight*, 53–71.
9. Roland Greene, Stephen Cushman, et al., eds., "Deep Image," in *Princeton Encyclopedia of Poetry and Poetics*, 4th ed. (Princeton, NJ: Princeton University Press, 2012), 342. For Bly's role in promoting the ideas of Deep Image poetry through his magazines, essays, and poems, see 342–43. See also Peter Henry's excellent discussion of Deep Image poetry in "'The beautiful white ruins / of America': Surrealist Poetry and the Cold War," PhD diss., University of Virginia, 2013. In "'Close to Religious Aspirations': Notes on John Haines's Poetry," Robert DeMott comments tellingly on how Haines has been erased from literary histories of Deep Image poetry (*Gradual Twilight*, 81–101).
10. Writing to Haines on July 8, 1966, for example, Bly complains about the tone of Haines's latest letter as "condescending and touched with malice. It is the tone of a man working off a grudge, not of a man trying to help another man with his poetry" (JHP Box 1, Folder 18). Haines wrote brutally critical letters to Bly on April 24, 1972, and May 15, 1972, but he also admits that his own published criticisms are often too harsh. (JHP Box 1, Folder 18). Early letters from Haines to Bly are in JHP Box 5, Folder 37.
11. The phrase "more than human" was coined by David Abram in his seminal book, *The Spell of the Sensuous: Language and Perception in a More-than-Human*

World (New York, NY: Pantheon, 1996). Abram has a more recent book that develops similar arguments about human embeddedness and entanglement in the world of nature: *Becoming Animal: An Earthly Cosmology* (New York, NY: Pantheon, 2010). For a general introduction and bibliography about posthumanism and animal studies, see Bruce Clarke's article "Posthumanism" in *Johns Hopkins Guide to Literary Theory and Criticism*, 2nd ed. (2005). Web. 6 Aug. 2014. http://litguide.press.jhu.edu.ezproxy.wlu.edu/cgi-bin/view.cgi?eid=318&query=posthumanism>.

CHAPTER 2

1. "Experience" was first published in *Essays: Second Series* (1844) and is readily available in the edition *Essays and Lectures* (New York, NY: Library of America, 1983).
2. This summary owes much to Steven Rogers's chronology in *A Gradual Twilight: An Appreciation of John Haines* (Fort Lee, NJ: CavanKerry Press, 2003), 277–81. For Haines's most caustic view of the suburbs, see "The Great Barrier Reef" in *Michigan Quarterly Review* 11 (Summer 1972): 159–60.
3. JHP Box 10, Folder 5. The notes are for Everett Edwards Poetry Tapes, and they include commentaries on nine particular poems from the volume as well as the introductory remarks.
4. See Henry Taylor's persuasive analysis in "Form of Patience," *A Gradual Twilight*, 67–69.
5. In "Ecopoetries in America," Nick Selby reviews the critical definitions of ecopoetry over the past thirty years or more; discusses major poets from Robert Frost to Haines's contemporaries Wendell Berry, W. S. Merwin, Gary Snyder, A. R. Ammons, and Lorine Niedecker; and argues that contemporary American ecopoetry is marked by a persistent, complex sense of connection between the text and the environment, engagement between the poet and the natural world, and awareness of ecological crises engendered by human activities. The bibliography is also very helpful. Jennifer Ashton, ed., *The Cambridge Companion to American Poetry since 1945* (Cambridge, UK: Cambridge University Press, 2013), 127–42.
6. Haines describes his father's death as the origin of the poem in the 1990 essay "The Far Country of Sleep," in *Fables and Distances: New and Selected Essays* (Saint Paul, MN: Graywolf Press, 1996), 249–52. *Cicada* is dedicated to the poet's parents.

7. Several poems in *Leaves and Ashes* seem to be addressed to Jane McWhorter, not always in flattering terms. For the correspondence between two strong-willed people, see JHP Box 2, Folders 16–18, and Box 21, Folders 11 and 13. Diane Smith's correspondence with Haines is in JHP Box 4, Folder 32, and Box 23, Folder 42. Daphne Enslow's correspondence with Haines took place in 1974–1975, while she was a student at the University of Washington (JHP Box 20, Folder 17).
8. For analysis and full text of the Dawes Act, see "History Timeline, Nebraska Studies." Web. 4 June 2015. <http://nebraskastudies.org/0600/frameset.html>.
9. The poem was retitled "At Slim's River" in the 1993 collected poems *The Owl in the Mask of the Dreamer*. The revised title refers to Slim's River Bridge at the south shore of Kluane Lake. According to the much-consulted annual travel planner for roads in the Far North, the river was named for a packhorse that drowned at the bridge site during the 1903 Kluane gold rush. *The Milepost 2014* (Anchorage, AK: Morris Communications Company, 2014), 197.
10. See Haines's essay in Alberta T. Turner, ed., *Fifty Contemporary Poets: The Creative Process* (New York, NY: David McKay Co., 1977), 115–25. The quoted material appears on page 122. Haines's drafts (115–20) give the place-names I use in my description. The sixth stanza (25–28) describes the narrow bridge in the distance.
11. Walker's letters to Haines suggest that the volume was a commercial and critical success as well, and at one point in October 1978 they discussed bringing out a second, expanded edition of the book (JHP Box 21, Folders 6, 7).
12. Haines wrote an essay on the genesis and composition of "The Eye in the Rock" for Alberta T. Turner, ed., *45 Contemporary Poems: The Creative Process* (London: Longman, 1985) and reprinted it in *Fables and Distances*, 231–38.
13. Many partial specimens were known before Blue Babe was discovered at a placer gold mine near Fairbanks in 1979, but the poem could be describing many of the details of the famous specimen. See R. Dale Guthrie, *Frozen Fauna of the Mammoth Steppe: The Story of Blue Babe* (Chicago, IL: University of Chicago Press, 1990) and Mary Lee Guthrie, *Blue Babe: The Story of a Steppe Bison Mummy from Ice Age Alaska* (Fairbanks, AK: White Mammoth, 1988).
14. For an influential, contemporary theoretical treatment of the pastoral, see Terry Gifford, *Pastoral* (New York, NY: Routledge, 1999). Also helpful are the entries on "elegy" and "pastoral" in the most recent *Princeton Encyclopedia of Poetry and Poetics*, 4th ed., edited by Roland Green, Stephen Cushman, et al. (Princeton: Princeton University Press, 2012). The modern sense of pastoral and pastoral elegy suggests that Haines's closest predecessor in these modes might be Rainer Maria Rilke in the *Duino Elegies* (1923).

15. The classic treatment is Sacvan Bercovitch, *The American Jeremiad* (Madison, WI: University of Wisconsin Press, 1978).
16. Fitzgerald was Haines's student at the University of Montana in 1974 and maintained contact with him through letters until at least 1980. See JHP Box 20, Folder 22.
17. See the website of the Montana Natural History Center, accessed 1 May 2014. <http://www.glaciallakemissoula.org/>.

CHAPTER 3

1. For a suggestive account of the poem in relation to William Carlos Williams's *Paterson*, see Claire Bowen, "Frames of Reference: Paterson in 'In the Waiting Room,'" in *Twentieth Century Literature* 54, no. 4 (2008): 472+. *Literature Resource Center*. Web. 14 May 2014. <http://go.galegroup.com/ps/i.do?id=GALE%7CA203955356&v=2.1&u=vic_wlu&it=r&p=LitRC&sw=w&asid=3be2adfda6e64de1a1dc6eb47d6e27c8>.
2. Hayden Carruth (1921–2008) gave crucial friendship and support to Haines, especially evident in their regular correspondence of 1977–1988. As poetry editor at *Harper's*, Carruth was able to broker Haines's essays and poems for publication in the magazine, but perhaps even more important were the positive critical responses Carruth gave to Haines's work over these productive years. Carruth's considerable papers are available at the Special Collections Library of the University of Vermont. For more on this friendship, see chapter 6.
3. A short version of the essay appears as "Notes from an Interrupted Journal" in *Fables and Distances: New and Selected Essays* (Saint Paul, MN: Graywolf Press, 1996), 169–76.
4. Dragon Press was a private company founded by Chris and Frances Brann in 1978. It is profiled in *Envoy* (September 1982), the newsletter of the Alaska Association for the Arts, based in Fairbanks.
5. See *Alaska Fish and Game* 17 (November–December 1985): 18–19; *Alaska Fish and Game* 18 (January–February 1986): 18–19.
6. For a comprehensive, well-written guide to the flora and fauna of the Far North, see Ronald L. Smith, *Interior and Northern Alaska: A Natural History* (Bothell, WA: Book Publishers Network, 2008). See also the *Alaska Wildlife Notebook Series* published by the Alaska Department of Fish and Game (2008). Haines published a shortened version of the first two parts of the essay as "Shadows" in *Alaska Fish and Game* 18 (July–August 1986): 18–19.

That makes three distinct versions of "Shadows" published in the magazine within a few months.

7. The essay appears in *permafrost* 1 (October 1977): 8–9. The magazine version differs slightly from the final version; Haines cut one brief paragraph, probably because of some repetitious phrasing.

CHAPTER 4

1. The best source for information about John Luther Adams, with biography, discography, and selected links for listening, is www.johnlutheradams.com. Over the years, Adams has set other Haines poems to music, notably "Little Cosmic Dust Poem" (2007) and "Poem of the Forgotten" (2004). The "firm structure" of the sequence must have been altered, by the way, because in the final published version there are fifteen poems, not eighteen. Adams has recently published a long essay on his friendship with Haines and with the Fairbanks conductor Gordon Wright. See "They Were My People," *Alaska Quarterly Review* 32 (Fall–Winter 2015): 5–82.
2. The British Museum and Smithsonian Institution have tested crystal skulls in their collections and have been unable to authenticate them as of ancient origin. From marks left by polishing tools, the skulls appear to be nineteenth-century forgeries. See http://en.wikipedia.org/wiki/Crystal_skull for an overview with full bibliography.
3. Matthew Cooperman, "Wilderness and Witness: An Interview with John Haines," in *A Gradual Twilight: An Appreciation of John Haines*, ed. Steven B. Rogers (Fort Lee, NJ: CavanKerry Press, 2003), 127–45. The quotation appears on page 134.
4. "The Dreamtime of John Haines," *Interdisciplinary Studies in Literature and Environment* 13, no. 1 (Winter 2006): 147–48. As the quotation suggests, the essay as a whole (147–65) is a wide-ranging and insightful discussion of Haines's vision.

CHAPTER 5

1. Haines sent Wendell Berry a three-page beginning to the essay "What Are Poets For?" on November 25, 1990, noting that he had taken the title from Berry's "What Are People For?" As he continued to work on the essay in 1991

to 1995, Haines sent drafts to Berry and enlisted his aid in publishing the essay. See Wendell Berry Collection, Kentucky Historical Society, Correspondence: Box 7, Folder 5; Box 9, Folder 9; Box 16, Folder 6; and Box 19, Folder 2.

2. The book was inspired by Forché's stay in El Salvador during the civil war that lasted from 1980 to 1992. For the complete text of "The Colonel" and other poems, as well as a good biography of the poet, see "Poetry Foundation: Carolyn Forché." Web. 8 July 2014. <http://www.poetryfoundation.org/bio/carolyn-forche#about>.
3. "The View from Buckeye Dome" tells the story of Haines's return to the Richardson homestead on a camping trip in July 1980, and the narrative spine of the essay allows Haines to reflect on the changes Alaska has undergone since he left the homestead in 1969. These changes include the passing of the old settlers of Richardson and the industrialization of Alaska because of the oil boom and the building of the Alyeska Pipeline. Less gentle and lyrical than the essays of *The Stars, the Snow, the Fire*, "The View from Buckeye Dome," still unpublished in its entirety, is a stirring hybrid essay that ranges widely across the Alaskan landscape. Like such long draft essays as "Shadows," it became a source for shorter, partial essays. "Notes from an Interrupted Journal" is the longest and most nearly complete published version.
4. For a scholarly introduction to Goya's work, see James Voorhies, "Francisco de Goya (1746–1828) and the Spanish Enlightenment," in *Heilbrunn Timeline of Art History* (New York, NY: The Metropolitan Museum of Art, 2000). Web. 11 June 2015. <http://www.metmuseum.org/toah/hd/goya/hd_goya.htm>. See also "Francisco Goya: The Complete Works." Web. 11 June 2015. <http://www.franciscodegoya.net/>.
5. For a comprehensive survey of Rodin's career and artworks, see "Artble: Auguste Rodin." Web. 10 July 2014. <http://www.artble.com/artists/auguste_rodin>. This is also my source for the information about "The Vanquished" and its relation to the Franco-Prussian War.
6. The volume is the first in the Pacific Northwest Poetry Series, published by University of Washington Press, 2001.
7. The language of "In the House of Wax" will remind many contemporary readers of such political and psychoanalytical thinkers as Jacques Lacan, Michel Foucault, Louis Althusser, and Slavoj Žižek. For an introduction to the discussion of the "Big Other," see the article "Slavoj Žižek" in the *Johns Hopkins Guide to Literary Theory* (2005). Web. 3 August 2014. <http://litguide.press.jhu.edu.ezproxy.wlu.edu/cgi-bin/view.cgi?eid=264>. Žižek discusses Lacan and the concept of the "Big Other" in his *Looking Awry: An Introduction to Jacques Lacan through Popular Culture* (Cambridge: MIT Press, 1991); an

entertaining recent introduction is Sophie Fiennes's documentary film *A Pervert's Guide to Ideology* (2012).

8. The essay was delivered as a paper at a conference in Atlanta in 1999. It appears in the late miscellany of prose works, *Descent: Selected Essays, Reviews, and Letters* (Fort Lee, NJ: CavanKerry Press, 2010), 11–22. Haines gives the date of his reading and of his work on the essay and poem on pages 16 and 22.

   The definitive edition of the epic is Andrew R. George, trans., *The Babylonian Gilgamesh Epic: Critical Edition and Cuneiform Texts*, 2 vols. (Oxford, UK: Oxford University Press, 2003). See also Stephen Mitchell, trans., *Gilgamesh: A New English Version* (New York, NY: Free Press, 2004). For a good summary of the scholarship and the Standard Version of the epic, see "Wikipedia: Epic of Gilgamesh." Web. 5 August 2014. <http://en.wikipedia.org/wiki/Epic_of_Gilgamesh>.

CHAPTER 6

1. University of Minnesota. Robert Bly Papers. Correspondence, Box 4, Folder 2.
2. John Meade Haines Papers, Ohio University. Series II: Correspondence, Box 1, Folder 41.
3. Robert Bly Papers, University of Minnesota MSS. Division, Series 16. Miscellaneous. Box 278, Folder 1.
4. Graywolf Press Archives, University of Minnesota, Box 10 Editorial, Folder 2. Further references to this archive appear in parenthetical citations.
5. John Meade Haines Papers, Ohio University. Series II: Correspondence. Box 2, Folders 16 and 17. References to this collection are cited parenthetically as "Ohio JHP."
6. E-mail message from Scott Walker to author, 16 December 2013.
7. The essay was reprinted in the volume *Can Poetry Matter?* (Saint Paul, MN: Graywolf Press, 1992) and can also be accessed on Gioia's website, <http://www.danagioia.net/essays/ecpm.htm>.
8. That quotation comes from a postscript to the essay, added for the tenth anniversary edition of *Can Poetry Matter?* See also the recent essay "Telling Jeffers's Story" on Gioia's website, <http://www.danagioia.net/essays/ejeffers.htm>.
9. Ohio University, John Haines Collection, Series 1.2. Outgoing Correspondence, Folder 10. This collection, arranged in eight series, is cited parenthetically as "Ohio JHC."
10. Gioia seems to have read an early version of the book, dating from August 1988. The Berg Collection at the New York Public Library has a copy of Gioia's

reading typescript, with his table of contents on the title page. The typescript does not have "Water of Night" or "In the Forest Without Leaves" in final form, with proper titles, and it does not include the three important poems "Of Michelangelo, His Question," "The Owl in the Mask of the Dreamer," and "Paolo and Francesca." Backlog Box 52. John Haines, *New Poems, 1980–88*, [71] leaves, typescript (photocopy) with MS annotations. The Henry W. and Albert A. Berg Collection of English and American Literature, The New York Public Library, Astor, Lenox and Tilden Foundations.

11. John Luther Adams, "I Do Not Expect to See His Kind Again," unpublished TS. Provided to author by Adams. For a more recent, revised account of the friendship, see John Luther Adams, "They Were My People," *Alaska Quarterly Review* 32 (Fall–Winter 2015): 5–82.
12. This early draft eventually became a series of pieces on "Forest Without Leaves," a lecture given in conjunction with performances of the cantata, a publication in *Ear* magazine, liner notes for the sound recording, and the essay "Forest Without Leaves (1984)" in Adams's *Winter Music: Composing the North* (Middletown, CT: Wesleyan University Press, 2004), 36–39.
13. Hayden Carruth Papers, University of Vermont Special Collections. Carton 8, Folder 34.
14. David Budbill Papers. University of Vermont Special Collections. Carton 33, Folder 24. See letter of June 25, 1970, to Budbill.
15. Reprinted in Kevin Bezner and Kevin Walzner, eds., *The Wilderness of Vision: On the Poetry of John Haines* (Brownsville, OR: Story Line Press, 1996), 222–23.
16. These letters and dozens more from Carruth to Haines, most from 1993 to 2000, are in Ohio JHP II, Box 1, Folders 39–42.
17. Wendell Berry, *Imagination in Place* (Counterpoint: Berkeley, CA, 2010), 49–53. First published in Kevin Bezner and Kevin Walzner, eds., *The Wilderness of Vision: On the Poetry of John Haines* (Brownsville, OR: Story Line Press, 1996), 25–28, with a final sentence omitted in the 2010 printing: "I acknowledge here my own debt and gratitude." Reprinted in *Sewanee Review* 104, no. 1 (Winter 1996): 108–10, along with four sections of "In the House of Wax."
18. As noted in *Imagination in Place*, a shortened version of "My Friend Hayden" was published in *American Poet* (Fall 2007). The version here ends with a postscript, several paragraphs taken from Berry's memorial tribute, "Hello, Hayden," published in the *Sewanee Review* (Fall 2009).
19. Haines's letter is contained in the Wendell Berry Collection at the Kentucky Historical Society, Correspondence, Box 14, Folder 5. Over two hundred letters from Haines to Berry, from 1989 to 2010, are housed here. References to the letters are cited parenthetically as WBC, with box and folder. For Berry's

account of the first meeting and his reading of "The Traveler" and other texts, see *Imagination in Place*, 49–50.

20. The *Exxon Valdez* oil spill took place on March 24, 1989, with somewhere between 11 million and 32 million gallons of crude oil being spilled into Prince William Sound in Alaska. Until the 2010 Deepwater Horizon oil spill, it was the worst environmental disaster in U.S. history.

CONCLUSION

1. Ralph Waldo Emerson, "The Transcendentalist," in *Emerson's Prose and Poetry*, ed. Joel Porte and Saundra Morris (New York, NY: Norton Critical Edition, 2001), 93.
2. "Introduction" in *Ecopoetry: A Critical Introduction*, ed. J. Scott Bryson (Salt Lake City, UT: University of Utah Press, 2002), 5–6.
3. Bernard Quetchenbach, *Back from the Far Field: American Nature Poetry in the Late Twentieth Century* (Charlottesville, VA: University of Virginia Press, 2000), 1–54.
4. See Gifford's "Gary Snyder and the Post-Pastoral" in *Ecopoetry: A Critical Introduction*, ed. J. Scott Bryson (Salt Lake City, UT: University of Utah Press, 2002), 77–87. See also Terry Gifford, *Pastoral* (New York, NY: Routledge, 1999). Nick Selby reads ecopoetry as politically and socially engaged in Jennifer Ashton, ed., "Ecopoetries in America," *The Cambridge Companion to American Poetry since 1945* (Cambridge, UK: Cambridge University Press, 2015), 127–42.

ABOUT THE AUTHOR

James Perrin Warren has taught American literature and environmental literature at Washington and Lee University for over 32 years. He has published several books and dozens of articles on nineteenth-century American literature, focusing on figures like Walt Whitman, Ralph Waldo Emerson, Henry David Thoreau, Frederick Douglass, Margaret Fuller, John Burroughs, John Muir, and Theodore Roosevelt. His most recent work has focused on modern and contemporary environmental writers. He edited the collected poems of Mary Austin, *The Road to the Spring* (Syracuse UP, 2014) and recently published the first book-length study of contemporary writer Barry Lopez: *Other Country: Barry Lopez and the Community of Artists* (U of Arizona Press, 2015). His work on John Haines's poetry emerged from the friendship of Haines, composer John Luther Adams, and Barry Lopez.

Currently Warren is beginning a project on "New Topographers," examining the emergence of contemporary environmental writers in the United Kingdom and Ireland. This book will focus on the work of writers like Nan Shepherd, Tim Robinson, Roger Deakin, Kathleen Jamie, and Robert Macfarlane.

INDEX